Microsoft Windows® Me Millennium Edition For Dummies®

Cheat Sheet

Helpful Hints

- Don't turn off your computer without giving Windows Me fair warning. First, click the Start button and choose Shut Down from the menu. Choose Shut down from the next menu, if needed, and click the OK button. When Windows Me says it's okay to turn off your computer, go ahead and turn it off.

- Don't know what a certain button does in a program? Rest your mouse pointer over the button for a few seconds. A helpful box often pops up to explain the button's purpose.

- If you're baffled, try pressing F1, that "function key" on your keyboard's upper, left corner. A "help" window appears, often bringing hints about your current problem.

- To quickly organize the windows on the desktop, click the taskbar's clock with your *right* mouse button. When the menu appears, click one of the Tile options, and all your open windows neatly tile across the screen.

- To keep icons organized in neat rows across a folder, right-click the folder's background. When the menu pops up, choose Auto Arrange from the Arrange Icons menu.

Click these words to see helpful menus

Click here to shrink the window

Click here for a helpful menu

Click here to enlarge the window

Click here to close the window

Helpful Hints Dept. - WordPad

File   Edit   View   Insert   Format   Help

Push the mouse across your desk, and the mouse's arrow will move across your screen.

Push the mouse's left button with your finger to "click" the mouse. Push the button twice in rapid succession to "double-click."

By pointing to different parts of the window and either "clicking" or "double-clicking," you can perform different chores.

For Help, press F1   NUM

Click here to move up the page

Click here to move down the page

Click the arrows to move up or down a single line

Point here, hold down the mouse button, and move the mouse to change the window's size

Handling Files within a Program

To Do This . . .	Do This . . .
Start a new file	Press Alt, F, N.
Open an existing file	Press Alt, F, O.
Save a file	Press Alt, F, S.
Save a file under a new name	Press Alt, F, A.
Print a file	Pres Alt, F, P.

For Dummies®: Bestselling Book Series for Beginners

Microsoft Windows® Me Millennium Edition For Dummies®

Cheat Sheet

Organizing a Pile of Windows

To Do This . . .	Do This . . .
See a list of all open windows	Look at the names on the taskbar.
Move from one window to another window	Press Alt+Tab+Tab or click the window's name on the taskbar.
Tile the windows across the screen	Click the taskbar's clock with the *right* mouse button and then click Tile <u>H</u>orizontally or Tile <u>V</u>ertically.
Cascade the windows across the screen	Click the taskbar's clock with the *right* mouse button and then click <u>C</u>ascade.
Shrink all open windows	Click the little pencil-and-pad icon near your Start button.
Make a window fill the screen	Double-click on the title bar along its top edge.

Cut and Paste Stuff

To Do This . . .	Hold Down These Keys . . .
Copy highlighted stuff to the Clipboard	Ctrl+C or Ctrl+Insert
Cut highlighted stuff to the Clipboard	Ctrl+X or Shift+Delete
Paste stuff from the Clipboard to the current window	Ctrl+V or Shift+Insert
Copy an entire screen to the Clipboard	PrintScreen (Shift+PrintScreen on some keyboards)
Copy the current window to the Clipboard	Alt+PrintScreen

DOS Window Stuff

To Do This . . .	Do This . . .
Toggle DOS program from a full-screen display to a window-sized display	Press Alt+Enter
Change a DOS program from a taskbar button to a full screen	Click the program's icon on the taskbar.
Close a DOS window	Use that program's normal exit command and then click the X in the window's upper-right corner.

Windows Explorer and My Computer Programs

To Do This . . .	Do This . . .
Copy a file to another location on the *same* disk drive	Hold down Ctrl and drag it there.
Copy a file to a *different* disk drive	Hold down Shift and drag it there.
Remember how to copy or move files	Hold down the *right* mouse button while dragging and then choose <u>C</u>opy or <u>M</u>ove from the menu.
Select several files	Hold down Ctrl and click the filenames
Look at a different folder	Double-click that folder's icon.

The IDG Books Worldwide logo is a registered trademark under exclusive license to IDG Books Worldwide, Inc., from International Data Group, Inc. The ...For Dummies logo is a trademark, and For Dummies is a registered trademark of IDG Books Worldwide, Inc. All other trademarks are the property of their respective owners.

For Dummies®: Bestselling Book Series for Beginners

Microsoft® Windows® Me Millennium Edition FOR DUMMIES®

by Andy Rathbone

IDG Books Worldwide, Inc.
An International Data Group Company

Foster City, CA ◆ Chicago, IL ◆ Indianapolis, IN ◆ New York, NY

Microsoft® Windows® Me Millennium Edition For Dummies®

Published by
IDG Books Worldwide, Inc.
An International Data Group Company
919 E. Hillsdale Blvd.
Suite 400
Foster City, CA 94404
www.idgbooks.com (IDG Books Worldwide Web site)
www.dummies.com (Dummies Press Web site)

Library of Congress Control Number: 00-102506

ISBN: 0-7645-0735-4

Printed in the United States of America

10 9 8 7 6 5 4 3 2 1

1B/SV/QX/QQ/IN

Distributed in the United States by IDG Books Worldwide, Inc.

Distributed by CDG Books Canada Inc. for Canada; by Transworld Publishers Limited in the United Kingdom; by IDG Norge Books for Norway; by IDG Sweden Books for Sweden; by IDG Books Australia Publishing Corporation Pty. Ltd. for Australia and New Zealand; by TransQuest Publishers Pte Ltd. for Singapore, Malaysia, Thailand, Indonesia, and Hong Kong; by Gotop Information Inc. for Taiwan; by ICG Muse, Inc. for Japan; by Intersoft for South Africa; by Eyrolles for France; by International Thomson Publishing for Germany, Austria and Switzerland; by Distribuidora Cuspide for Argentina; by LR International for Brazil; by Galileo Libros for Chile; by Ediciones ZETA S.C.R. Ltda. for Peru; by WS Computer Publishing Corporation, Inc., for the Philippines; by Contemporanea de Ediciones for Venezuela; by Express Computer Distributors for the Caribbean and West Indies; by Micronesia Media Distributor, Inc. for Micronesia; by Chips Computadoras S.A. de C.V. for Mexico; by Editorial Norma de Panama S.A. for Panama; by American Bookshops for Finland.

For general information on IDG Books Worldwide's books in the U.S., please call our Consumer Customer Service department at 800-762-2974. For reseller information, including discounts and premium sales, please call our Reseller Customer Service department at 800-434-3422.

For information on where to purchase IDG Books Worldwide's books outside the U.S., please contact our International Sales department at 317-596-5530 or fax 317-572-4002.

For consumer information on foreign language translations, please contact our Customer Service department at 1-800-434-3422, fax 317-572-4002, or e-mail rights@idgbooks.com.

For information on licensing foreign or domestic rights, please phone +1-650-653-7098.

For sales inquiries and special prices for bulk quantities, please contact our Order Services department at 800-434-3422 or write to the address above.

For information on using IDG Books Worldwide's books in the classroom or for ordering examination copies, please contact our Educational Sales department at 800-434-2086 or fax 317-572-4005.

For press review copies, author interviews, or other publicity information, please contact our Public Relations department at 650-653-7000 or fax 650-653-7500.

For authorization to photocopy items for corporate, personal, or educational use, please contact Copyright Clearance Center, 222 Rosewood Drive, Danvers, MA 01923, or fax 978-750-4470.

is a registered trademark under exclusive license to IDG Books Worldwide, Inc. from International Data Group, Inc.

About the Author

Andy Rathbone started geeking around with computers in 1985 when he bought a boxy CP/M Kaypro 2X with lime-green letters. Like other budding nerds, he soon began playing with null-modem adapters, dialing up computer bulletin boards, and working part-time at Radio Shack.

In between playing computer games, he served as editor of the *Daily Aztec* newspaper at San Diego State University. After graduating with a comparative literature degree, he went to work for a bizarre underground coffee-table magazine that sort of disappeared.

Andy began combining his two main interests, words and computers, by selling articles to a local computer magazine. During the next few years, he started ghostwriting computer books for more-famous computer authors, as well as writing several hundred articles about computers for technoid publications like *Supercomputing Review, CompuServe Magazine, ID Systems, DataPro,* and *Shareware.*

In 1992, Andy and *DOS For Dummies* author/legend Dan Gookin teamed up to write *PCs For Dummies.* Andy subsequently wrote the award-winning *Windows For Dummies, Upgrading & Fixing PCs For Dummies,* and *MP3 For Dummies,* and *Windows 2000 Professional For Dummies* with Sharon Crawford.

Today, he has more than 11 million copies of his books in print, which have been translated into more than 30 languages.

Andy lives with his most-excellent wife, Tina, and their cat in Southern California. He wants a new LCD panel monitor for his main computer, but then the cat wouldn't have any where to sleep. Feel free to drop by his Web site at www.andyrathbone.com.

ABOUT IDG BOOKS WORLDWIDE

Welcome to the world of IDG Books Worldwide.

IDG Books Worldwide, Inc., is a subsidiary of International Data Group, the world's largest publisher of computer-related information and the leading global provider of information services on information technology. IDG was founded more than 30 years ago by Patrick J. McGovern and now employs more than 9,000 people worldwide. IDG publishes more than 290 computer publications in over 75 countries. More than 90 million people read one or more IDG publications each month.

Launched in 1990, IDG Books Worldwide is today the #1 publisher of best-selling computer books in the United States. We are proud to have received eight awards from the Computer Press Association in recognition of editorial excellence and three from Computer Currents' First Annual Readers' Choice Awards. Our best-selling ...For Dummies® series has more than 50 million copies in print with translations in 31 languages. IDG Books Worldwide, through a joint venture with IDG's Hi-Tech Beijing, became the first U.S. publisher to publish a computer book in the People's Republic of China. In record time, IDG Books Worldwide has become the first choice for millions of readers around the world who want to learn how to better manage their businesses.

Our mission is simple: Every one of our books is designed to bring extra value and skill-building instructions to the reader. Our books are written by experts who understand and care about our readers. The knowledge base of our editorial staff comes from years of experience in publishing, education, and journalism — experience we use to produce books to carry us into the new millennium. In short, we care about books, so we attract the best people. We devote special attention to details such as audience, interior design, use of icons, and illustrations. And because we use an efficient process of authoring, editing, and desktop publishing our books electronically, we can spend more time ensuring superior content and less time on the technicalities of making books.

You can count on our commitment to deliver high-quality books at competitive prices on topics you want to read about. At IDG Books Worldwide, we continue in the IDG tradition of delivering quality for more than 30 years. You'll find no better book on a subject than one from IDG Books Worldwide.

IDG BOOKS WORLDWIDE

John Kilcullen
Chairman and CEO
IDG Books Worldwide, Inc.

VIII
WINNER
*Eighth Annual
Computer Press
Awards 1992*

IX
WINNER
*Ninth Annual
Computer Press
Awards 1993*

1995 COMPUTER CURRENTS READERS CHOICE

X
WINNER
*Tenth Annual
Computer Press
Awards 1994*

XI
WINNER
*Eleventh Annual
Computer Press
Awards 1995*

IDG is the world's leading IT media, research and exposition company. Founded in 1964, IDG had 1997 revenues of $2.05 billion and has more than 9,000 employees worldwide. IDG offers the widest range of media options that reach IT buyers in 75 countries representing 95% of worldwide IT spending. IDG's diverse product and services portfolio spans six key areas including print publishing, online publishing, expositions and conferences, market research, education and training, and global marketing services. More than 90 million people read one or more of IDG's 290 magazines and newspapers, including IDG's leading global brands — Computerworld, PC World, Network World, Macworld and the Channel World family of publications. IDG Books Worldwide is one of the fastest-growing computer book publishers in the world, with more than 700 titles in 36 languages. The "...For Dummies®" series alone has more than 50 million copies in print. IDG offers online users the largest network of technology-specific Web sites around the world through IDG.net (http://www.idg.net), which comprises more than 225 targeted Web sites in 55 countries worldwide. International Data Corporation (IDC) is the world's largest provider of information technology data, analysis and consulting, with research centers in over 41 countries and more than 400 research analysts worldwide. IDG World Expo is a leading producer of more than 168 globally branded conferences and expositions in 35 countries including E3 (Electronic Entertainment Expo), Macworld Expo, ComNet, Windows World Expo, ICE (Internet Commerce Expo), Agenda, DEMO, and Spotlight. IDG's training subsidiary, ExecuTrain, is the world's largest computer training company, with more than 230 locations worldwide and 785 training courses. IDG Marketing Services helps industry-leading IT companies build international brand recognition by developing global integrated marketing programs via IDG's print, online and exposition products worldwide. Further information about the company can be found at www.idg.com.   1/26/00

Dedication

To my wife, parents, sister, and cat.

Author's Acknowledgments

Special thanks to Dan Gookin and his wife Sandy Gookin, Matt Wagner, the Kleskes, the Tragesers, Darren Meiss, Rev Mengle, and Donna Frederick.

Publisher's Acknowledgments

We're proud of this book; please register your comments through our IDG Books Worldwide Online Registration Form located at `http://my2cents.dummies.com`.

Some of the people who helped bring this book to market include the following:

Acquisitions, Editorial, and Media Development

Project Editor: Darren Meiss

   (Previous Edition: Jennifer Erhlich)

Acquisitions Editor: Steven H. Hayes

Copy Editor: Donna S. Frederick

   (Previous Edition: Michael Bolinger)

Proof Editor: Dwight Ramsey

Technical Editors: Jamey Marcum, Lee Musick

Editorial Manager: Rev Mengle

Editorial Assistant: Candace Nicholson

Production

Project Coordinator: Maridee Ennis

Layout and Graphics: Amy Adrian, Tracy Oliver, Julie Trippetti, Jacque Schneider

Proofreaders: Vickie Broyles, Susan Moritz, Marianne Santy, York Production Services, Inc.

Indexer: York Production Services, Inc.

Special Help

   Diana Conover, Amy Pettinnella, Mica Johnson, Beth Parlon

General and Administrative

IDG Books Worldwide, Inc.: John Kilcullen, CEO

IDG Books Technology Publishing Group: Richard Swadley, Senior Vice President and Publisher; Walter R. Bruce III, Vice President and Publisher; Joseph Wikert, Vice President and Publisher; Mary Bednarek, Vice President and Director, Product Development; Andy Cummings, Publishing Director, General User Group; Mary C. Corder, Editorial Director; Barry Pruett, Publishing Director

IDG Books Consumer Publishing Group: Roland Elgey, Senior Vice President and Publisher; Kathleen A. Welton, Vice President and Publisher; Kevin Thornton, Acquisitions Manager; Kristin A. Cocks, Editorial Director

IDG Books Internet Publishing Group: Brenda McLaughlin, Senior Vice President and Publisher; Sofia Marchant, Online Marketing Manager

IDG Books Production for Branded Press: Debbie Stailey, Director of Production; Cindy L. Phipps, Manager of Project Coordination, Production Proofreading, and Indexing; Tony Augsburger, Manager of Prepress, Reprints, and Systems; Laura Carpenter, Production Control Manager; Shelley Lea, Supervisor of Graphics and Design; Debbie J. Gates, Production Systems Specialist; Robert Springer, Supervisor of Proofreading; Trudy Coler, Page Layout Manager; Troy Barnes, Page Layout Supervisor, Kathie Schutte, Senior Page Layout Supervisor; Michael Sullivan, Production Supervisor

Packaging and Book Design: Patty Page, Manager, Promotions Marketing

◆

The publisher would like to give special thanks to Patrick J. McGovern, without whom this book would not have been possible.

◆

Contents at a Glance

Cartoons at a Glance

By Rich Tennant

page 7

page 185

page 321

page 293

page 63

Fax: 978-546-7747
E-mail: richtennant@the5thwave.com
World Wide Web: www.the5thwave.com

Table of Contents

Introduction

· ·

Welcome to *Microsoft Windows Me Millennium Edition For Dummies!*

This book boils down to this simple fact: Some people want to be Windows wizards. They love interacting with dialog boxes. While sitting in front of their computers, they randomly press keys on their keyboards, hoping to stumble onto a hidden, undocumented feature. They memorize long strings of computer commands while rinsing dishes to go in the dishwasher.

And you? Well, you're no dummy, that's for sure. In fact, you're much more developed than most computer nerds. You can make casual conversation with a neighbor without mumbling about ordering pizzas over the Internet, for example. But when it comes to Windows and computers, the fascination just isn't there. You just want to get your work done, feed the cat, and relax for a while. You have no intention of changing, and there's nothing wrong with that.

That's where this book comes in handy. It won't try to turn you into a Windows wizard, but you'll pick up a few chunks of useful computing information while reading it. Instead of becoming a Windows Me expert, you'll know just enough to get by quickly, cleanly, and with a minimum of pain so that you can move on to the more pleasant things in life.

About This Book

Don't try to read this book in one sitting; there's no need to. Instead, treat this book like a dictionary or an encyclopedia. Turn to the page with the information you need and say, "Ah, so that's what they're talking about." Then put down the book and move on.

Don't bother trying to remember all the Windows Me buzzwords, such as "Select the menu item from the drop-down list box." Leave that stuff for the computer gurus. In fact, if anything technical comes up in a chapter, a road sign warns you well in advance. That way, you can either slow down to read it or speed on around it.

You won't find any fancy computer jargon in this book. Instead, you'll find subjects like these, discussed in plain old English:

- Why did they choose a dumb name like "Windows Me"?
- Finding the file you saved yesterday
- Moving those little windows around on the screen with the mouse
- Making Windows Me run a little better
- Performing chores in Windows Me that you used to do in older versions of Windows
- Starting and closing programs by clicking the mouse button

There's nothing to memorize and nothing to learn. Just turn to the right page, read the brief explanation, and get back to work. Unlike other books, this one enables you to bypass the technical hoopla and still get your work done.

How to Use This Book

Something in Windows Me will eventually leave you scratching your head. No other program brings so many buttons, bars, and babble to the screen. When something in Windows Me has you stumped, use this book as a reference. Look for the troublesome topic in this book's table of contents or index. The table of contents lists chapter and section titles and page numbers. The index lists topics and page numbers. Page through the table of contents or index to the spot that deals with that particular bit of computer obscurity, read only what you have to, close the book, and apply what you've read.

If you're feeling spunky and want to learn something, read a little further. You can find a few completely voluntary extra details or some cross-references to check out. There's no pressure, though. You won't be forced to learn anything that you don't want to or that you simply don't have time for.

If you have to type something into the computer, you'll see easy-to-follow text like this:

```
http://www.vw.com
```

In the preceding example, you type the cryptic string of letters **http://www. vw.com** and then press the keyboard's Enter key. Typing words into a computer can be confusing, so a description of what you're supposed to type usually follows. That way, you can type the words exactly as they're supposed to be typed.

Whenever I describe a message or information that you see on-screen, I present it in the same way, as follows:

```
This is a message on-screen.
```

This book doesn't wimp out by saying, "For further information, consult your manual." No need to pull on your wading boots. This book covers everything you need to know to use Windows Me. You won't find information about running specific Windows software packages, such as Microsoft Office. Windows Me is complicated enough on its own! Luckily, other ...*For Dummies* books mercifully explain most popular software packages.

Don't feel abandoned, though. This book covers Windows in plenty of detail for you to get the job done. Plus, if you have questions or comments about *Microsoft Windows Me For Dummies,* feel free to drop me a line on my Web site at www.andyrathbone.com.

Finally, keep in mind that this book is a *reference*. It's not designed to teach you how to use Windows Me like an expert, heaven forbid. Instead, this book dishes out enough bite-sized chunks of information so that you don't *have* to learn Windows.

When you're ready for some more-advanced Windows Me information, pick up a copy of *MORE Microsoft Windows Me For Dummies.* It grabs you gently by the hand where this book left off, and leads you through some of the Windows Me program's more tumultuous ground.

Please Don't Read This!

Computers thrive on technical stuff. Luckily, you're warned in advance when you're heading for something even vaguely obtuse. Chances are, it's just more minute detail concerning something you've already read about. Feel free to skip any section labeled Technical Stuff. Those niblets of information aren't what this book is about. But if you're feeling particularly ornery, keep reading, and you may learn something. (Just don't let anybody see you do it.)

And What about You?

Well, chances are that you have a computer. You have Windows Me or are thinking about picking up a copy. You know what *you* want to do with your computer. The problem lies in making the *computer* do what you want it to do. You've gotten by one way or another, hopefully with the help of a computer guru — either a friend at the office, somebody down the street, or your fourth-grader. Unfortunately, though, that computer guru isn't always around. This book can be a substitute during your times of need. Keep a doughnut or Pokémon card nearby, however, just in case you need a quick bribe.

How This Book Is Organized

The information in this book has been well sifted. This book contains five parts, and each part is divided into chapters related to the part's theme. Each chapter is divided into short sections to help you navigate the stormy seas of Windows Me. Sometimes, you may find what you're looking for in a small, boxed tip. Other times, you may need to cruise through an entire section or chapter. It's up to you and the particular task at hand.

Here are the categories (the envelope, please):

Part I: Bare-Bones Windows Me Stuff

This book starts out with the basics. You find out how to turn on your computer and how to examine your computer's parts and what Windows Me does to them. It explains all the Windows Me stuff that everybody thinks that you already know. It explains the new features in Windows Me, separating the wheat from the chaff while leaving out any thick, technical oatmeal. You discover whether your computer has enough oomph to run Windows Me. And you end this part (with great relief) by turning off your computer.

Part II: Making Windows Me Do Something

The program sits on the screen, playing jazzy tunes and flashing exciting pictures. But how do you make the darn thing do something _useful?_ Here, you find ways to overcome the frustratingly playful tendencies of Windows Me and force it to shovel the walkway or blow leaves off the driveway.

Part III: Using Windows Me Applications (And Surfing the Web, Should the Mood Strike)

Windows Me comes with a whole bunch of free programs. In this part, you find practical information about your new word processor and WebTV for Windows, as well as ways to start playing with that World Wide Web thing everyone is mumbling about suspiciously. You discover what the funky, new Windows Me Active Desktop is all about and why your computer screen looks like a billboard for Microsoft products. In fact, punching the right buttons turns your desktop's background — its wallpaper — into customized Internet Web pages. Zounds!

Part IV: Help!

Although glass doesn't shatter when Windows Me crashes, it still hurts. In this part, you find some soothing salves for the most painful irritations. Plus, you find ways to unleash the Windows Me program's wise new team of powerful Troubleshooting Wizards. Imagine: A computer that can finally wave a wand and fix itself!

Part V: The Part of Tens

Everybody loves lists (except during tax time). This part contains lists of Windows-related trivia — ten aggravating things about Windows Me (and how to fix them), ten ways to fix confusing Internet problems, ten confusing Windows Me icons and what they mean, ten expensive things that make Windows Me easier, and other shoulder-rubbing solutions for tense problems.

Appendixes

Windows Me didn't come preinstalled on your computer? Flip to the back of the book for tips on transferring the software from the box onto your computer. The official Windows Me glossary lurks back here, too, ready to explain funky computer terms like "32-bit."

Icons Used in This Book

Already seen Windows? Then you've probably noticed its *icons,* which are little pictures for starting various programs. The icons in this book fit right in. They're even a little easier to figure out:

Watch out! This signpost warns you that pointless technical information is coming around the bend. Swerve away from this icon, and you'll be safe from the awful technical drivel.

This icon alerts you about juicy information that makes computing easier. For example, remove your new Windows CE palmtop from your back pants pocket *before* sitting down at the bar.

Don't forget to remember these important points. (Or at least dog-ear the pages so that you can look them up again a few days later.)

The computer won't explode while you're performing the delicate operations associated with this icon. Still, wearing gloves and proceeding with caution is a good idea when this icon is near.

Already familiar with Windows 98, the predecessor to Windows Me? This icon marks information that can ease the transition from the two systems.

Where to Go from Here

Now, you're ready for action. Give the pages a quick flip and maybe scan through a few sections that you know you'll need later. Oh, and this is *your* book — your weapon against the computer criminals who've inflicted this whole complicated computer concept on you. So pretend you're back in grade school and you can't get caught: Circle any paragraphs you find useful, highlight key concepts, cover up the technical drivel with sticky notes, and draw gothic gargoyles in the margins next to the complicated stuff.

The more you mark up your book, the easier it will be for you to find all the good stuff again.

Part I
Bare-Bones
Windows Me Stuff

The 5th Wave   By Rich Tennant

"HEY DAD, IS IT ALL RIGHT IF I WINDOW YOUR COMPUTER?"

In this part . . .

Windows Me is an exciting, new way to use the computer. That means it's as confusing as a new car's dashboard. Even the most wizened old computer buffs stumble in this strange new land of boxes, bars, and bizarre oddities like push technology.

Never used a computer before but bought Windows Me because it's "easy to use"? Well, Windows Me can be intuitive, but that doesn't mean that it's as easy to figure out as a steak knife.

In fact, most people are dragged into Windows Me without a choice. Your new computer probably came with a version of Windows Me already installed. Or maybe you had Windows Me installed at the office, where everyone has to learn it except for Jerry, who moved over to the Art Department and got his own Macintosh. Or perhaps the latest version of your favorite program, like Microsoft Word, requires Windows Me, so you've had to learn to live with the darn thing.

No matter how you were introduced, you can adjust to Windows Me, just like you eventually learned to live comfortably with that funky college roommate who kept leaving hair clogs in the shower.

Whatever your situation, this part keeps things safe and sane, with the water flowing smoothly. If you're new to computers, the first chapter answers the question you've been afraid to ask around the lunch room: "Just what is this Windows Me thing, anyway?"

Chapter 1

What Is Windows Me?

*O*ne way or another, you've probably already heard about Microsoft Windows. Windows posters line the walls of computer stores. While you're stuck in traffic, the Microsoft roadside billboards cheerfully ask, "Where do you want to go today?" Everybody who's anybody talks breezily about Windows, the Internet, and the World Wide Web. Weird code words, like www.vw.com, stare out cryptically from magazine, newspaper, and television advertisements.

To help you play catch-up in the world of Windows, this chapter fills you in on the basics of the latest version of Windows, called *Windows Me*. The chapter explains what Windows Me is and what it can do. This chapter also shows that Windows Me works with your older Windows programs.

What Are Windows and Windows Me?

Windows is just another piece of software, like the zillions of others lining the store shelves. But it's not a program in the normal sense — something that lets you write letters or lets your coworkers play Bozark the Destroyer over the office network after everybody else goes home. Rather, Windows controls the way you work with your computer.

For years, computers have clung to a typewriter-style of work. Just as on a typewriter, people type letters and numbers into the computer. The computer listens and then places letters and numbers onto the screen. This time-tested system works well. But it takes a long time to learn, and it's as boring as reading the ingredients on a jar of reduced-fat mayonnaise.

The method is boring because computer engineers designed computers for other computer engineers many moons ago. They thought that computers would be forever isolated in narrow hallways where somber youngsters with crewcuts, clipboards, and white lab coats jotted down notes while the big reels whirled. Nobody expected normal people to use computers — especially not in their offices, their dens, or even in their kitchens.

✔ Windows software dumps the typewriter analogy and updates the *look* of computers. Windows replaces the words and numbers with pictures and fun buttons. It's smooth and shiny, like an expensive new coffeemaker.

✔ Windows Me is the most powerful personal computer version of Windows software — software that's been updated many times since starting to breathe in January 1985. It's short for Windows *Millennium,* but Microsoft labels it "Windows Me." I don't know why. Nobody else likes the name, either.

✔ Programmer types say Windows software is big enough and powerful enough to be called an *operating system.* That's because Windows "operates" your computer. Most computer users, however, call Windows lots of other names, including some that my editor won't let me publish here.

✔ *Windows 2000* is Microsoft's biggest, most powerful version of Windows. Stronger and more full-featured than Windows Me, Windows 2000 is favored mostly by large office networks so all the computers can talk to each other. In fact, Microsoft eventually plans to discontinue its Windows Me line in favor of its Windows 2000 series. (That means it also gets its own book, *Windows 2000 Professional For Dummies,* written by me and Sharon Crawford, and published by IDG Books Worldwide, Inc.)

Windows 2000 isn't the replacement for Windows 98, even though its name sounds like it's the logical next step. No, Windows 2000 is the latest version of Windows NT, the corporate version of Windows used for networking. Windows Me — also known as Windows Millennium — is the replacement for Windows 98, even though the two names have nothing in common.

What Does Windows Do?

Like the mother with the whistle in the lunch court, Windows controls all the parts of your computer. You turn on your computer, start Windows, and start running programs. Each program runs in its own little *window* on-screen, as shown in Figure 1-1. Yet Windows keeps things safe, even if the programs start throwing food at each other.

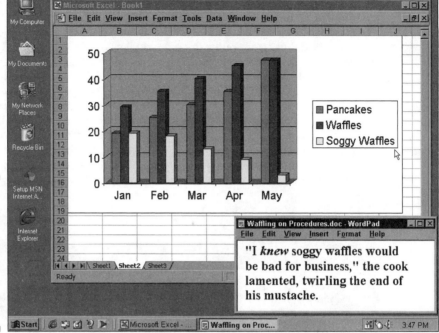

Figure 1-1:
The
Windows
Me desktop
runs
programs
in little
on-screen
windows.

Windows gets its name from all the cute little windows on-screen. Each window shows some information: a picture, perhaps, or a program that you're running. You can put several windows on-screen at the same time and jump from window to window, visiting different programs.

Some people say that colorful windows and pictures make Windows easier to use; others say that Windows is a little too arty. To write a letter in Windows Me, for example, do you select the picture of the notepad, the quill, or the clipboard? And what potential problems can emerge with the icons of the spinning globe and the bomb?

> ✔ A computer environment that uses little pictures and symbols is called a *graphical user interface,* or *GUI.* (It's pronounced *gooey,* believe it or not.) Pictures require more computing horsepower than letters and numbers, so Windows Me requires a relatively powerful computer. (You can find a list of its requirements in Chapter 2.)

> ✔ When the word *Windows* starts with a capital letter, it refers to the Windows program. When the word *windows* starts with a lowercase letter, it refers to windows you see on-screen. When the word *Windows* ends with the letters "Me", it refers to the latest version of the Windows software, Windows Me.

Because Windows uses graphics, it's much easier to use than to describe. To tell someone how to move through a Windows document you say, "Click in the vertical scroll bar beneath the scroll box." Those directions sound awfully weird, but after you've done it, you'll say, "Oh, is that all? Golly!" (Plus, you can still press the PgDn key in Windows. You don't have to "click in the vertical scroll bar beneath the scroll box" if you don't want to.)

With Windows Me, your desktop doesn't have to look like a typewritten page *or* a desktop. Now, it can look like an Internet Web page, as shown in Figure 1-2. (You can find more about Web pages and the Internet in Chapter 13.) In fact, the chameleonlike Windows Me can run like a Web page, use the "Classic Windows 95" settings, or let you customize it with any combination. That introduces many more ways for things to go wrong.

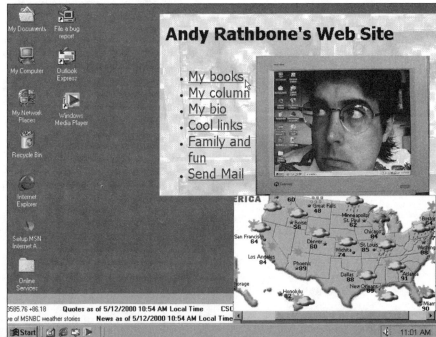

Figure 1-2: Windows Me enables "Web surfers" to fill their desktop with pages from the Internet.

How Does Windows Me Affect My Older Programs?

Windows Me can still run most of your older Windows programs, too, thank goodness. So after upgrading to Windows Me, you won't have to buy expensive new software immediately. It runs almost all Windows 98 and Windows 95 programs, as well as many Windows 3.1 programs.

If you're finally upgrading from an old computer that uses DOS, Windows Me can probably still run your old DOS programs. (Your dusty old computer probably won't have enough oomph to run Windows Me, but you probably wanted a new one, anyway.)

✔ When people say *Windows 3.1,* they're often referring to several older versions of Windows: *Windows 3.11, Windows for Workgroups 3.1,* and *Windows for Workgroups 3.11.* Each version is just a slightly improved reworking of its predecessor, however. *Windows 3.1* is easiest to say, so that's the phrase most people use. (Some programmers use the term Windows 3.*x,* however, just to add a scientific touch.)

✔ Most programs from the Windows 3.0 generation or earlier simply can't keep up with Windows Me: Retire them.

✔ You can't take Windows Me, install it onto your five-year-old computer, and expect it to run well. No, Windows Me is a big operating system for a big computer. You'll probably have to buy a new one or add bigger shoulders to your older one. (In computer language, *big shoulders* translate to a faster CPU chip, more memory, a larger hard drive, and a CD-ROM drive.) Unfortunately, adding bigger shoulders often costs more than buying a new PC.

When people say that Windows Me is *backward compatible,* they just mean that it can run software that was written for older versions of Windows. You can still run most Windows 95 and Windows 3.1 software on Windows Me, for example, as well as most DOS software. (Don't even think about running Macintosh software, though.)

Should I Bother Using Windows Me?

Windows 95 and Windows 98 users are elbowing each other nervously by the water cooler and whispering the Big Question: Why bother buying Windows Me, going through the hassle of installing it, and learning all its new programs?

Here's why: Windows Me comes preinstalled on most new computers, so many people are simply stuck with it. Also, Windows Me offers quite a few improvements over earlier versions, as you'll find out in the next two sections.

Basically, the upgrade question boils down to this answer: If your computer crashes a lot when using Windows 95 or Windows 98, it may be time to upgrade. But if you're happy with your current computer setup, don't bother. After all, why buy new tires if your old ones still have some life left?

Upgrading from Windows 95

Upgrading from Windows 95? Then you'll find Windows Me easier to install. Plus, it handles files faster and more efficiently on today's powerhouse PCs.

It can automatically run background maintenance tasks to keep itself "tuned up" and ready to run. If you have access to the Internet, Windows Me can diagnose itself to see if it's up to date and then automatically grab the latest files it needs to keep running smoothly.

Technolusters who like the latest and greatest gadgets will like the new "TV Tuner" programs for watching TV on their monitors (provided they shell out a hundred bucks or so for a TV card). Or if your desk is big enough, splurge on another monitor. Windows Me lets you arrange your desktop across both monitors, doubling your workspace. Whoopee!

If you're an Internet devotee, you'll like the way Windows Me wraps itself around Microsoft's Web browser, Internet Explorer. Not only can you make your computer look like a Web page, but you can also have parts of Web pages embedded in your desktop and running in the background — where the boss can't notice 'em as much.

Finally, Windows makes the Internet act more like a television, with easily switchable — and customizable — Channels. You'll find Channels for Disney, America Online, Warner Brothers, and other large corporate conglomerations.

Upgrading from Windows 3.1

Windows 3.1 users who skipped Windows 95 will be pleasantly surprised: They won't have to point and click as much to find files and start programs. For example, Windows Me remembers the names of files or programs you've recently used and stores their names in a special spot. Do you want to load the file again? Just click on the file's name from the pop-up list — no wading through menus or opening programs: White-gloved Windows Me opens the car door and lets you start moving immediately.

You see lots more little buttons with pictures on them — *icons* — used in Windows Me programs. You don't know what the icon with the little butterfly picture is supposed to do? Then just rest your mouse pointer over the icon; after a few seconds, a message often pops up on-screen, explaining the butterfly button's role among the fields of Windows. The most helpful messages appear when you rest the pointer over the unlabeled buttons that hang out along the tops of programs, such as word processors and spreadsheets, in their *toolbar* areas.

Should I upgrade from Windows 98 to Windows Me?

Here's the ugly truth about Windows Me that you may not hear anyplace else. Windows Me is really just a slightly polished version of Windows 98. Although Microsoft gave it a face-lift, Windows Me really acts almost identically to its cousin.

The big difference? Microsoft changed lots of the icons so they look like its other, corporate-level program called Windows 2000. The changes are more than cosmetic, too. Windows Me makes it easier to work with today's digital cameras by including a video editor. The Media

Player has been enhanced to tune in Internet radio stations and to create categorized playlists of your MP3, audio CDs, and video clips. In short, it's competing with RealAudio, WinAmp, and other third-party programs catering to today's multimedia-craving users.

Some people will be excited by these new-tech changes. Others won't bother installing them, because they prefer the third-party programs. And others will wonder if Windows Me is even worth the upgrade in the first place. Only you can decide.

Windows Me allows longer filenames, just like Windows 95 and Windows 98. After 15 years of frustration, PC users can call their files something more descriptive than RPT45.TXT. In fact, Windows offers you 255 characters to describe your creations.

✔ Ready to upgrade your computer? Windows Me can give you a hand with its upgraded "Plug and Play" concept. A new Windows Me "Wizard" keeps better track of the parts inside your computer and can alert you when internal brawls start. Better yet, it prevents many brawls from even starting by making sure that two computer parts aren't assigned the same areas of your computer's memory.

✔ Windows Me automates many computing chores. To install a program, for example, just push the floppy disk (or compact disc) into the drive and click the Control Panel's Add/Remove Programs button (which I cover in Chapter 9, by the way). Windows searches all your drives for the installation program and runs it automatically. Windows Me can automatically search for any new hardware you've installed as well, recognizing quite a few of the most popular upgrades.

✔ Are you tired of twiddling your thumbs while Windows formats a floppy? Windows Me can handle floppy chores in the background so that you can continue playing your card game. (The card game, FreeCell, is an incredibly delicious time-waster.)

Bracing Yourself (and Your Computer) for Windows Me

With Windows, everything happens at the same time. Its many different parts run around like hamsters with an open cage door. Programs cover each other up on-screen. They overlap corners, hiding each other's important parts. Occasionally, they simply disappear.

Be prepared for a bit of frustration when things don't behave properly. You may be tempted to stand up, bellow, and toss a nearby stapler across the room. After that, calmly pick up this book, find the trouble spot listed in the index, and turn to the page with the answer.

- Windows software may be accommodating, but that can cause problems, too. For example, Windows Me often offers more than three different ways for you to perform the same computing task. Don't bother memorizing each command. Just choose one method that works for you and stick with it. For example, Andrew and Deirdre Kleske use scissors to cut their freshly delivered pizza into slices. It stupefies most of their houseguests, but it gets the job done.

- Windows Me runs best on a powerful new computer with the key words *Pentium II, Pentium III, K6-III, AMD Athlon,* or *testosterone* somewhere in the description. Look for as much *RAM* (Random-Access Memory) and as many *gigabytes* as you can afford. You can find the detailed rundown of the Windows Me finicky computer requirements in Chapter 2.

Chapter 2

Ignore This Chapter on Computer Parts

. . . .

In This Chapter

▶ Finding out the names for the gizmos and gadgets on the computer

▶ Understanding what all those things do

▶ Finding out what stuff your computer needs in order to use Windows Me

. . . .

*T*his chapter introduces computer gizmos and gadgets. Go ahead and ignore it. Who cares about what all your PC gadgetry is called? Unless your PC's beeping at you like a car alarm (or not beeping when it's supposed to beep), don't bother messing with it. Just dog-ear the top of this page, say, "So, that's where all that stuff is explained," and keep going.

In Windows Me, you just press the buttons. Windows Me does the dirty work, scooting over to the right part of your computer and kick-starting the action. In case Windows Me stubs a toe, this chapter explains where you may need to put the bandages. And, as always, the foulest-smelling technical chunks are clearly marked; just hold your nose while stepping over them gingerly.

The Computer

The computer is that box with all the cables. Officially, it probably answers to one of two names: IBM (called *True Blue* when people try to dump their old ones in the classifieds) or an *IBM compatible* or *clone.*

However, most people just call their computers *PCs* because that's what IBM called its first *personal computer* back in 1981. In fact, the first IBM PC started this whole personal computing craze, although some people lay the blame on video games.

The concept of a small computer that could be pecked on in an office or den caught on well with the average Joe, and IBM made gobs of money. So much money, in fact, that other companies immediately ripped off the IBM design.

They *cloned,* or copied, IBM's handiwork to make a computer that worked just like it. Made by companies like Dell and Gateway, they're *compatible* with IBM's own PC; they can all use the same software as an IBM PC without spitting up.

IBM-compatible computers generally have an obscure brand name and a lower price on their invoice, but they often work just as well (or better) than IBM's own line of computers. In fact, more people own compatibles than own IBM's own line of personal computers.

- ✔ Windows Me runs equally well on IBM-compatible computers and on IBM's own computers; the key word is *IBM.* Computers from other planets, like the Macintosh, don't run Windows Me, but their owners don't care. They just smile pleasantly when you try to figure out how to create a Windows Me "file association."

- ✔ Okay, so a Macintosh can *run* some third-party versions of Windows software, but you need a special (and expensive) breed of Windows-emulating software. These days, you're probably better off sticking with either a Mac or a PC — don't try to interbreed their brands of software.

- ✔ Older computers lay flat across a desktop; newer computers, called *tower* PCs, stand upright, usually on the floor. The tilt doesn't affect the computer's performance, but it does make them look cool and commanding. In fact, some muscular people heft their old desktop PCs onto one side and put them in a special stand so they look cool, too.

- ✔ As other companies built *compatible* computers, they strayed from the original IBM design. They added sound, color, and dozens of exciting new internal parts. Luckily, Windows Me identifies what computer parts it's dealing with automatically, so it knows what tone of voice to use when speaking with them. Most identification problems pop up when first installing Windows Me — a topic covered step by step in this book's Appendix A.

- ✔ Laptop and notebook computers can run Windows Me with no problems. Palmtops and other handheld computers can't; they run an itty-bitty version of Windows called Windows CE. (Windows CE Version 3.0 runs on Microsoft's new "Pocket PCs," designed to compete with the much more successful PalmPilots.)

The Microprocessor (CPU)

The computer's brain is a chunk of silicon buried deep inside the computer's case; it's grown from the size of a cracker to a mammoth chocolate bar. This flat computer chip is the *microprocessor,* but nerds tend to call it a *central processing unit,* or *CPU.* (You may have seen flashy microprocessor TV commercials that say "Intel Inside." Intel is a leading CPU developer.)

The computer's microprocessor determines how fast and powerful the computer can toss information around. Refer to Table 2-1 for a look at the power of your particular computer.

Table 2-1	Microprocessor Power Ratings
Computer	*Comments*
XT, AT, 386SX, 386DX	Nearly obsolete, these chips can't handle Windows Me. These computers make great gifts to friends and charities.
486SX, 486DX	A few of these chips can barely run Windows Me, but much too slowly. Get rid of 'em.
Pentium (sometimes called 586 or AMD-K6)	A Pentium runs Windows Me much faster than a 486, meaning less thumb-twiddling while opening programs and files. (Computer games play much smoother, too.)
Pentium Pro	The Pentium Pro was designed specifically to run the more-powerful versions of Windows, like Windows 98 and Windows NT. So it runs Windows Me faster than a plain old Pentium. (But not by much.)
Pentium II	These are basically fast Pentium Pros with special "MMX" technology tossed in for faster graphics and videos. (MMX once stood for *Multi Media eXtensions,* but Intel registered the acronym as a brand name so nobody could rip it off.)
Pentium III, Itanium	Intel's stoked up the power of these, its latest CPUs, and sprinkled more speedy graphics technology on top. Windows Me screams in ecstasy over these CPUs. (Although Microsoft says Windows Me works with a fast Pentium, all of its software won't run well until you use a Pentium III.)
"Celeron", "Xeon", and Mobile	Pentium chips labeled "Celeron" are the budget models without as much oomph as the more luxurious and powerful Xeon chips. These Mobile models, designed for laptops, are small, cool, and power-conscious. Windows Me works reasonably well with these CPUs.
AMD and Cyrix chips	Intel isn't the only chipmaker, just the most expensive. AMD (Advanced Micro Devices) and Cyrix grab the budget market with chips that deliver high performance, a low price, and no big name. Windows Me prefers AMD's K6-3 or Athalon CPU or the latest from Cyrix (whenever Cyrix comes up with their new power CPU.)

- ✔ A microprocessor is the current evolution of the gadget that powered those little 1970s pocket calculators. It performs all the computer's background calculations, from juggling spreadsheets to swapping dirty jokes through office e-mail.

- ✔ Microprocessors are described by several numbers. Generally, the bigger the numbers, the faster and more powerful the chip.

- ✔ Intel assigns three numbers to its Pentium chips. The chip's model number — Pentium, Pentium II, Pentium III — comes in Roman numerals. The chip's processing speed is measured in *megahertz*, or *MHz*. The *cache* size (pronounced "cash") is measured in *kilobytes*, like 512K. When comparing Pentiums, just remember that the bigger the number, the faster Windows performs.

Disks and Disk Drives

The computer's *disk drive*, that thin slot in its front side, is like the drawer at the bank's drive-up teller window. That disk drive enables you to send and retrieve information from the computer. Instead of making you drop information into a cashier's drawer, the computer makes you send and receive your information from disks. The most popular types — the floppy disk, the compact disc, the hard disk, the DVD, and the Zip drive — appear in the next five sections.

Not sure what kilobyte (K), megabyte (MB), and gigabyte (GB) mean? Head for that section a few pages later on in this chapter.

Floppy disks

You can shove anything that's flat into a floppy drive, but the computer recognizes only one thing: *floppy disks.* Things get a little weird here, so hang on tight. See, by some bizarre bit of mechanical wizardry, computers store information on disks as a stream of magnetic impulses.

A disk drive spits those little magnetic impulses onto the floppy disk for safe storage. The drive can slurp the information back up, too. You just push the disk into the disk drive and tell Windows whether to spit or slurp information. That's known as *copy to* or *copy from* in computer parlance.

Floppy disks are sturdy 3½-inch squares that are losing popularity in favor of the compact disc, or CD, which I describe next.

- A disk drive automatically grabs the 3½-inch disk when you push it in far enough. You hear it *clunk,* and the disk sinks down into the drive. If it doesn't, you're putting it in the wrong way. (The disk's silver edge goes in first, with the little round silver thing in the middle facing down.) To retrieve the disk, push the button protruding from around the drive's slot and then grab the disk when the drive kicks it out.

- Computer stores sell blank floppy disks so that you can copy your work onto them. Unless your new box of blank disks has the word *preformatted,* you can't use them straight out of the box. They must be *formatted* first. I cover this merry little chore in Chapter 11.

- Computers love to *copy* things. When you're copying a file from one disk to another, you aren't *moving* the file. You're just placing a copy of that file onto that other disk. (Of course, you can *move* the files over there, if you want, as I describe in Chapter 11.)

Compact discs (CD-ROM drive stuff)

Computer technicians snapped up compact disc technology pretty quickly when they realized that the shiny discs could store numbers as well as music. Today, most companies sell their programs and information on compact discs. A single compact disc holds more information than hundreds of floppy disks.

To use a disc, however, your computer needs its own compact disc drive. The CD player with your stereo won't cut it. Luckily, most compact disc drives let you access programs *and* play music through your PC. Now you can sell the CD player attached to your stereo. (It's getting old anyway.)

CDs enter your computer in a more dignified way than a floppy disk. Push a button on your compact disc drive, and the drive spits out a little platter. Place the CD on the platter, label side up, and push the little button again. The computer grabs the CD, ready for action. (If the button's too hard to reach, just nudge the platter, and it'll retreat.)

- For years, you couldn't copy files onto a compact disc — you could only read information from them. Only the people at the CD factory could copy files to CDs, and that's because they had a whoppingly expensive machine. Now, many cheap compact disc drives let you read *and* copy files and music to your own discs. In fact, copyright attorneys are holding international conferences to make sure that nobody can create copies of their favorite Pearl Jam albums and give them to their friends.

- A CD that stores information until it's full is known as a CD-R. A CD that can read, write, erase, and then write more information is called a CD-RW. Naturally, the CD-RW discs cost much more than their limited cousins.

✓ Compact disc is spelled with a *c* to confuse people accustomed to seeing disk ending with a *k*.

✓ Multimedia computers need a sound card as well as a compact drive; the drive alone isn't enough. This requirement is the computer industry's special way of making people spend more money. And, of course, most of today's computers come with a built-in CD-ROM drive and sound card.

✓ The Windows Me Sound Recorder can record lousy sounding MP3 files — cool little files containing songs from your CDs. For the latest information about MP3, pick up my book, *MP3 For Dummies,* published by IDG Books Worldwide, Inc. (in case you had any doubt about the publisher of all these black-and-yellow-covered books).

✓ The latest compact disc drives play both CDs and *DVD discs* — the CDs with movies on them. DVD players get their own section coming up next.

✓ Windows Me offers technology called *Autoplay.* Just pop the CD into the CD-ROM drive, and Windows Me automatically revs it up, whether the disc contains music, programs, or trendy videos of glassblowers in Italy. Autoplay is one more step toward eliminating installation hassles. If Windows Me doesn't Autoplay your CD, see Chapter 18 for the fix.

DVD discs

Although it's hard to tell the difference between a DVD disc and a compact disc by looking, the computer certainly knows. A DVD disc holds *much* more information — enough information to hold an entire movie in several languages and extra perks, such as a director's voiceover explaining why a certain actress giggled during certain shots.

A DVD player costs a bit more, but it plays back music CDs as well as DVDs (the kind you rent or buy in video stores).

They're great for computer nerds who love watching movies on a 15-inch computer monitor with tiny speakers. Nearly everybody else prefers watching DVDs on their living room TV or home theater.

Although nearly every sound card works with a DVD player, only special DVD-compatible sound cards can play the extra "surround sound" stored on a DVD.

Iomega drives

The robotic-sounding Zip, Jaz, and the laptop-ready Clik drives from Iomega are thick plastic disks that hold 100MB or more of information, making them convenient for backing up garage-sized boxes of data.

They're very convenient — not only for people who always run out of data space, but also for people who've been burned a few times and always like to keep plenty of backups.

✔ Iomega's Zip drives are the small, portable gadgets that look sort of like a Sony Walkman. The Jaz drives hold up to 2 gigabytes; they fit into the computer like a regular floppy drive, but with a bigger slot. The portable Clik drives fit into a shirt pocket, ready to store 40 megabytes of information from a laptop or digital camera.

✔ Zip, Jaz, and Clik drives provide an easy way to move large amounts of data from the office to home and back — if you're forced to even consider such a thing.

Hard disks

Not every computer has a compact disc drive, Iomega drive, or even a floppy drive, but just about everybody has a hard disk: thick little Frisbees inside the computer that can hold thousands of times more information than floppy disks. Hard disks are also much quicker at reading and writing information. (They're a great deal quieter, too, thank goodness.) Windows Me insists on a hard disk because it's such a huge program.

The programs that run under Windows Me can be pretty huge, too. The Microsoft Monster Truck Madness game grabs 200MB of hard disk space if you install all the coolest options. Microsoft recommends a 1-gigabyte hard drive for video cards that let you watch TV.

✔ The point? Buy the largest hard disk you can afford. If you're shopping for a computer, make sure that it has room to add a second hard disk. Windows loves two disks, and you'll eventually need the room.

✔ If a program has a lot of *multimedia* — sounds, graphics, or movies — you need a huge hard disk or perhaps a second one. That type of information eats up the most space on a hard disk.

Windows Me comes with "DriveSpace 3," but that program no longer compresses hard drives. It now works only with floppies and other removable drives. Don't bother with it, though. Save disk tweaking for people who *like* to play with their computer's ailing innards.

What disk drives does Windows Me like?

Windows Me can easily eat up 500MB of space, depending on how much of it you choose to install. Your Windows Me programs can eat up even more space. Nobody will laugh if you buy an 8-gigabyte or larger hard drive for Windows Me and your Windows Me programs. (A single gigabyte equals roughly 1,000 megabytes.)

You also want a CD-ROM drive, or you won't be able to use most of today's programs. In fact, buy one that can both read and write to the CD-R compact discs explained a few sections ago. Those discs only cost a few dollars, and they're a quick and easy way to back up your computer, store digital photos, or save those special things you don't want to lose.

What does write-protected mean?

Write protection is supposed to be a helpful safety feature, but most people discover it through an abrupt bit of computer rudeness: Windows Me stops them short with the threatening message shown in Figure 2-1 while they are trying to copy a file to a floppy disk.

Figure 2-1:
Windows 98
sends an
error
message if
the disk is
write-
protected.

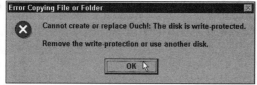

A *write-protected disk* has simply been tweaked so that nobody can copy to it or delete the files it contains. Write protection is a simple procedure, surprisingly enough, requiring no government registration. You can write-protect and unwrite-protect disks in the privacy of your own home.

- ✔ To write-protect a 3½-inch floppy disk, look for a tiny black sliding tab in a square hole in its corner. Slide the tab with a pencil or your thumbnail so that the hole is uncovered. The disk is now write-protected.

- ✔ To remove the write protection on a 3½-inch disk, slide the little black plastic thingy so that the hole is covered up.

- ✔ If you encounter the write-protect error shown in Figure 2-1, wait until the drive stops making noise. Remove the disk, unwrite-protect the disk, and put it back in the drive. Then repeat what you were doing before you were so rudely interrupted.

Disk do's and doughnuts

✔ Do label your disks so that you know what's on them. (You can write on the top side of compact discs with a permanent felt pen.)

✔ Do at least make a valiant effort to peel off a disk's old label before sticking on a new one. (After a while, those stacks of old labels make the disk too fat to fit into the drive.)

✔ Do feel free to write on the label after it has been placed on the disk.

✔ Do not write on the disk's sleeve instead of the label. Disks always end up in each other's sleeves, leading to mistaken identities and faux pas.

✔ Do copy important files from your hard disk to floppy disks or compact discs on a regular basis. (This routine is called *backing up* in computer lingo. Windows comes with special backup software to make this chore a little easier — not much, but a little.)

✔ Do not leave disks lying in the sun.

✔ Do not place 3½-inch disks next to magnets. Don't place them next to magnets disguised as paper clip holders, either, or next to other common magnetized desktop items, such as older telephones.

✔ Do handle compact discs and DVDs by their edges, not their surfaces. Keep the backside of the disc as clean as possible.

The Mouse and That Double-Click Stuff

The *mouse* is that rounded plastic thing that looks like a child's toy. Marketing people thought that the word *mouse* sounded like fun, so the name stuck. Actually, think of your mouse as your electronic finger, because you use it in Windows Me to point at stuff on-screen.

A mouse has a little roller, or mouse ball, embedded in its belly. (Where were the animal-rights people?) When you move the mouse across your desk, the ball rubs against electronic sensor gizmos. The gizmos record the mouse's movements and send the information down the mouse's tail, which connects to the back of the computer.

As you move the mouse, you see an *arrow,* or *pointer,* move simultaneously across the computer screen. Here's where your electronic finger comes in: When the arrow points at a picture of a button on-screen, you press and release, or *click,* the left button on the mouse. The Windows Me button is selected, just as if you'd pressed it with your finger. It's a cool bit of 3-D computer graphics that makes you want to click buttons again and again.

✔ You control just about everything in Windows Me by pointing at it with the mouse and clicking the mouse button. (The mouse pitches in with a helpful clicking noise when you press its button.)

✔ The plural of mouse is *mice,* just like the ones cats chew on. It's not *mouses.*

✔ Some laptops come with a *touch-pad* — a little square thing for you to slide your finger over. As you move the tip of your finger across the pad, you move the mouse pointer across the screen. Other laptops, like IBM's suave black Thinkpads, have a *Trackpoint,* a little pencil eraser that sticks up out of the keyboard, wedged above the b key and below the g and h. Just push the eraser in the direction you want the mouse to move, and the mouse pointer scurries.

✔ If your mouse doesn't work with Windows Me (it gets the shivers, it scurries around at random, or the arrow doesn't move), visit Chapter 14 for help.

✔ Microsoft's IntelliMouse has what looks like a tiny waterwheel protruding from the mouse's neck. By slowly rolling the waterwheel back and forth with your index finger, you can scroll up or down in your current work, line by line. Fun! Plus, pushing down once on the waterwheel is equivalent to an automatic double-click.

✔ Here's a bit of Windows Me upgrade ugliness: For years, a mouse worked fairly simply in Windows. You pointed at something on the screen — a button for a program, for instance — and clicked twice in rapid succession to load that particular program. Now, Windows Me comes with three different mouse "modes." Sometimes a single click loads a program; other times it takes two clicks. Still other times, the click factor depends on the program's lineage — whether it hails from the Internet. See Chapter 5 for the rundown on these new complications and how to choose your Mouse behavior.

The mouse arrow changes shape, depending on what it's pointing at in Windows Me. When it changes shape, you know that it's ready to perform a new task. Table 2-2 is a handy reference for the different uniforms the mouse pointer wears for different jobs.

Table 2-2	**The Various Shapes of the Mouse Pointer**	
Shape	*What It Points At*	*What to Do When You See It*
	Just about anything	Use this pointer for moving from place to place on-screen. Then click to bring that place to Windows' attention.
	A single window	Uh-oh. You've somehow selected the annoying size or move option from the Control menu. Moving the mouse or pressing the cursor-control keys now makes the current window bigger or smaller. Press Enter when you finish, or press Esc if you want to get away from this uncomfortable bit of weirdness.
	The top or bottom edge of a window	Hold down the mouse button and move the mouse back and forth to make the window grow taller or shorter. Let go when you like the window's new size.
	The left or right side of a window	Hold down the mouse button and move the mouse back and forth to make the window fatter or skinnier. Let go when you like the window's new size.
	The corner of a window	Hold down the mouse button and move the mouse anywhere to make the window fat, skinny, tall, or short. Let go when you're through playing.
	A program or box that accepts text (this pointer is called an I-beam)	Put the pointer where you want words to appear, click the button, and start typing the letters or numbers.
	A word with a hidden meaning in the Windows' help system	Click the mouse, and Windows Me trots out some more helpful information about that particular subject.
	Nothing (Windows is busy ignoring you)	Move the mouse in wild circles and watch the hourglass spin around until Windows catches up with you. This shape usually appears when you are loading files or copying stuff to a floppy disk.
	Anything	Keep working. This pointer means that Windows Me is doing something in the background, so it may work a little more slowly.

(continued)

Table 2-2 (continued)

Shape	What It Points At	What to Do When You See It
☒	Anything	By clicking the little question mark found in the top-right corner of some boxes, you create this pointer. Click confusing on-screen areas for helpful informational handouts.
⊘	Something forbidden	Press the Esc key, let go of the mouse button, and start over. (You're trying to drag something to a place where it doesn't belong.)

Don't worry about memorizing all the various shapes that the pointer takes on. The pointer changes shape automatically at the appropriate times. I describe the shapes here so that you won't think that your pointer's goofing off when it changes shape.

The Microsoft IntelliMouse — the one with the little wheel — comes with bunches of cutesy pointers. Open the Mouse icon in the Windows Control Panel to see them all. When all the cutesy stuff becomes overwhelming, choose None to return to the more reassuring arrow pointer.

Video Cards and Monitors

The *monitor* is the thing you stare at all day until you go home to watch TV. The front of the monitor, called its *screen* or *display,* is where all the Windows Me action takes place. The screen is where you can watch the windows as they bump around, cover each other up, and generally behave like nine people eyeing a recently delivered eight-slice pizza.

Monitors have *two* cords so they won't be mistaken for a mouse. One cord plugs into the electrical outlet; the other heads for the *video card,* a special piece of electronics poking out from the computer's back. The computer tells the video card what it's doing; the card translates the events into graphics information and shoots it up the cable into the monitor, where it appears on-screen.

Ignore these awful graphics terms

Some people describe their monitors as "boxy" or "covered with cat hair;" others use the following strange scientific terms:

Pixel: A pixel is a fancy name for an individual dot on-screen. Everything on-screen is made up of bunches of dots, or pixels. Each pixel can be a different shade or color, which creates the image. (Squint up close and you may be able to make out an individual pixel.) If your thin new LCD monitor has a tiny dot that doesn't match the colors on the rest of your screen, that pixel is "out." Complain, loudly. It occasionally results in a replacement.

Resolution: The resolution is the number of pixels on a screen — specifically, the number of pixels across (horizontal) and down (vertical). More pixels mean greater resolution: smaller letters and more information packed onto the same-sized screen. People with small monitors usually use 640 x 480 resolution. People with larger monitors often switch to 800 x 600 or 1024 x 768 resolution so that they can fit more windows on-screen.

Color: This term describes the number of colors the card and monitor display on-screen. Today's speedy video cards can easily display Windows Me in millions of colors.

Mode: A predetermined combination of pixels, resolution, and colors is described as a graphics *mode*. Right out of the box, Windows Me uses a mode that works for just about everybody. You don't need to know any of this stuff, though. If you're feeling particularly modular, however, you can change the Windows Me graphics modes after reading Chapter 9.

✔ Like herbivores and cellulose-digesting gut microorganisms, monitors and video cards depend upon each other. Neither can function without the other. In fact, your monitor only displays pictures as nicely as your video card can dish them out. Also, LCD monitors require special cards capable of feeding them the right signals.

✔ Unlike other parts of the computer, the video card and monitor don't require any special care and feeding. Just wipe the dust off the screen every once in a while. (And at least *try* to keep the cat off the monitor.)

✔ Spray plain old glass cleaner on a rag and then wipe off the dust with the newly dampened rag. If you spray glass cleaner directly on the screen, it drips down into the monitor's casing, annoying the trolls who sleep under the bridge.

✔ Some glass cleaners contain alcohol, which can cloud the antiglare screens found on some fancy new monitors. When in doubt, check your monitor's manual to see if glass cleaner is allowed. My Nanao monitor came with its own special rag for cleaning the glass.

✔ When you first install Windows Me, it interrogates the video card and monitor until they reveal their brand name and orientation. Windows Me almost always gets the correct answer from them and sets itself up automatically so that everything works fine the first time.

✔ Windows Me may be dominating, but it's accommodating, too. It can handle a wide variety of monitors and cards. In fact, most monitors and cards can switch to different *modes,* putting more or fewer colors on-screen and shrinking the text so that you can cram more information onto the screen. Windows Me enables you to play around with all sorts of different video settings, if you're in that sort of mood. (If you are, check out Chapter 9.)

Hallelujah! If you have lots of money, a big desk, and a case of Windows Lust, Windows Me lets you do two things: First, you can plug a special TV card inside your computer that lets you watch TV on the monitor. Second, you can plug a second video card inside your computer, heft a second monitor onto your desk, and watch Windows on two monitors — *at the same time!* Scurry to Chapter 17 for the lowdown on both new features.

Keyboards

Computer keyboards look pretty much like typewriter keyboards with a few dark growths around the perimeter. In the center lie the familiar white typewriter keys. The grayish keys with obtuse code words live along the outside edges. They're described next.

Can I load Windows Me with the Num Lock key turned off?

If you're not a zippy-fingered banker, you may want to use the number pad as cursor-control keys. Luckily, your Num Lock key's settings can be toggled through your computer's BIOS in its Setup area, which can usually be accessed by pressing Delete, Esc, or a special key combination when you first turn on your computer.

After you find the Setup screen's Keyboard area, look for a Num Lock key setting and set it either on or off. If that doesn't work, here's another thing to try: Your computer keeps some settings in another special place, a file called CONFIG.SYS. To edit that file, type **SYSEDIT** into your Start button's Run box. When the Sysedit program loads, click in the CONFIG.SYS window and add the line NUMLOCK = OFF or NUMLOCK = ON (depending on your preference). Although you need to use a separate line, that line can appear anywhere in the file.

When your computer boots up, it should set your Num Lock key to the position you prefer.

Groups of keys

Obtuse code-word sorters divvy those outside-edge keys into key groups:

Function keys: These keys either sit along the top of the keyboard in one long row or clump together in two short rows along the keyboard's left side. Function keys boss around programs. For example, you can press F1 to demand help whenever you're stumped in Windows Me.

Numeric keypad: Zippy-fingered bankers like this thingy: a square, calculator-like pad of numbers along the right edge of most keyboards. (You have to press a key called Num Lock above those numbers, though, before they'll work. Otherwise, they're *cursor-control keys,* which I describe next.)

Cursor-control keys: If you *haven't* pressed the magical Num Lock key, the keys on that square, calculatorlike pad of numbers are the cursor control keys. These keys have little arrows that show which direction the cursor moves on-screen. (The arrowless 5 key doesn't do anything except try to overcome its low self-esteem.) Some keyboards have a second set of cursor control keys next to the numeric keypad. Both sets do the same thing. Additional cursor control keys are Home, End, PgUp, and PgDn (or Page Up and Page Down). To move down a page in a word-processing program, for example, you press the PgDn key.

Pressing the cursor keys doesn't move the little mouse-pointer arrow around on the screen. Instead, cursor keys control your position inside a program, letting you type information in the right place.

The Windows Key: Eager to make money from selling keyboards *and* software, Microsoft came out with a bold new design: a keyboard with a special key marked "Windows." (The key's little "Windows" icon looks like the icon on your Start button.) What does the key do? It opens the Start menu, which can be done at the click of a mouse, anyway. Ho hum. Table 2-3 shows more things the Windows key can do — if you can remember them.

Table 2-3	Windows Key Shortcuts
To Do This	*Press This*
Display Windows Me Help	<Windows Key>+F1
Display the Start menu	<Windows Key>
Cycle through the taskbar's buttons	<Windows Key>+Tab
Display Windows Explorer	<Windows Key>+E

(continued)

Table 2-3 *(continued)*

To Do This	Press This
Find files	<Windows Key>+F
Find other computers on the network	Ctrl+<Windows Key>+F
Display your computer's properties	<Windows Key>+Break
Minimize or restore all windows	<Windows Key>+D
Undo minimize all windows	Shift+<Windows Key>+M

More key principles

These keyboard keys may sound confusing, but Windows still makes you use them a lot:

Shift: Just as on a typewriter, this key creates uppercase letters or the symbols %#@$ — the traditional G-rated swear words.

Alt: Watch out for this one! When you press Alt (which stands for *Alternate*), Windows moves the cursor to the little menus at the top of the current window. If you're trapped up there and can't get out, you probably pressed Alt by mistake. Press Alt again or Esc to free yourself.

Ctrl: This key (which stands for *Control*) works like the Shift key, but it's for weird computer combinations. For example, holding down the Ctrl key while pressing Esc (described next) brings up the Windows Me Start menu. (Check out Chapter 6 for more Ctrl key fun.)

Esc: This key (which stands for *Escape*) was a pipe dream of the computer's creators. They added Esc as an escape hatch from malfunctioning computers. By pressing Esc, the user was supposed to be able to escape from whatever inner turmoil the computer was currently going through. Esc doesn't always work that way, but give it a try. It sometimes enables you to escape when you're trapped in a menu or a dastardly dialog box. (Those traps are described in Chapter 5.)

Scroll Lock: This one's too weird to bother with. Ignore it. (It's no relation to a *scroll bar,* either.) If a little keyboard light glows next to your Scroll Lock key, press the Scroll Lock key to turn it off. (The key's often labeled Scrl Lk or something equally obnoxious.)

Delete: Press the Delete key (sometimes labeled Del), and the unlucky character sitting to the *right* of the cursor disappears. Any highlighted information disappears as well. Poof.

Backspace: Press the Backspace key, and the unlucky character to the *left* of the cursor disappears. The Backspace key is on the top row, near the right side of the keyboard; it has a left-pointing arrow on it. Oh, and the Backspace key deletes any highlighted information, too.

If you've goofed, hold down Alt and press the Backspace key. This action undoes your last mistake in most Windows Me programs.

Insert: Pressing Insert (sometimes labeled Ins) puts you in Insert mode. As you type, any existing words are scooted to the right, letting you add stuff. The opposite of Insert mode is Overwrite mode, where everything you type replaces any text in its way. Press Insert to toggle between these two modes.

Ugly disclaimer: Some Windows Me programs — Notepad, for example — are always in Insert mode. There's simply no way to move to Overwrite mode, no matter how hard you pound the Insert key.

Enter: This key works pretty much like a typewriter's Return key, but with a big exception: Don't press Enter at the end of each line when typing documents. A word processor can sense when you're about to type off the edge of the screen. It herds your words down to the next line automatically. So just press Enter at the end of each paragraph.

You'll also want to press Enter when Windows Me asks you to type something — the name of a file, for example, or the number of pages you want to print — into a special box. (Clicking a nearby OK button often performs the same task.)

Caps Lock: If you've mastered the Shift Lock key on a typewriter, you'll be pleased to find no surprises here. (Okay, there's one surprise: Caps Lock affects only your letters. It has no effect on punctuation symbols or the numbers along the top row.)

Tab: There are no surprises here, either, except that Tab is equal to five spaces in some word processors and eight spaces in others. Still, other word processors enable you to set Tab to whatever number you want. Plus, a startling Tab Tip follows.

Press Tab to move from one box to the next when filling out a form in Windows Me. (Sometimes these forms are called *dialog boxes.*)

✔ A mouse works best for most Windows Me tasks, like starting programs or choosing among various options. Sometimes the keyboard comes in handy, however. Windows Me comes with *shortcut keys* to replace just about anything you can do with a mouse. Sometimes pressing a few keys can be quicker than wading through heaps of menus with a mouse. (I describe the shortcut keys in Chapter 4 in the section on when to use the keyboard.)

✔ If you don't own a mouse or a trackball, you can control Windows Me exclusively with a keyboard. But it's awkward, like when Freddy from *Nightmare on Elm Street* tries to floss his back molars.

✔ Finally, some keyboards come with special keys installed by the manufacturer. My Gateway's keyboard lets me adjust the sound, log onto the Internet, control my CD or DVD, or make the computer go to sleep. Information about these keys lives in my computer's Control Panel under an icon named "Multi-function Keyboard."

Print Screen: The one, fun, weird code key

Windows fixed something dreadfully confusing about an IBM computer's keyboard: the Print Screen key (sometimes called PrtScr, Print Scrn, or something similar). In the old days of computing, pressing the Print Screen key sent a snapshot of the screen directly to the printer. Imagine the convenience!

Unfortunately, nobody bothered to update the Print Screen key to handle graphics. If a screen showed anything other than straight text, pressing the Print Screen key sent a wild jumble of garbled symbols to the printer. And, if the printer wasn't connected, turned on, and waiting, the computer would stop cold.

Windows fixes those Print Screen woes — sort of. Pressing the Print Screen key now copies a picture of the screen to a special place in Windows Me that is known as the *Clipboard*. When the image is on the Clipboard, you can *paste* it into your programs or save it to disk. You can even print the screen's picture if you call up the Paint program in Windows and choose Paste from the Edit menu in Paint.

✔ Want to capture just a particular window, not the entire screen? Then click in your desired window and hold down Alt while pressing the PrintScreen key. That window immediately heads for the Clipboard for later action.

✔ With some older computers, you have to hold down Shift while you press Print Screen, or you get just an asterisk on-screen — not nearly as much fun.

✔ The Clipboard is described in Chapter 8. You'll find all that cut, copy, and paste stuff explained there, too.

✔ Want to peek onto your Clipboard and see what you've copied there? Use the Clipbook Viewer, a program also covered in Chapter 8. (Windows Me doesn't automatically install Clipbook Viewer onto every computer, though.) If you can't find Clipboard Viewer listed on your Start menu's Accessories page, head for Chapter 9. That chapter shows how to use Control Panel's Add/Remove Programs feature to install the Clipbook Viewer onto your own computer.

Modems and the Internet

I admit it. I used my modem the other night to order Cuban food from the place down the street. How? My wife and I dialed up "Gourmet on the Road" through the Internet, chose our items from the on-screen menu, and punched in our phone number. A few minutes later, the plantains were steaming on the dining room table.

Modems are little mechanical gadgets that translate a computer's information into squealing sounds that can be sent and received over plain, ordinary phone lines. We clicked on the check mark next to Baked Plantain on our computer, a modem at the credit card company tabulated the whole process, and the electric registers started ringing.

Most new computers come with modems in order to take advantage of the Internet's World Wide Web. In fact, if you bought a new computer, you probably already have everything you need to jump on the Internet bandwagon. Not wanting to be left out, Microsoft made sure that Windows Me comes with software called Internet Explorer. You can choose to let it blanket your desktop, as shown in Figure 2-2, giving it an ultramodern look of a Web page. Elaborate Web site art will fill your desktop like posters along the walls of Parisian streets.

Figure 2-2: Windows Me enables your desktop to look like a Web page.

- Chapter 13 covers the Internet and the Web. It doesn't say what baked plantains taste like, though.

- The computers on both ends of the phone lines need modems in order to talk to each other. Luckily, most online services have hundreds, or even thousands, of modems for your computer's modem to talk to over the phone lines.

- Modems need special *communications software* to make them work. Windows Me comes with Internet Explorer to access the Internet; it also comes with software for America Online (AOL), Earthlink, Prodigy Internet, and Microsoft's own offering, The Microsoft Network.

- Yes, all this software comes free with Windows Me. But you have to pay monthly fees in order to use any of these services.

- Your computer doesn't have a modem? You'll find complete installation instructions in one of my other books, *Upgrading and Fixing PCs For Dummies,* 5th Edition (IDG Books Worldwide, Inc.). And, if you're *really* curious about modems, check out my wife Tina's epic tome, *Modems For Dummies,* 3rd Edition.

Printers

Realizing that the paperless office still lies several years down the road, Microsoft made sure that Windows Me can shake hands and send friendly smoke signals to hundreds of different types of printers. When you install Windows Me, you need to click the name and manufacturer of your printer. Windows checks its dossiers, finds your printer, and immediately begins speaking to it in its native language.

That's all there is to it. Unless, of course, your printer happens to be one of the several hundred printers *left off* the Windows Me master list. In that case, cross your fingers that your printer's manufacturer is still in business. You may need to get a *driver* from the manufacturer before your prose can hit the printed page. (For information on printers, see Chapter 9.)

- Printers must be turned on before Windows Me can print to them. (You'd be surprised how easily you can forget this little fact.)

- Windows Me prints in a *WYSIWYG* (What You See Is What You Get) format, which means that what you see on-screen is reasonably close to what you'll see on the printed page.

Networks

Networks connect PCs so that people can share information. They can all send stuff to a single printer, for example, or send messages to each other asking whether Marilyn has passed out the paychecks yet.

Some networks are relatively small — less than ten computers in an office or school, for example. Other networks span the world; the Internet runs on a huge computer network that sprawls through nearly every country.

✔ You're probably on a network if you can answer "yes" to any of these questions: Can you and your friends or coworkers share a printer, data, or messages without standing up or yelling across the room? When your computer stops working, does everybody else's computer stop working, too?

✔ When networks are running correctly, you usually don't notice them. But for tips on what to do when you *do* notice them, see the section on networks in Chapter 3. And if you're trying to set up one of the darn things, check out this book's sequel, *MORE Microsoft Windows Me For Dummies*, published by — you guessed it — IDG Books Worldwide, Inc.

Sound Cards (Making Barfing Noises)

For years, PC owners looked enviously at Macintosh owners — especially when their Macs ejected a disk. The Macintosh would simultaneously eject a floppy disk from its drive and make a cute barfing sound. Macs come with sound built in; they can barf, giggle, and make *really* disgusting noises that I won't mention here.

But the tight shirts at IBM decided there was no place for sound on a Serious Business Machine. Microsoft fixed that mistake, and Windows Me can make the accounting department's computers barf as loudly as the ones in the art department down the hall.

✔ Before your computer can barf, it needs a *sound card.* A sound card looks just like a video card. In fact, all cards look alike: long green or brown flat things that nestle into long flat slots inside the computer. Speakers plug into sound cards like monitors plug into video cards.

✔ Windows works with a wide variety of sound cards, but you'll do best with cards that are compatible with Creative Labs' Sound Blaster card. Although most new computers come with sound cards already installed, most companies constantly release new software for making them work better. (Chapter 14's section on installing a driver can help knock a miscreant sound card back into action.)

✔ Windows Me comes with a wide variety of noises, but it doesn't have any barf noises. Most computer gurus can either find a copy for you or personally record one. In fact, most new sound cards come with a microphone, and the Windows Me Sound Recorder program is ready to capture your own efforts. Check out my sequel to this book, *MORE Microsoft Windows Me For Dummies,* for plenty of information on sound and video recording.

✔ The latest, fanciest computers come with DVD drives, special sound cards, software, and extra speakers so that you can hear "surround sound" when watching DVD movies. Better clear off your desk for the big woofer and extra speakers that go with it.

✔ Just like the Macintosh, Windows enables you to assign cool sounds to various Windows Me functions. For example, you can make your computer scream louder than you do when it crashes. For more information, refer to the section in Chapter 9 on making cool sounds with multimedia.

Ports

The back of your computer contains lots of connections for pushing out and pulling in information. The deeper you fall into the Windows lifestyle, the more likely you'll hear the following words bantered about. Plus, when something falls out of the back of your computer, Table 2-4 shows you where it should plug back in.

Table 2-4	What Part Plugs into What Port?	
This Port . . .	*. . . Looks Like This . . .*	*. . . And Accepts This*
Keyboard	New Style Old Style (Pre-1994)	Your keyboard — old style or new. (Some laptops let a mouse plug into the new style keyboard ports, too.)
Mouse	New Style	Your mouse. (Some laptops let a keyboard plug into it, too.)
Video		Your monitor's smallest cable. (The monitor's biggest cable plugs into the power outlet.)
Serial (COM)	Old Style (Pre-1952) New Style	External modems.

This Port . . .	. . . Looks Like This . . .	. . . And Accepts This
Parallel (LPT)		Your printer.
USB		Universal Serial Bus gadgets. (Used mostly by digital cameras and gamepads.)
Sound		A sound card has three of these ports for this tiny plug: one for headphones, one for the microphone, and the other for an external sound source like a radio, tape recorder, camcorder, TV card, and so on.
Cable TV		TV cards accept your TV cable here; cable modems use an identical port.
Telephone		Run a telephone line from the wall to here on a modem. (The modem's second jack lets you plug in the telephone. Look closely for a label.)

Parts Required by Windows Me

Table 2-5 compares what Windows Me asks for on the side of the box with what you *really* need before it works well.

Table 2-5	What Windows Me Requires	
Requirements Politely Touted by Microsoft	**What You Really Need**	**Why?**
A Pentium 150 MHz microprocessor	A Pentium II	While at the store, compare Windows Me running on different computers. The faster the computer, the less time you spend waiting for Windows Me to do something exciting. (Besides, a mere Pentium can't handle the multimedia aspects of Windows Me, as seen in the upcoming section.)

(continued)

Table 2-5 *(continued)*

Requirements Politely Touted by Microsoft	What You Really Need	Why?
32MB of memory (RAM)	At least 64MB of memory	Windows Me crawls across the screen with only 16MB and moves much more comfortably with 32MB. RAM is cheap; if you plan to run several large programs or use WebTV, quickly bump that to 128MB. Power users may want to consider 256MB or more, especially if they're into multimedia.
500MB to 575MB of hard disk space	At least 4GB	A full installation of Windows Me requires 675MB; Windows programs quickly rope off their sections of the hard drive, too. Plus, all that sound and video you're going to be grabbing off the Internet and your digital camera will take a whole lotta space. (You'll need at least a gigabyte to watch WebTV.) Don't be afraid to buy a hard disk that's 20GB (20 gigabytes) or larger so your computer will be useful for a long time.
A 3½-inch high-density disk drive	You don't need this to install Windows Me.	However, an occasional Windows program still comes packaged on high-density, 3½-inch floppy disks. Plus, floppy disks are a handy way to move your files to other computers.
Color VGA card	Super VGA	Because Windows Me tosses so many colorful little boxes on-screen, get an AGP VGA card with at least 8MB of RAM.
Windows 98 or Windows 95	Same	Microsoft is selling Windows Me as an upgrade to its existing products. If you're not upgrading from an earlier version of Windows, you need to buy the "complete," more expensive version of Windows Me.

Requirements Politely Touted by Microsoft	What You Really Need	Why?
14,000 modem	56K Modem	You don't need a modem, but if your computer isn't on a network, you need a modem to dial up the online services that come packaged with Windows Me. Without a modem, you can't play with Internet Explorer.
Microsoft Mouse	Any PS/2 mouse	Microsoft makes some darn good mice, though, with much better warranties than Microsoft's software. I prefer the Intellimouse — the kind with the little spinning wheel on its back.
Miscellaneous	A 15-inch monitor or larger	The bigger your monitor, the bigger your desktop: Your windows won't overlap so much. Unfortunately, super-large monitors are super-expensive.
Miscellaneous	CD-ROM or DVD drive	You may be able to find Windows Me on disks, but it's a lot easier to install off a compact disc than off of handfuls of floppy disks. (A DVD drive can read normal CDs, so it'll work fine.)

Other Computer Parts You'll Probably Need

Can your computer handle the requirements in Table 2-5? Unfortunately, there's more. Windows Me will work at its most basic level with that type of muscle, but it needs more before it reaches full capacity.

For instance, in order to hear anything from your computer, you need a sound card and speakers or headphones. (If you choose USB speakers, your computer needs USB ports.)

In order to watch video from DVD, you need a DVD-ROM drive and a compatible DVD decoder card (best) or DVD decoder software (not as good).

To watch TV on your monitor, you need a compatible TV tuner card. (Check your cable TV connection, too. Most TV tuner cards don't pick up much without cable TV.)

If you plan on using Windows Movie Maker, make sure that your computer's beefed up with at *least* the following goodies recommended by Microsoft:

    300-megahertz (MHz) Pentium II processor or equivalent

    64MB of RAM

    Two gigabytes (GB) of free hard-disk space to capture video

    A sound card for capturing audio

    A video capture card for capturing video

    An Internet Service Provider and e-mail account

Want to use Windows Media Player? Microsoft says you'll need at least this:

    266-megahertz (MHz) Pentium II processor or equivalent

    64MB of RAM

    SuperVGA (SVGA) monitor

To dump music from Windows Media Player into a portable music device, you need either:

    (a) Microsoft Windows CE-based Palm-size or Pocket PC or . . .

    (b) An MP3 player that handles Microsoft's proprietary WMA sound format.

You also need:

    ActiveSync 3.0 or higher (a freebie)

    Microsoft Windows CE Version 2.11 or greater (It comes with the newer players.)

    Windows Media Player for Palm-size PC (another freebie)

    You'll want a CompactFlash card to store tunes, too.

Chapter 3

Windows Me Stuff Everybody Thinks You Already Know

. . . .

In This Chapter

▶ Explanations of the strange terms used in Windows Me

▶ Information on where to look for more details on these strange terms

. . . .

*W*hen Windows first hit the market in 1985, it failed miserably. The over-priced, under-powered computers of the day busted a bearing over Windows' attempts at fancy graphics. Back then, Windows was not only slow, but it also looked dorky and awkward with ugly colors.

Today's best-selling computers come with custom-rigged V8 engines: They can easily whip Windows into shape. With faster computers, perseverance, and a dozen fashionably trendy color schemes, such as Lilac, Rose, and Rainy Day, Windows has turned into a trendy best-seller installed on nearly every new computer.

Because Windows has been around for so long, a lot of computer geeks have had a head start. To help you catch up, this chapter is a tourist's guidebook to those Windows words the nerds have been batting around for 15 years.

Backing Up a Disk

Computers store *bunches* of files on their hard drives. And that multitude of files can be a problem. When the computer's hard drive eventually dies (nothing lives forever), it takes all your files down with it. Pfffft. Nothing left.

Computer users who don't like anguished *pfffft* sounds *back up* their hard drives religiously. They do so in three main ways.

Some people copy all their files from the hard disk to a bunch of floppy disks. Although backup programs make this task easier, it's still a time-consuming chore. Who wants to spend half an hour backing up computer files *after* finishing work?

Other people buy a *tape backup* unit. This special computerized tape recorder either lives inside your computer like a floppy disk or plugs into the computer's rear. Either way, the gizmo tape-records all the information on your hard disk. Then, when your hard disk dies, you still have all your files. The faithful tape backup unit plays back all your information onto the new hard drive. No scrounging for floppy disks.

Finally, some people buy special *cartridge* storage units. These mechanisms work like hard drives you can slide in and out of your computer. Iomega's Jaz drives, for example, can store up to 2 gigabytes of information on a single cartridge. That can take up a *lot* less space than hundreds of floppies. (More information about Iomega's drives lurks in Chapter 2.)

- ✔ Don't use old backup programs with Windows Me. Unless the backup software specifically states that it's compatible with Windows Me, the backup might not be reliable.

- ✔ The average cost of a backup unit runs from $150–$400, depending on the size of your computer's hard drive. Some people back up their work every day, using a new tape or backup disk for each day of the week. If they discover on Thursday that last Monday's report had all the best stuff, they can pop Monday's backup into the unit and grab the report.

Clicking

Computers make plenty of clicking sounds, but one click counts the most: the one that occurs when you press a button on a mouse. You'll find yourself clicking the mouse hundreds of times in Windows Me. For example, to push the on-screen button marked Push Me, you move the mouse across your desk until the little on-screen arrow rests over the Push Me button and then click the mouse button.

- ✔ When you hear people say, "Press the button on the mouse," they leave out an important detail: *Release* the button after you press it. Press the button with your index finger and release it, just as you press a button on an elevator.

- ✔ Most mice have 2 buttons; some have 3, and some esoteric models for traffic engineers have more than 32. Windows Me listens mostly to clicks coming from the button on the *left* side of your mouse. It's the one under your index finger if you're right-handed. Refer to Chapter 9 for more mouse button tricks. (Windows Me also lets left-handed folks swap their left and right mouse button controls.)

> ✔ Windows Me listens to clicks coming from both the left *and* the right buttons on your mouse. The older Windows 3.1 listens only to clicks coming from the button on the *left* side of your mouse.
>
> ✔ Don't confuse a *click* with a *double-click*. For more rodent details, see the sections "The Mouse," "Double-Clicking," and "Pointers/Arrows," later in this chapter. The insatiably curious can find even more mouse stuff in Chapter 2, including the new Microsoft IntelliMouse with the little spinning wheel doohickey.

The Cursor

Typewriters have a little mechanical arm that strikes the page, creating the desired letter. Computers don't have little mechanical arms (except in science fiction movies), so they have *cursors:* little blinking lines that show where that next letter will appear in the text.

> ✔ Cursors appear only when Windows Me is ready for you to type text, numbers, or symbols — usually when you write letters or reports.
>
> ✔ The cursor and the mouse pointer are different things that perform different tasks. When you start typing, text appears at the cursor's location, not at the pointer's location.
>
> ✔ You can move the cursor to a new place in the document by using the keyboard's *cursor-control keys* (the keys with little arrows). Or you can point to a spot with the mouse pointer and click the button. The cursor leaps to that new spot.

Filling out a form? Here's a trick for the lazy: Press Tab after filling out each blank. At each press, the Tab key kicks the cursor to the next line on the form. That saves a lot of pointing and clicking to get the cursor to the right place. Hold down Shift while pressing Tab to move in reverse.

You can distinguish between the cursor and the mouse pointer with one look: Cursors always blink steadily; mouse pointers never blink.

For more information, check out the section "Pointers/Arrows" in this chapter or Table 2-2 in Chapter 2.

Defaults (And the Any Key)

Finally, a computer term that you can safely ignored. Clap your hands and square dance with a neighbor! Here's the lowdown on the, er, hoedown: Some programs present a terse list of inexplicable choices and casually suggest that you select the only option that's not listed: the *default option.*

Don't chew your tongue in despair. Just press Enter.

Those wily programmers have predetermined what option works best for 99 percent of the people using the program. So, if people just press Enter, the program automatically makes the right choice and moves on to the next complicated question.

- ✔ The default option is similar to the oft-mentioned *Any key* because neither of them appears on your keyboard (or on anybody else's, either — no matter how much money they paid).

- ✔ *Default* can also be taken to mean *standard option* or *what to select when you're completely stumped.* For example, strangers riding together in elevators stare at their shoes by default.

- ✔ When a program says to press any key, simply press the spacebar. (The Shift keys don't do the trick, by the way.)

Desktop (And Wallpapering It)

To keep from reverting to revolting computer terms, Windows Me uses familiar office lingo. For example, all the action in Windows Me takes place on the Windows Me desktop. The *desktop* is the background area of the screen where all the windows pile up.

Windows Me comes with a simple, sky-blue desktop. To jazz things up, cover the desktop with pictures, or *wallpaper.* Windows Me comes with several arty pictures you can use for wallpaper (and Chapter 9 can help you hang it up).

You can customize the wallpaper to fit your own personality: pictures of kittens, for example, or centipedes. You can draw your own wallpaper with the built-in Windows Me Paint program, which saves your work in one of the special wallpaper formats.

Internet Explorer and other Internet browsers let you automatically grab any picture you find on a Web site and turn it into your desktop's wallpaper. Right-click the cool picture and choose the Set as Wallpaper option.

The Windows Me Active Desktop option lets you use your favorite Web page as your desktop: Your stock market quotes or pictures of French poodles can be just a click away!

The DOS prompt

Some people haven't switched to the newer, Windows breed of programs. They're still using the programs they bought nearly a decade ago, when it was trendy to use a DOS program. To placate the old-timers, Windows Me still runs DOS programs.

It even contains an age-old DOS prompt for the needy. Click the Start button, click the word Programs, and choose Accessories. Finally, choose the MS-DOS Prompt option, and the prompt appears inside a reassuring window.

Not an old-timer? *The DOS prompt* rhymes with *the boss chomped,* and it's a symbol that looks somewhat like this:

C:\>

Type the name of your program at the DOS prompt, press Enter, and the program begins.

If you've been rudely dumped at the DOS prompt, you can scoot quickly to Windows Me by typing the following no-nonsense word:

C:\> EXIT

That is, you type **EXIT** (lowercase works, too) and follow it with a press of the Enter key.

To appease the DOS hounds, Windows Me waits in the background while you run a DOS session.

Double-Clicking

Windows Me places a great significance on something pretty simple: pressing a button on the mouse and releasing it. Pressing and releasing the button once is known as a *click.* Pressing and releasing the button twice in rapid succession is a *double-click.*

Windows Me watches carefully to see whether you've clicked or double-clicked on its more sensitive parts. The two actions are completely different.

- A click and a double-click often mean two different things to Windows programs. They're not the same.

- A double-click can take some practice to master, even if you have fingers. If you click too slowly, Windows Me thinks that you're simply clicking twice — not double-clicking. Try clicking a little faster next time, and Windows Me will probably catch on.

- Can't click fast enough for Windows Me to tell the difference between a mere click and a rapid-fire double-click? Grab the office computer guru and say that you need to have your Control Panel called up and your clicks fixed. If the guru is at the computer store, tiptoe to the section on tinkering with the Control Panel in Chapter 9.

Windows Me now emulates the Web, if you prefer, so it can banish the double-click. Simply pointing at an icon selects it; then, when you click it, the program leaps into action. (To fiddle with these settings — the ever-confusing Windows lets you configure it in more than three different ways — march to Chapter 9.)

Dragging and Dropping

Although the term *drag and drop* sounds as if it's straight out of a hitman's handbook, it's really a nonviolent mouse trick in Windows Me. Dragging and dropping is a way of moving something — say, a picture of an egg — from one part of your screen to another.

To *drag*, put the mouse pointer over the egg and *hold down* the left or right mouse button. (I prefer the right mouse button.) As you move the mouse across your desk, the pointer drags the egg across the screen. Put the pointer/egg where you want it and release the mouse button. The egg *drops*, uncracked.

✔ Big Tip Dept.: If you hold down the *right* mouse button while dragging, Windows Me tosses a little menu in your face when you let go, asking if you're sure that you want to move that egg across the screen. Always hold down your right mouse button when dragging.

✔ For more mouse fun, see the sections, "Clicking," "Double-Clicking," "The Mouse," and "Pointers/Arrows" in this chapter and, if you're not yet weak at the knees, the information on the parts of your computer in Chapter 2.

✔ Started dragging something and realized in midstream that you're dragging the wrong thing? Breathe deeply like a yoga instructor and press Esc. Then let go of your mouse button. Whew! (If you've dragged with your right mouse button and already let go of the button, there's another option: Choose Cancel from the pop-up menu.)

Drivers

Although Windows Me performs plenty of work, it hires help when necessary. When Windows Me needs to talk to unfamiliar parts of your computer, it lets special *drivers* do the translation. A driver is a piece of software that enables Windows Me to communicate with parts of your computer.

Hundreds of computer companies sell computer attachables, from printers to sound cards to sprinkler systems. Microsoft requires these companies to write drivers for their products so that Windows Me knows the polite way to address them.

✔ Sometimes computer nerds say that your *mouse driver* is all messed up. They're not talking about your swerving hand movements. They're talking about the piece of software that helps Windows Me talk and listen to the mouse.

✔ Computer products often require new, improved drivers. The best way to get these new drivers is from the Web, usually on the Web site of the company that made the gadget. Sometimes, the Microsoft Web page itself will have the proper driver, too.

✔ If you send a begging letter to the company that made your mouse, the company may mail you a new, updated driver on a floppy disk. Occasionally, you can get these new drivers from the wild-haired teenager who sold you your computer. Find a computer guru to install the driver, however, or check out the section on installing drivers in Chapter 14.

✔ Windows Me comes with an aptly named program called "Windows Update." Described in Chapter 12, the program dials a special spot on the Internet, where a stethoscope examines your computer's internal parts and inserts updated software where needed.

Files

A *file* is a collection of information in a form that the computer can play with. A *program file* contains instructions telling the computer to do something useful, like adding up the number of quarters the kids spent on SweeTARTS last month. A *data file* contains information you've created, like a picture of an obelisk you drew in the Windows Me Paint program.

✔ Files can't be touched or handled; they're invisible, unearthly things. Somebody figured out how to store files as little magnetic impulses on a round piece of specially coated plastic, or *disk*. (Yep, these are the disks I cover in Chapter 2.)

✔ A file is referred to by its *filename*. Older computers made people call files by a single word containing no more than eight characters. For example, FILENAME could be the name of a file, as could REPORT, SPONGE, or X. Yes, it was difficult to think up descriptive filenames.

✔ It's so difficult that Windows breaks the barrier: It lets you call files by bunches of words, as long as they don't total more than 255 characters.

✔ Filenames have optional *extensions* of up to three letters that usually refer to the program that created them. For example, the Windows Me Paint program automatically saves files with the extension BMP. Microsoft realized that most people don't care about file extensions, so Windows Me no longer lists a file's extension when it's displaying filenames. (You can make it display them, however, if you're curious enough to struggle through the file-and-folder display details in Chapters 9 and 11.)

✔ Be careful if you're transferring files between a Windows Me computer and a Windows 3.1 computer. Your Windows Me file that's named Kayaking in the Rockies will be automatically renamed KAYAKI˜1 on the Windows 3.1 computer. The filename's ending is simply truncated, never to be seen again.

✔ Filenames still have more rules and regulations than the Jacuzzi at the condo's clubhouse.

✔ For more information than you'll ever want to know about filenames, flip to Chapter 11.

Folders (Directories)

In your everyday paper world, files are stored in folders in a cabinet. In the computer world, files are stored in a *directory* on a disk. Dusty old file cabinets are boring, but directories are even more dreadfully boring: They *never* hold any forgotten savings bonds.

So Windows Me swapped metaphors. Instead of storing files in directories, Windows Me holds files in *folders.* You can see the little pictures of the folders on your monitor.

The folders in Windows Me are *really* just directories, if you've already grown used to working with directories.

Maintaining fil∋s and working with folders can be painful experiences, so they're explained in Chapter 11. In the meantime, just think of folders as separate work areas to keep files organized. Different folders hold different projects; you move from folder to folder as you work on different things with your computer.

✔ A file cabinet's Vegetables folder could have an Asparagus folder nested inside for organizing material further. In fact, most folders contain several other folders in order to organize information even more. You need to be pretty fastidious around computers; that's the easiest way of finding your work again.

✔ Technically, a folder in a folder is a nested *subdirectory* that keeps related files from getting lost. For example, you can have folders for Steamed Asparagus and Raw Asparagus in the Asparagus folder, which lives in the Vegetables folder.

Graphical User Interfaces

The way people communicate with computers is called an *interface*. For example, the *Enterprise*'s computer used a *verbal interface*. Captain Kirk just told it what to do.

Windows Me uses a *graphical user interface*. People talk to the computer through *graphical symbols,* or pictures. A graphical user interface works kind of like travel kiosks at airports — you select some little button symbols right on the screen to find out which hotels offer free airport shuttles.

- ✔ A graphical user interface is called a *GUI,* pronounced *gooey,* as in *Huey, Dewey, Louie,* and *GUI.*

- ✔ Despite what you read in the Microsoft full-page ads, Windows Me isn't the only GUI for a personal computer. The Apple Macintosh has used a graphical user interface for years.

- ✔ You'll eventually hear people raving about a new operating system called Linux (usually pronounced LINE-uhx, after Linus, the operating system's creator). Programmers and computer tweakers love Linux, but this new operating system can't run nearly as many programs as Windows. Don't buy a new PC with Linux installed unless you're a professional programmer or married to one.

- ✔ The little graphical symbols or buttons in a graphical user interface are called *icons.*

- ✔ Some computers with sound cards can talk to us. A few of the best software packages can actually speak a few words, but even they stumble when asked to comment on the sacrifice of Isaac in Kierkegaard's *Fear and Trembling.*

Hardware and Software

Alert! Alert! Fasten your seat belt so that you don't slump forward when reading about these two particularly boring terms: hardware and software.

Your CD player is *hardware;* so are the stereo amplifier, speakers, and batteries in the boom box. By itself, the CD player doesn't do anything but hum. It needs music to disturb the neighbors. The music is the *software,* or the information processed by the CD player.

- ✔ Now you can unfasten your seat belt and relax for a bit. Computer *hardware* refers to anything you can touch, including hard things like a printer, a monitor, disks, and disk drives.

✔ *Software* is the ethereal stuff that makes the hardware do something fun. A piece of software is called a *program*. Programs come on disks (or CDs, too, if you've anted up for the latest computer gear).

✔ Software has very little to do with lingerie.

✔ When somber technical nerds (STNs) say, "It must be a hardware problem," they mean that something must be wrong with your computer itself: its disk drive, keyboard, or central processing unit (CPU). When they say, "It must be a software problem," they mean that something is wrong with the program you're trying to run from the disk.

Here's how to earn points with your computer gurus: When they ask you the riddle, "How many programmers does it take to change a light bulb?," pretend that you don't know this answer: "None; that's a hardware problem."

Icons

An *icon* is a little picture. Windows Me fills the screen with little pictures, or icons. You choose among them to make Windows Me do different things. For example, you'd choose the Printer icon, the little picture of the printer, to make your computer print something. Icons are just fancy names for cute buttons.

✔ Windows Me relies on icons for nearly everything from opening files to releasing the winged monkeys.

✔ Some icons have explanatory titles, like Open File or Terrorize Dorothy. Others make you guess; for example, the Little Juggling Man icon opens the network mail system.

✔ For more icon stuff, see the section "Graphical User Interfaces," earlier in this chapter.

The Internet

In the late 1960s, the U.S. government worried that enemies could drop bombs on its main cluster of Department of Defense computers, quickly turning circuits into slosh. So, the scientists moved the computers away from each other, connecting them globally with high-speed phone lines and a unique system of information forwarding.

If a computer in Hawaii blew up, for example, the data chain from surrounding computers wouldn't simply stop there. The other computers would automatically reroute their information to other computers in the network, and everybody would still have e-mail waiting the next morning (except for the folks in Hawaii, of course).

With this sprawling chain of new networks running automatically in the background, enemies no longer have a single target to destroy. The system has proven quite durable, and thousands of other networks have hopped on for a ride. Many academic institutions climbed aboard as well, helping the system grow to gigantic proportions. Now known as the *Internet*, the information chain's built-in independence keeps it difficult to use, completely uncensored, and rampantly random in quality.

Anybody can use the Internet and its trendy World Wide Web to sample the information strewn about the globe. Windows Me includes most of the tools you need to jump aboard.

  ✔ In fact, Windows Me includes tools to create your own spot — a Web page — on the Internet for everybody to visit. It includes software for cruising the Web, creating Web pages, watching video clips, and listening to radio stations from around the world.

  ✔ There's one problem. In order to use Windows Me's tools and visit the Web, you need to sign up with an Internet Service Provider (ISP). These businesses usually charge a monthly fee, just like any other utility company.

  ✔ For more Internet fun, see Chapter 13. To turn off any of the Windows Me Internet components, such as the Active Desktop, flip forward to Chapter 21.

Kilobytes, Megabytes, and So On

Figuring out the size of a real file folder is easy: Just look at the thickness of the papers stuffed in and around it. But computer files are invisible, so their size is measured in bytes (which is pronounced like what Dracula does).

A *byte* is pretty much like a character or letter in a word. For example, the word *sodium-free* contains 11 bytes. (The hyphen counts as a byte.) Computer nerds picked up the metric system much more quickly than the rest of us, so bytes are measured in kilos (1,000), megas (1,000,000), and gigas (way huge).

A page of double-spaced text in Notepad is about 1,000 bytes, known as 1 kilobyte, which is often abbreviated as 1K. One thousand of those kilobytes is a megabyte, or 1MB. One thousand megabytes is a gigabyte, which brings us to your computer's sales slip: Most hard drives today are 2 gigabytes or larger.

  ✔ Just about all floppy disks these days can hold 1.44MB. Today's programs are huge, so they usually come on compact discs, which hold more than 600MB.

✔ All files are measured in bytes, regardless of whether they contain text. For example, the Tiles wallpaper that some people put on their Windows Me desktop takes up 16,384 bytes. (For information on placing wallpaper on your desktop, see Chapter 9.)

✔ A page of double-spaced text in Notepad takes up about 1K, but that same page in Microsoft Word consumes much more space. That's because Word sticks in lots more information: font size, the author's name, bookmarks, spell-check results, and just about anything else you can think of.

✔ The Windows Me Explorer and My Computer programs tell you how many bytes each of your files consumes. To find out more, check out the information on Explorer in Chapter 11. (***Hint for anxious users:*** Right-click any file's name and choose P̲roperties from the menu that pops up; you will find more information about a file than you want to know.)

One kilobyte doesn't *really* equal 1,000 bytes. That would be too easy. Instead, this byte stuff is based on the number two. One kilobyte is really 1,024 bytes, which is 2 raised to the 10th power, or 210. (Computers love mathematical details, especially when a 2 is involved.) For more byte-size information, see Table 3-1.

Table 3-1	Ultra-Precise Details from the Slide-Rule Crowd		
Term	*Abbreviation*	*Rough Size*	*Ultra-Precise Size*
Byte	byte	1 byte	1 byte
Kilobyte	K or KB	1,000 bytes	1,024 bytes
Megabyte	M or MB	1,000 kilobytes	1,048,576 bytes
Gigabyte	G or GB	1,000 megabytes	1,073,741,824 bytes

Loading, Running, Executing, and Launching

Files are yanked from a file cabinet and placed onto a desk for easy reference. On a computer, files are *loaded* from a disk and placed into the computer's memory so that you can do important stuff with them. You can't work with a file or program until it has been loaded into the computer's memory.

When you *run, execute,* or *launch* a program, you're merely starting it up so that you can use it. *Load* means pretty much the same thing, but some people fine-tune its meaning to describe when a program file brings in a data file.

Picture lovers can start programs by clicking pictures — icons — on the Windows Me desktop. Word-oriented people can start programs by clicking on names in a list with Explorer (although Explorer lets you click icons, too, if you prefer).

Memory

Whoa! How did this complicated memory stuff creep in here? Luckily, it all boils down to one key sentence:

The more memory a computer has available, the more pleasantly Windows Me behaves.

> ✔ Memory is measured in bytes, just like a file. The computer at the garage sale probably came with 640 kilobytes, or 640K, of memory. Last year's computer models usually came with at least 32MB of memory. Today's computers often come with at least 64MB of memory installed.

> ✔ Windows Me requires computers to have at least 32 megabytes, or 32MB, of memory, or it won't even bother to come out of the box.

Memory and hard disk space are both measured in bytes, but they're two different things: *Memory* is what the computer uses for quick, on-the-fly calculations when programs are up and running on-screen. *Hard disk space* is what the computer uses to store unused files and programs.

Everybody's computer contains much more hard disk space than memory because hard disks — also known as *hard drives* — are so much cheaper. Also, a hard disk remembers things even when the computer is turned off. A computer's memory, on the other hand, is washed completely clean whenever someone turns it off or pokes its reset button.

Not sure about all that kilobyte and MB stuff? Skip a few pages back to the "Kilobytes, Megabytes, and So On" section.

The Mouse

A *mouse* is a smooth little plastic thing that looks like Soap on a Rope. It rests on a little roller, or *ball,* and its tail plugs into the back of the PC. When you push the mouse across your desk, the mouse sends its current location through its tail to the PC. By moving the mouse around on the desk, you move a corresponding arrow across the screen.

You can wiggle the mouse in circles and watch the arrow make spirals. Or, to be practical, you can maneuver the on-screen arrow over an on-screen button and click the mouse button to boss Windows Me around. (Refer to the sections "Clicking," "Double-Clicking," and "Pointers/Arrows," and, if you haven't run out of steam, turn to Chapter 2 for information on the parts of your computer.)

Multitasking and Task Switching

Windows Me can run two or more programs at the same time, but computer nerds take overly tedious steps to describe the process. So skip this section because you'll never need to know it.

Even though the words *task switching* and *multitasking* often have an exclamation point in computer ads, there's nothing really exciting about them.

When you run two programs, yet switch back and forth between them, you're *task switching*. For example, if Jeff calls while you're reading a book, you put down the book and talk to Jeff. You are task switching: stopping one task and starting another. The process is similar to running your word processor and then stopping to look up a phone number in your handy business card database program.

But when you run two programs simultaneously, you're *multitasking*. For example, if you continue reading your book while listening to Jeff talk about the Natural History Museum's new Grecian urns, you're multitasking: performing two tasks at the same time. In Windows Me, multitasking can be playing a solitaire game or adding a huge spreadsheet while you print something in the background.

These two concepts differ only subtly, and yet computer nerds make a big deal out of the difference. Everybody else shrugs and says, "So what?"

Networks

Networks connect PCs with cables so that people can share equipment and information. Every computer can send stuff to one printer, for example, or people can send messages back and forth talking about Jane's new hairstyle.

You, as a Windows Me beginner, are safely absolved from knowing anything about networks. Leave network stuff to that poor person in charge.

- ✔ This book provides more information about networks in case you need to know about the subject. Chapter 4, for example, explains logging on and off. Chapter 11 shows how to push and pull files off of other computers that may be networked with your own computer.

- ✔ Unless you're working on a computer in an office, however, you probably won't have to worry about networks.

- ✔ For information about dial-up networks, like connecting to the Internet through the Windows Me Internet Explorer, head for Chapter 13.

Pointers/Arrows

This idea sounds easy at first. When you roll the mouse around on your desk, you see a little arrow move around on-screen. That arrow is your *pointer,* and it is also called an *arrow.* (Almost everything in Windows Me has at least two names.)

The pointer serves as your *electronic index finger.* Instead of pushing an on-screen button with your finger, you move the pointer over that button and click the left button on the mouse.

So what's the hard part? Well, that pointer doesn't always stay an arrow. Depending on where the pointer is located on the Windows Me screen, it can turn into a straight line, a two-headed arrow, a four-sided arrow, an hourglass, a little pillar, or a zillion other things. Each of the symbols makes the mouse do something slightly different. Luckily, I cover these and other arrowheads in Chapter 2.

Plug and Play

Historically, installing new hardware devices has required substantial technical expertise to configure and load hardware and software. Basically, that means that only geeks could figure out how to fix their computers and add new gadgets to them.

So, a bunch of computer vendors hunched together around a table and came up with *Plug and Play* — a way for Windows Me to set up new gadgets for your computer automatically, with little or no human intervention. You plug in your latest gadget, and Windows Me "interviews" it, checking to see what special settings it needs. Then Windows Me automatically flips the right switches.

Because Windows Me keeps track of which switches are flipped, none of the parts argue over who got the best settings. Better yet, users don't have to do anything but plug the darn thing into their computers and flip the On switch.

 - Of course, the process couldn't be *that* simple. Only gadgets that say "Plug and Play" on the box allow for this automatic switch flipping. With the others, you probably need to flip the switches yourself. (But at least they still work when the right switches are flipped.)

 - Plug-and-Play laptops and palmtops often work well with "docking stations." For example, when you plug the laptop into the docking station, Windows Me automatically detects the new monitor, keyboard, mouse, sound card, and whatever other goodies the owner could afford. Then Windows Me automatically sets itself up to use those new goodies — without the owner having to fiddle with the settings.

 - Some people call Plug and Play "PnP."

 - Other, more skeptical, people refer to Plug and Play as "Plug and Pray." (It can't recognize everything, particularly older computer parts.)

Quitting or Exiting

When you're ready to throw in the computing towel and head for greener pastures, you need to stop, or quit, any programs you've been using. The terms *quit* and *exit* mean pretty much the same thing: making the current program on-screen stop running so that you can go away and do something a little more rewarding.

Luckily, exiting Windows Me programs is fairly easy because all of them are supposed to use the same special exit command. You simply click the little X in the upper-right corner of the program's window. Or, if you prefer using the keyboard, you hold down the Alt key (either one of them, if you have two) and press the key labeled F4. (The F4 key is a *function key;* function keys are either in one row along the top of your keyboard or in two rows along its left-most edge.)

Never quit a program by just flicking off your computer's power switch. Doing so can foul up your computer's innards. Instead, you must leave the program responsibly, so that it has time to perform its housekeeping chores before it shuts down.

 - When you press Alt+F4 or click the little X in the upper-right corner, the program asks whether you want to save any changes you've made to the file. Normally, you click the button that says something like, "Yes, by all means, save the work I've spent the last three hours trying to create." (If you've muffed things up horribly, click the No button. Windows Me disregards any work you've done and lets you start over from scratch.)

✔ If, by some broad stretch of your fingers, you press Alt+F4 by accident, click the button that says Cancel, and the program pretends that you never tried to leave it. You can continue as if nothing happened.

✔ Windows Me still lets you close most Windows programs by double-clicking on the icons in their uppermost left corners. However, it's usually easier to single-click the X in the program's uppermost *right* corner. But either action tells the program that you want to close it down.

✔ Save your work before exiting a program or turning off your computer. Computers aren't always smart enough to save it automatically.

Save Command

Save means to send the work you've just created on your computer to a disk for safekeeping. Unless you specifically save your work, your computer thinks that you've just been fiddling around for the past four hours. You need to specifically tell the computer to save your work before it will safely store the work on a disk.

Thanks to Microsoft's snapping leather whips, all Windows Me programs use the same Save command, no matter what company wrote them. Press and release the Alt, F, and S keys in any Windows Me program, and the computer saves your work.

If you're saving something for the first time, Windows Me asks you to think up a filename for the work and pick a folder to stuff the new file into. Luckily, I cover this stuff in Chapter 4.

✔ You can save files to a hard disk or a floppy disk; some people save files on Zip drives or on writable compact discs. (Check out Chapter 2 for more drive specifics.) Or if you're working in a networked office, you can often save files onto other computers.

✔ If you prefer using the mouse to save files, click the word *File* from the row of words along the top of the program. After a menu drops down, choose Save. Some programs even have a little picture of a floppy disk along their top edge; clicking the picture saves the file.

✔ Choose descriptive filenames for your work. Windows Me gives you 255 characters to work with, so a file named "June Report on Squeegee Sales" is easier to relocate than one named "Stuff."

✔ Some programs, such as Microsoft Word for Windows, have an *autosave* feature that automatically saves your work every five minutes or so.

Save As Command

Huh? Save as *what?* A chemical compound? Naw, the Save As command just gives you a chance to save your work with a different name and in a different location.

Suppose that you open the Random Musings file in your Miscellaneous Stuff directory and change a few sentences around. You want to save the changes, but you don't want to lose the original stuff. So you select Save As and type the new name, **Additional Random Musings.**

- ✔ The Save As command is identical to the Save command when you're first trying to save something new: You can choose a fresh name and location for your work.
- ✔ The world's biggest clams can weigh up to 500 pounds.

ScanDisk

You've probably seen this program, usually abruptly, and at the worst times. When your computer crashes — or when it's turned off without using the Start button's Shut Down command — the ScanDisk program hops onto the big blue screen.

Greet it with relief. ScanDisk is a disk detective that examines your hard drive for errors and then repairs them before allowing Windows Me to reappear on the screen.

In fact, if your computer is behaving oddly, run ScanDisk yourself. Open My Computer, right-click on a disk drive, and choose Properties. Click the Check Now button to bring ScanDisk to life. Highlight all your disk drives, click the Standard and Automatically fix errors boxes, and click the box's Start button.

ScanDisk will examine your hard drives for anything askew and automatically repair it. It's not a cure-all; it merely restores the way information is stored on your disk. But if your computer often freezes, it's worth a try.

Shortcuts

The shortcut concept is familiar to most people: Why bother walking around the block to get to school when a shortcut through Mr. McGurdy's backyard can get you there twice as fast?

It's the same with Windows Me. Instead of wading through a bunch of menus to get somewhere, you can create a shortcut and assign it to an icon. Then, when you double-click the shortcut icon, Windows Me immediately takes you to that location.

You can create a shortcut to your word processor, for example, and leave the shortcut icon sitting on your desktop within easy reach. Double-click the word processor's shortcut icon, and Windows Me automatically wades through your computer's folders and files, grabs the word processor, and throws it onto the screen.

A *shortcut* is simply a push button that loads a file or program. You can even make shortcuts for accessing your printer or a favorite folder.

To create a desktop shortcut to your favorite program, open My Computer or Explorer and right-click on your coveted program's icon. Drag it to your desktop and let go of the button. Then choose Create Shortcut(s) Here from the pop-up menu. Fun!

Here's the important thing to remember about Windows Me: Deleting a shortcut doesn't delete the file or program that the shortcut points to. It merely deletes one of the push buttons that quickly brings up that file or program. You can still get to the program by moving through the menus on the Start button or using Windows Explorer.

✔ Internet-crazy Windows Me even lets you create shortcuts to your favorite spots on the Internet and sprinkle them around your desktop for easy access. Just point at the icon next to the Internet site's address and drag it to the desktop.

✔ The ever-helpful Start button automatically makes a shortcut to the last 15 documents you've opened. Click the Start button, click the word Documents, and you see shortcuts waiting for you to discover them.

✔ Unfortunately, the Start button only keeps track of the last 15 documents you've opened. If you're looking for the *16th* one, you won't find a shortcut waiting. Also, not all programs tell the Start button about recently opened documents; the shortcuts then don't appear on the list. (It's not your fault, if that makes you feel better.)

✔ A shortcut isn't a program. It's a push button that starts a program. If you delete a shortcut, you haven't deleted the program; you've just removed a button that started that program.

Temp Files

Like children who don't put away the peanut butter jar, Windows Me also leaves things lying around. They're called *temp files* — secret files Windows

Me creates to store stuff in while it's running. Windows Me normally deletes them automatically when you leave the program. It occasionally forgets, however, and leaves them cluttering up your hard drive. Stern lectures leave very little impression.

✓ Temp files usually (but not always) end with the letters TMP. Common temp filenames include ~DOC0D37.TMP, ~WRI3F0E.TMP, the occasional stray ~$DIBLCA.ASD, and similar-looking files that usually start with the wavy ~ thing. (Typographically correct people call it a *tilde*.)

✓ If you exit Windows Me the naughty way — by just flicking the computer's off switch — Windows Me won't have a chance to clean up its temp file mess. If you keep doing it, you'll eventually see hundreds of TMP files lying around your hard drive. Be sure to exit Windows Me the Good Bear way: by clicking the Start button and choosing Shut Down from the menu that pops up.

✓ To free up wasted disk space, use Windows Me's Disk Cleanup option. Open My Computer, right-click on a disk drive, and click the Disk Cleanup button. It lets you delete bunches of old, unnecessary maintenance files, including temporary files.

The Windows

Windows Me enables you to run several programs at the same time by placing them in *windows*. A window is just a little on-screen box.

You can move the boxes around. You can make them bigger or smaller. You can make them fill your entire screen. You can make them turn into little icons at the bottom of your screen. You can spend hours playing with windows. In fact, most frustrated new Windows Me users do.

✓ You can put as many windows on-screen as you want, peeping at all of them at the same time or just looking into each one individually. This activity appeals to the voyeur in all of us.

✓ For instructions on how to move windows or resize them, head to Chapter 6. To retrieve lost windows from the pile, head immediately to Chapter 7.

The World Wide Web

The World Wide Web, known simply as the Web, is merely a way for sending and receiving pictures, sound, and other information on the Internet network. (See the section "The Internet" earlier in this chapter, or see Chapter 13 if you're *really* interested.)

Part II
Making Windows
Me Do Something

The 5th Wave   By Rich Tennant

"THE PHONE COMPANY BLAMES THE MANUFACTURER, WHO SAYS IT'S THE SOFTWARE COMPANY'S FAULT, WHO BLAMES IT ON OUR MOON BEING IN VENUS WITH SCORPIO RISING."

In this part . . .

*W*indows Me is more fun than cheap tattoos from the bottom of a Cracker Jack box. It's especially fun to show friends the built-in screen savers, like the one that cruises past the stars at warp speed. You can even adjust the ship's pace by using the Control Panel.

Unfortunately, some spoilsport friend will eventually mutter the words that bring everything back to Earth: "Let's see Windows Me do something useful, like balance a checkbook or teach the kids to rinse off their plates and put them in the dishwasher."

Toss this eminently practical part at them to quiet 'em down.

Chapter 4

Starting Windows Me

· ·

In This Chapter

▶ Revvin' up Windows Me

▶ Starting a program

▶ Finding the secret pull-down menus

▶ Loading a file

▶ Putting two programs on the screen

▶ Using the keyboard

▶ Printing your work

▶ Saving your work

▶ Quitting Windows Me

· ·

*H*old on to your hat! Then try to type at the same time. No, let the hat fly by the wayside because this is a hands-on Windows Me chapter that demonstrates some dazzling special effects. First, you make Windows Me leap to your screen, ready to load a program!

Then, at the click of the mouse, you launch a second program, running at the same time as the first! Plus, you discover secret magic tricks to bypass the mouse and use the keyboard instead!

Finally, you find out how to print your work so that you'll have some hard copy to show those doubting friends of yours.

Oh, and you also find out how to save your work so that you can find it again the next day. So warm up those fingers, shake out your sleeves, and get ready for action.

Beware, however, that you can set up Windows Me in a zillion different ways. Because I describe most of them here, you'll have to ignore the ones that don't apply to your own computer. (Luckily, most people are happiest when ignoring their computers.)

Revvin' Up Windows Me

If your PC came with Windows Me already installed (most of them do these days), Windows Me probably leaps to your screen automatically when you first turn on the computer. Its Start button is ready for action. Windows Me is like an elevator that moves around your computer, and the Start button is like a panel of elevator buttons. By pushing the Start button, you tell Windows Me where to go and what to do.

✔ When you start Windows Me, you may hear pleasant synthesizer sounds singing from the computer's sound card. If you don't have a sound card, you don't hear anything but a strong inner urge driving you toward the computer store's sound-card aisles. (Sound cards range in price from $75–$250.)

✔ Can't hear cheery synthesized greetings when Windows Me loads itself? If the desktop speakers are turned up, Windows Me may have its sound options turned off. To activate the sounds yourself, choose the Sounds icon from the Control Panel and select a new sound Scheme, a not-too-laborious process that I describe in Chapter 9.

It wants me to enter a password!

Your computer may be part of a *network* — a bunch of computers linked with cables or through the phone lines. A network lets you sit at your own computer in your own cubicle but swap files with Grace's computer in her cubicle — and neither of you has to get up.

But how do you make sure nobody uses your computer to steal Grace's files? How can you set up your computer so that nobody else can mess with your own files? Or if several people share the same computer, how can they make sure that their Windows Me desktop is customized to their own special needs?

Typing a password solves some of those problems. After Windows Me wakes up and figures out that it's part of a network, it cautiously sends out the box shown in Figure 4-1.

Figure 4-1:
Type your
name in
the box,
press Tab,
type any
assigned
password
into the
bottom box,
and click OK
to log on
to your
computer.

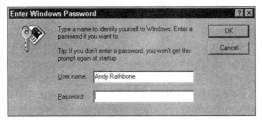

Figure 4-1:
Type your
name in
the box,
press Tab,
type any
assigned
password
into the
bottom box,
and click OK
to log on
to your
computer.

Running Windows Me for the first time

Just installed Windows Me or turned on your new computer for the first time? Then you're treated with a few extra Windows Me spectacles.

First, a hip little box appears on the screen, demonstrating that Windows Me can indeed create cool colors and noises.

Then Windows Me leaves you at a box with the following four buttons:

✔ **Digital Media:** Click here to check out Windows fun multimedia stuff. It contains tours of Media Player, a program for playing CDs, videos, Internet radio stations and more. You'll also find information about the built-in video editor, Movie Maker, and the digital camera connector, My Pictures.

✔ **Rich Internet Experience:** Nothing really new here: tours of Windows Me Web browser, Internet Explorer, and the e-mail program, Outlook Express. There's also a plug for MSN Messenger, a program for tracking down buddies on the Internet.

✔ **Home Networking:** On your second or third computer? Perhaps it's time to link them together with cables, run the easy Home Networking software, and add the words Network Administrator to your business card. (It's a great pickup tool in Silicon Valley.)

✔ **Improved User Experience:** These buzzwords merely refer you to Windows Help program. Yawn.

To access any of the information mentioned above, let the mouse pointer hover above the button. Then click on either the words "try it" or "learn more" to head to that particular program. "Try it" takes you to the program itself; "learn more" takes you to the program's help menu.

By typing your name in the User name box and making up a password to type into the Password box, you enable your computer to immediately recognize you: You're logged on.

- ✔ Depending on your network's level of security, a password can let you do many things. Sometimes, entering the password merely lets you use your own computer. Other times, it lets you share files on a network.

- ✔ Because networks can be notoriously difficult to set up, most networked offices have a full-time network administrator who tries to make the darn thing work. (That's the person to bug if something goes wrong.)

- ✔ If you are not working on a network where security is an issue, don't type anything in the Password box shown in Figure 4-1. If you leave the box blank and click the OK button, Windows Me just lets you type in your name to log on to the computer — nothing to remember and nothing to forget.

- ✔ Have you forgotten your password already? Just click on the Cancel button shown in Figure 4-1. Unless you're on a strict network, Windows Me still lets you in. Because it doesn't recognize you, however, you may not be able to see your favorite wallpaper, desktop, and other Windows Me accoutrements. (Plus, you probably won't be able to access your network connections.)

- ✔ Keep your password short and sweet: the name of your favorite vegetable, for example, or the brand of your dental floss. (See your network administrator if Windows Me doesn't accept your password.)

- ✔ Passwords are case-sensitive. That means that a password of *caviar* is different from *Caviar.* The computer notices the capital C, and considers caviar and Caviar to be two different words.

Make Windows stop asking me for a password!

Windows asks for your name and password only when it needs to know who's tapping on its keys. And it needs that information for only two reasons:

- ✔ Your computer is part of a network, and your identity determines what goodies you can access.

- ✔ You share your computer with other people, and each person customizes how Windows Me looks and behaves.

If you're not working on a network, disable the network password request by double-clicking the Control Panel's Network icon and choosing Windows Logon in the Primary Network Logon box. Click the OK button and follow any instructions.

If you don't share your machine with other users — or everybody uses the same desktop — head for the Control Panel's Passwords icon. Under the User Profiles tab, choose the button marked All users of this computer use same preferences and desktop settings.

By choosing these two settings, you cause Windows Me to never ask for a password again.

It wants me to choose whether to click or double-click!

We are entering a historical moment in the computing world as programmers ponder the big question: Should we click or double-click the mouse to get things done on-screen?

For years, Windows owners have double-clicked to make things happen; Macintosh owners have single-clicked. Internet aficionados do both, sometimes clicking and sometimes double-clicking. To please everybody, Microsoft presents Windows Me users with a form to determine how their mouse buttons should behave.

For example, when you choose Folder Options from any folder's Tools menu (or open the Folder icon in Windows Control Panel), Windows Me presents you with a stunningly detailed form, as shown in Figure 4-2.

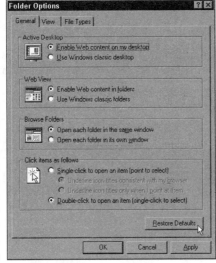

Figure 4-2:
Windows Me lets you choose between single-clicking or double-clicking.

The bottom of the form lets you choose whether you want to single-click or double-click on items to boss them around. I cover the rest of this form's weirdness in Chapter 21. (Windows refers to these decisions as the *Active Desktop.* Many people prefer their desktop to remain *inactive,* thank you very much.)

Windows Me can mimic Web software on the Internet. And with the Web, a simple click on a button makes things happen — just like controlling an elevator. So, if you enjoy using the Internet's Web — and you want your desktop to look and act like the Web — this page lets you make the changes.

Keep this in mind: The single-click/double-click choice only applies to the folders and icons on the Windows Me desktop. Even if you choose to single-click folders and icons in Windows Me, you still end up double-clicking occasionally when inside most Windows programs.

If you're not a big Web user — or you don't even know what the Web is — then don't bother with this form. Or if something weird has happened, choose the Restore Defaults button to remain with the Windows traditional double-click option, called, sentimentally enough, Classic style.

Because Windows Me now lets people customize the desktop to such an extreme, Windows Me can act very differently on different people's computers. Be prepared.

Starting your favorite program with the Start button

When Windows Me first takes over your computer, it turns your screen into a desktop. However, the desktop is merely a fancy name for a plate of buttons with labels underneath them. Click a button, and programs hop to the screen in their own little windows. Click the Start button in the bottom-left corner of the screen, and you'll have even more buttons to choose from, as shown in Figure 4-3.

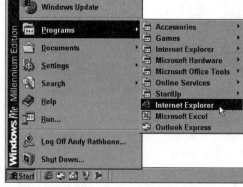

Figure 4-3: The Start button in Windows Me hides dozens of menus for starting programs.

Because the buttons have little pictures on them, they're called *icons*. Icons offer clues to the programs they represent. For example, the icon of the stamped envelope stands for Microsoft Outlook Express, a program that lets people send and receive electronic mail on their computers.

See the dark bar shading the Internet Explorer icon's title in Figure 4-3? The bar means that the Internet Explorer program is *highlighted:* It's queued up and ready to go. If you press the Enter key while Internet Explorer is highlighted, Explorer hops to the forefront. (Don't press Enter, though, because Explorer is too boring to play with right now.)

Look at the little arrow sitting by itself in the corner of your screen. Roll your mouse around until that arrow hovers over the button that says Start.

Click your mouse button, and the Start menu pops up on the screen, as shown in Figure 4-4. Next, click the Programs button, and another menu full of buttons shoots out, as shown in Figure 4-5. Click Games to see yet another menu, as shown in Figure 4-6. And, if this doesn't exhaust you, click Spider Solitaire (see Figure 4-7) to check out one of the new card games in Windows Me.

Figure 4-4: To start a program in Windows Me, click the Start button . . .

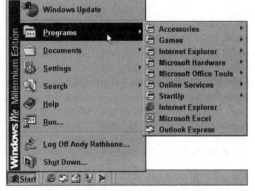

Figure 4-5: . . . and then click Programs and follow the menu as it grows.

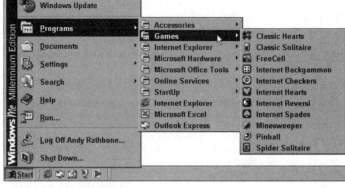

Figure 4-6:
Click the
type of
program
you'd like
to load . . .

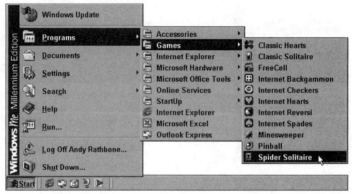

Figure 4-7:
. . . and then
click your
program's
name to
load it.

✔ The Start button is just a big panel of buttons. When you press one of the buttons by pointing at it and clicking with the mouse, the program assigned to that button heads for the top of the screen and appears in a little window.

✔ You don't have to click your way through all those buttons hiding beneath the Start button. Click the Start button and then just hover your mouse pointer over the other menu areas you want to open. Windows Me opens them without even waiting for your clicks.

✔ Icons can stand for files as well as for programs. Clicking the Documents button usually brings up shortcut buttons that take you to 15 of your most recently used documents, as well as your My Documents and My Pictures folders.

✔ Microsoft has already set up the Start button to include icons for the most popular programs and files Windows Me found as it installed itself on your computer — stuff like Microsoft Word or Excel. If you want to add some other programs and files, however, check out the section in Chapter 10 on customizing your Start button.

TIP

✔ If you're kind of sketchy about all this _double-click_ stuff, head to the end of Chapter 5; you're not alone.

✔ Do you despise mice? You don't need a mouse for the Start button. Hold down Ctrl and press Esc to make the Start menu appear. Then push your arrow keys to navigate the various menus. Highlighted the program you want? Press Enter, and the program begins to run.

✔ If the thing you're after in the Start menu has a little black bar around its name, it's _highlighted_. If you just press Enter, the highlighted program loads itself into a little window. Or you can still double-click it to load it. Windows Me lets you do things in a bunch of different ways.

✔ This chapter gives you just a quick tour of Windows Me. You can find glowing descriptions of the Start button in Chapter 10.

Some of my menu options are missing!

After you've been using Windows Me for a little while, it pulls a fast one. That dastardly program thinks it knows you well enough to hide the menu options you haven't used for awhile. For example, Figure 4-5 shows what you normally see when you click your Start button's Programs area.

But a few days later, after Windows Me thinks it knows what menu options you choose, it hides the others, as shown in Figure 4-8.

Figure 4-8:
Windows
Me displays
your
frequently
used menu
items, but it
hides the
least-used
ones. To see
them, click
the two
little down
arrows at
the bottom
of the menu.

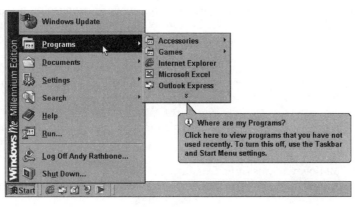

To make Windows Me show you *all* its menu options, click the two little downward-pointing arrows at the bottom of the menu. Windows immediately unveils all the menu options.

Windows Me does this all the time. Some people like it. They no longer have to wade through the useless items to get to the good stuff that they always use. Other people hate it: They always feel that they're missing something.

To make Windows Me stop hiding menu items, right-click on a blank part of your taskbar and choose Properties (or choose the Control Panel's Taskbar and Start icon). Then remove the check mark from the Use personalized menus setting. Click OK to cinch the deal. To make Windows Me keep hiding unused menu items, leave the check mark in the Use personalized menus setting.

Pull-Down Menus

Windows Me, bless its heart, makes an honest effort toward making computing easier. For example, the Start button puts a bunch of options on the screen in front of you. You just choose the one you want, and Windows Me takes it from there.

But if Windows Me put all its options on the screen at the same time, it would look more crowded than a 14-page menu at the Siam Thai restaurant. To avoid resorting to fine print, Windows Me hides some menus in special locations on the screen. When you click the mouse in the right place, more options leap toward you.

For example, begin loading Windows' simple word-processing program, WordPad, by clicking the Start button. When the Start menu pops up, choose Programs, click Accessories, and click WordPad to bring it to the screen.

See the row of words beginning with File that rests along the top edge of WordPad? You find a row of words across the top of just about every Windows Me program. Move your mouse pointer over the word File and click.

A menu opens from beneath File. This menu is called a *pull-down menu,* if you're interested, and it looks somewhat like what you see in Figure 4-9.

- ✔ Pull-down menus open from any of those key words along the top of a window. Just click the mouse on the word, and the menu tumbles down like shoeboxes falling off a closet shelf.
- ✔ To close the menu, click the mouse again, but click it someplace away from the menu.

✔ Different Windows Me programs have different words across the menu bar, but almost all of the bars begin with the word File. The File pull-down menu contains file-related options, like Open, Save, Print, and Push Back Cuticles.

✔ You find pull-down menus sprinkled liberally throughout Windows Me.

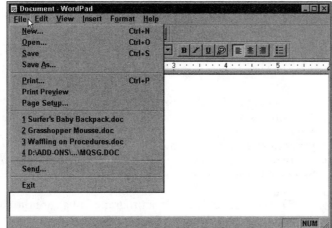

Figure 4-9:
Click a word along the top of any window to reveal a secret pull-down menu.

Loading a file

First, here's the bad news: Loading a file into a Windows Me program can be a mite complicated sometimes. Second, *loading* a file means the same thing as *opening* a file.

Now that those trifles have been dispensed with, here's the good news: All Windows Me programs load files in the exact same way. So after you know the proper etiquette for one program, you're prepared for all the others!

Here's the scoop: To open a file in any Windows Me program, look for the program's *menu bar,* that row of important-looking words along its top. Because you're after a *file,* click File.

A most-welcome pull-down menu descends from the word File. The menu has a list of important-looking words. Because you're trying to *open* a file, move the mouse to the word Open and click once again.

Yet another box hops onto the screen, as shown in Figure 4-10, and you see this box named *Open* appear over and over again in Windows Me.

Figure 4-10:
Almost
every
Windows
Me program
tosses this
box at you
when you
load or
save a file.

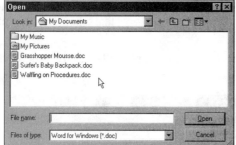

Open	? X

Look in: My Documents

- My Music
- My Pictures
- Grasshopper Mousse.doc
- Surfer's Baby Backpack.doc
- Waffling on Procedures.doc

File name: [   ] Open

Files of type: Word for Windows (*.doc) Cancel

See the list of filenames inside the box? Point at one of them with the mouse, click the button on the mouse, and that file's name shows up in the box called File name. Click the Open button, and WordPad opens the file and displays it on the screen. If you don't have a mouse, press the Tab key until a little square appears around one of the file's names. Then press the arrow keys until the file you want is highlighted, and press Enter.

You've done it! You've loaded a file into a program! Those are the same stone steps you walk across in any Windows Me program, whether it was written by Microsoft or by the teenager down the street. They all work the same way.

- Sometimes, you won't immediately spot the file you're after. It's just not listed in that little box. That means that you'll have to do a little spelunking. Just as most people store their underwear and T-shirts in different dresser drawers, most computers store their files in different places called folders. If you're having trouble finding a file for your program to open, head for the section on folders in Chapter 11.

- You can speed things up by simply double-clicking a file's name right from a menu; that action tells Windows Me to load the file as well. Or you can click the name once to highlight it (it turns black) and then press the Enter key. Windows Me is full of multiple options like that (different strokes for different folks and all).

  If you set up Windows Me to work with the single-click option (making your desktop work like Internet Explorer), then just single-clicking a file will load the file and the program that created it.

- Whenever you load a file into a program and change it, even by an accidental press of the spacebar, Windows Me assumes that you've consciously changed the file for the better. If you try to load another file into the program, Windows Me cautiously asks whether you want to save the changes you've made to the current file. Click the No button unless you do, indeed, want to save that version you've haphazardly changed.

✔ The Open box has a bunch of options in it. You can open files that are stored in different folders or on other disk drives. You can also call up files that were created by certain programs, filtering out the ones you won't be needing. Chapter 5 explains all this Open box stuff. *Tip:* Don't know what those little icons along the top are supposed to do? Let the mouse pointer rest over them, and a box will appear, announcing their occupation.

✔ Now, here's some more bad news: Only Windows Me, Windows 98, and Windows 95 programs can handle long filenames. If you're using Windows 3.1 programs in Windows Me, you are still stuck with the old versions of the Open and Save boxes, and the long filenames won't work right in these programs.

✔ If you're still a little murky on the concepts of *files, folders, directories,* and *drives,* flip to Chapter 11 for an explanation of Windows Explorer.

Putting two programs on-screen simultaneously

After spending all your money for Windows Me and a computer powerful enough to cart it around, you're not going to be content with only one program on your screen. You want to *fill* the screen with programs, all running in their own little windows.

How do you put a second program on the screen? Well, if you've opened WordPad by clicking its icon in the Start button's Accessories area (that area's listed under the Programs area), you're probably already itching to load Spider Solitaire, the new card game. Simply click the Start button and start moving through the menus, as I describe in the "Starting your favorite program with the Start button" section, earlier in this chapter.

✔ This section is intentionally short. When working in Windows Me, you almost always have two or more programs on the screen at the same time. There's nothing really special about it, so there's no need to belabor the point here.

✔ The special part comes when you move information between the two programs, which is explained in Chapter 8. (Moving information between windows is known as *cutting and pasting* in Windows parlance.)

✔ If you want to move multiple windows around on the screen, move yourself to Chapter 6.

✔ If you've started up Spider Solitaire, you're probably wondering where the WordPad window disappeared to. It's now hidden behind the Spider Solitaire window. To get it back, check out the information on retrieving lost windows in Chapter 7. (Or, if you see a button called WordPad along the bottom of your screen, click it to put WordPad back in front.)

✔ To switch between windows, just click them. When you click a window, it immediately becomes the *active* window — the window where all the activity takes place. For more information on switching between windows, switch to Chapter 6.

✔ Can't find Spider Solitaire *anywhere*? Unfortunately, Windows Me doesn't automatically install Spider Solitiare on everybody's computers. To correct this oversight, use the Control Panel's Add/Remove Programs icon, as I describe in Chapter 9.

Using the Keyboard

It's a good thing Microsoft doesn't design automobiles. Each car would have a steering wheel, a joystick, a remote control, and handles on the back for people who prefer to push. Windows Me offers almost a dozen different ways for you to perform the simplest tasks.

For example, check out the top of any window where that important-looking row of words hides above secret pull-down menus. Some of the words have certain letters underlined. What gives? Well, it's a secret way for you to open their menus without using the mouse. This sleight of hand depends on the Alt key, that dark key resting next to your keyboard's spacebar.

Press (and release) Alt and keep an eye on the row of words in the WordPad *menu bar*. The first word, File, darkens immediately after you release Alt. You haven't damaged it; you've selected it, just as if you'd pointed to it with the mouse. The different color means that it's highlighted.

Now, see how the letter F in File is underlined? Press the letter F, and the pull-down menu hidden below File falls recklessly down, like a mushroom off a pizza.

That's the secret underlined-letter trick! And pressing Alt and F is often faster than plowing through a truckload of mouse menus — especially if you think that the whole mouse concept is rather frivolous, anyway.

✔ You can access almost every command in Windows Me by using Alt rather than a mouse. Press Alt, and then press the key for the underlined letter. That option, or command, then begins to work.

✔ If you accidentally press Alt and find yourself trapped in Menu Land, press Alt again to return to normal. If that doesn't work, try pressing Esc.

✔ As pull-down menus continue to appear, you can keep plowing through them by selecting underlined letters until you accomplish your ultimate goal. For example, pressing Alt and then F brings down the File pull-down menu. Pressing O subsequently activates the Open files option from the File menu and immediately brings the Open file box to the front of the screen.

When you see a word with an underlined letter in a menu, press and release Alt. Then press that underlined letter to choose that menu item.

Printing Your Work

Eventually, you'll want to transfer a copy of your finely honed work to the printed page so that you can pass it around. Printing something from any Windows Me program (or application, or applet, whatever you want to call it) takes only three keystrokes. Press and release Alt, and then press the letters F and P. What you see on your screen will be whisked to your printer.

Pressing Alt activates the words along the top, known as the *menu bar*. The letter F wakes up the File menu, and the letter P tells the program to send its stuff to the printer — pronto. (Some fancier programs bring up a special Print box that makes you click the OK button first.)

✔ Alternatively, you can use the mouse to click the word File and then click the word Print from the pull-down menu. Depending on the RPM of your mouse ball and the elasticity of your wrist, both the mouse and the keyboard method can be equally quick.

✔ If nothing comes out of the printer after a few minutes, try putting paper in your printer and making sure that it's turned on. If it still doesn't work, cautiously tiptoe to Chapter 14.

✔ When you print something in Windows Me, you're actually activating yet another program, which sits around and feeds stuff to your printer. You may see the program as a little icon at the bottom of your screen. If you're curious about the new printing process, check out Chapter 8.

✔ Some programs, such as WordPad, have a little picture of a printer along their top. Clicking on that printer icon is a quick way of telling the program to shuffle your work to the printer.

Saving Your Work

Anytime you create something in a Windows Me program, be it a picture of a spoon or a letter to *The New York Times* begging for a decent comics page, you'll want to save it to disk.

Saving your work means placing a copy of it onto a disk, either the mysterious hard disk inside your computer or a floppy disk, one of those things you're always tempted to use as beverage coasters. (Don't try it, though.)

Luckily, Windows Me makes it easy for you to save your work. You need only press three keys, just as if you were printing your work or opening a file. To save your work, press and release Alt, press F, and then press S.

If you prefer to push the mouse around, click File from the Windows Me menu bar. When the secret pull-down menu appears, click Save. Your mouse pointer turns into an hourglass, asking you to hold your horses while Windows Me shuffles your work from the program to your hard disk or to a floppy disk for safekeeping.

That's it!

- ✔ If you're saving your work for the first time, you see a familiar-looking box: It's the same box you see when opening a file. See how the letters in the File name box are highlighted? The computer is always paying attention to the highlighted areas, so anything you type appears in that box. Type in a name for the file and press Enter.

- ✔ If Windows Me throws a box in your face saying something like A filename cannot contain any of the following characters, you haven't adhered to the ridiculously strict filename guidelines spelled out in Chapter 11.

- ✔ Just as files can be loaded from different directories and disk drives, they can be saved to them as well. You can choose between different directories and drives by clicking various parts of the Save box. All this stuff is explained in Chapter 5.

Quitting Windows Me

Ah! The most pleasant thing you'll do with Windows Me all day could very well be to stop using it. And you do that the same way you started: by using the Start button, that friendly little helper that popped up the first time you started Windows Me.

Other Windows Me programs come and go, but the Start button is always on your screen somewhere. (Sometimes you have to press Ctrl+Esc to bring the playful button out of hiding.)

First, make the Start menu pop to the forefront by clicking the Start button or holding down Ctrl and pressing Esc at the same time. Next, click the Shut Down command from the Start button's menu. Windows Me, tearful that you're leaving, sends out one last plea, as shown in Figure 4-11.

Figure 4-11:
Be sure to
shut down
Windows
Me before
turning off
your com-
puter. If you
mean busi-
ness, click
the OK
button or
press Enter.

🖝 Be sure to shut down Windows Me through its official Shut Down program before turning off your computer. Otherwise, Windows Me can't
properly prepare your computer for the event, leading to future troubles.

🖝 When you tell Windows Me that you want to quit, it searches through all
your open windows to see whether you've saved all your work. If it finds
any work you've forgotten to save, it tosses a box your way, letting you
click the OK button to save it. Whew!

🖝 Holding down Alt and pressing F4 tells Windows Me that you want to
stop working in your current program and close it down. If you press
Alt+F4 while no programs are running, Windows Me figures that you've
had enough for one day, and it acts as though you clicked its Shut Down
command.

🖝 If you happen to have any DOS programs running, Windows Me stops and
tells you to quit your DOS programs first. See, Windows Me knows how to
shut down Windows Me programs because they all use the same command.
But all DOS programs are different. You have to shut the program down
manually, using whatever exit sequence you normally use in that program.

🖝 You don't *have* to shut down Windows Me. In fact, some people leave
their computers on all the time. Just be sure to turn off your monitor;
those things like to cool down when they're not being used.

Chapter 5

Field Guide to Buttons, Bars, Boxes, Folders, and Files

. . . .

In This Chapter

▶ Looking at a typical window

▶ Getting into bars

▶ Changing borders

▶ Getting to know the button family

▶ Disregarding the dopey Control-menu button

▶ Exploring dialog box stuff: text boxes, drop-down list boxes, list boxes, and other gibberish

▶ Finding out how to open a file

▶ Changing your folder viewing options

▶ Knowing when to click and when to double-click

▶ Knowing when to use the left mouse button and when to use the right mouse button

. . . .

*A*s children, just about all of us played with elevator buttons until our parents told us to knock it off. An elevator gives such an awesome feeling of power: Push a little button, watch the mammoth doors slide shut, and feel the responsive push as the spaceship floor begins to surge upward . . . . What fun!

Part of an elevator's attraction still comes from its simplicity. To stop at the third floor, you merely press the button marked 3. No problems there.

Windows Me takes the elevator button concept to an extreme, unfortunately, and it loses something in the process. First, some of the Windows Me buttons don't even *look* like buttons. Most of the Windows Me buttons have ambiguous little pictures rather than clearly marked labels. And the worst part is the Windows Me terminology: The phrase *push the button* becomes *click the scroll bar above or below the scroll box on the vertical scroll bars.* Yuck!

When braving your way through Windows Me, don't bother learning all these dorky terms. Instead, treat this chapter as a field guide, something you can grab when you stumble across a confusing new button or box that you've never encountered before. Just page through until you find its picture. Read the description to find out whether that particular creature is deadly or just mildly poisonous. Then read to find out where you're supposed to poke it with the mouse pointer.

You'll get used to the critter after you've clicked it a few times. Just don't bother remembering the scientific name *vertical scroll bar,* and you'll be fine.

A Typical Window

Nobody wants a field guide without pictures, so Figure 5-1 shows a typical window with its most important parts labeled (all 11 of them, unfortunately).

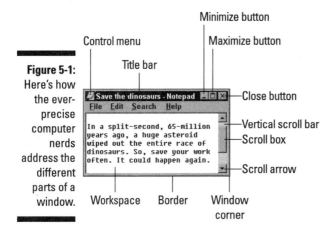

Figure 5-1:
Here's how the ever-precise computer nerds address the different parts of a window.

Just as boxers grimace differently depending on where they've been punched, windows behave differently depending on where they've been clicked. The following sections describe the correct places to click and, if that doesn't work, the best places to punch.

> ✔ Windows Me is full of little weird-shaped buttons, borders, and boxes. You don't have to remember their Latin or Greek etymologies. The important part is just finding out what part you're supposed to click. Then you can start worrying about whether you're supposed to single-click or double-click. (And that little dilemma is explained near the end of this chapter.)

✔ Not sure whether Windows Me is set up for single-clicking or double-clicking? This trick always works: Click cautiously once. If that doesn't do the trick — the click doesn't prod your program into action, for instance — then double-click by clicking twice in rapid succession.

✔ After you click a few windows a few times, you realize how easy it really is to boss them around. The hard part is finding out everything for the first time, just like when you stalled the car while learning how to use the stick shift.

Bars

Windows Me is filled with bars; perhaps that's why some of its programs seem a bit groggy and hung over. Bars are thick stripes along the edges of a window. You find several different types of bars in Windows Me.

The title bar

The title bar is that topmost strip in any window (see Figure 5-2). It lists the name of the program, as well as the name of any open file. For example, the title bar in Figure 5-2 comes from the Windows Me Notepad. It contains an untitled file because you haven't had a chance to save the file yet. (For example, the file may be full of notes you've jotted down from an energetic phone conversation with Ed McMahon.)

Figure 5-2:
A title bar
lists the
program's   `New Text Document - Notepad`
name along
the top of a
window.

Windows Me often chooses the name New Text Document for untitled Notepad files; you choose a more descriptive name for that file when you save it for the first time. That new filename then replaces the admittedly vague New Text Document in the title bar.

✔ In addition to displaying the name of your work, the title bar serves as a *handle* for moving a window around on-screen. Point at the title bar, hold down the mouse button, and move the mouse around. An outline of the window moves as you move the mouse. When you've placed the outline in a new spot, let go of the mouse button. The window leaps to that new spot and sets up camp.

✔ When you're working on a window, its title bar is *highlighted,* meaning that it's a different color from the title bar of any other open window. By glancing at all the title bars on-screen, you can quickly tell which window is currently being used.

To enlarge a window so that it completely fills the screen, double-click its title bar. It expands to full size, making it easier to read and covering up everything else. No mouse? Then press Alt, the spacebar, and then X. Maximized windows can't be moved, however; double-click their title bars once again to return them to window size. Then they can be moved once again.

The menu bar

Windows Me has menus *everywhere.* But if menus appeared all at once, everybody would think about deep-fried appetizers rather than computer commands. So Windows Me hides its menus in something called a *menu bar* (see Figure 5-3).

Figure 5-3:
A menu bar
provides
a handy
place for
Windows
Me to
hide its
cluttersome
menus.

| File | Edit | Search | Appetizer | Help |

Lying beneath the title bar, the menu bar keeps those little menus hidden behind little words. To reveal secret options associated with those words, click one of those words.

If you think that mice are for milksops, use the brawny Alt key instead. A quick tap of the Alt key activates the menu words across the top of the window. Press the arrow keys to the right or left until you've selected the word you're after and then press the down-arrow key to expose the hidden menu. (You can also press a word's underlined letter to bring it to life, but that tip is explained in Chapter 4 and later in more detail.)

For example, to see the entrees under Edit, click your mouse button on Edit (or press Alt and then E). A secret menu tumbles down from a trap door, as shown in Figure 5-4, presenting all sorts of *edit-related* options.

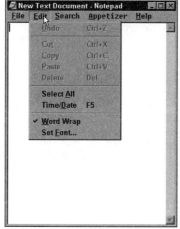

Figure 5-4:
Select any
word in
the menu
bar to
reveal its
secret
hidden
menu.

Keep the following points in mind when using menus:

- ✔ When you select a key word in a menu bar, a menu comes tumbling down. The menu contains options related to that particular key word.

- ✔ Just as restaurants sometimes run out of specials, a window sometimes isn't capable of offering all its menu items. Any unavailable options are *grayed out,* as the Undo, Cut, Copy, Paste, and Delete options are in Figure 5-4.

- ✔ If you accidentally select the wrong word, causing the wrong menu to jump down, just sigh complacently. (S-i-i-i-i-igh.) Then select the word you *really* wanted. The first menu disappears, and the new one appears below the new word.

✔ If you want out of a program's Menu Land completely, click the mouse pointer back down on your work in the window's *workspace* — usually the area where you've been typing stuff. (Or press your Alt key; whichever method comes to mind sooner.)

✔ Some menu items have *shortcut keys* listed next to them, such as the Ctrl+Z key combination next to the Undo option in Figure 5-4. Just hold down the Ctrl key and press the letter Z to undo your last effort. The Undo option takes place immediately, and you don't have to wait for the menu to tumble down.

If you find yourself performing the same task on a menu over and over, check to see whether a shortcut key is next to it. By pressing the shortcut key, you can bypass the menu altogether, performing that task instantly. (In fact, many shortcut keys do the same thing in every program.)

The scroll bar

The scroll bar, which looks like an elevator shaft, is along the edge of a window (see Figure 5-5). Inside the shaft, a little freight elevator (the *scroll box*) travels up and down as you page through your work. In fact, by glancing at the little elevator, you can tell whether you're near the top, the middle, or the bottom of a document.

Figure 5-5:
Scroll bars
enable you
to page
through
everything
that's in the
window.

For example, if you're looking at stuff near the *top* of a document, the elevator box is near the top of its little shaft. If you're working on the bottom portion of your work, the elevator box dangles near the bottom. You can watch the little box travel up or down as you press the PgUp or PgDn key. (Yes, it's easy to get distracted in Windows Me.)

Here's where the little box in the scroll bar comes into play: By clicking in various places on that scroll bar, you can quickly move around in a document without pressing the PgUp or PgDn key.

- Instead of pressing the PgUp key, click in the elevator shaft *above* the little elevator (the *scroll box*). The box jumps up the shaft a little bit, and the document moves up one page, too. Click *below* the scroll box, and your view moves down, just as with the PgDn key.

- To move your view up line by line, click the boxed-in arrow (*scroll arrow*) at the top of the scroll bar. If you hold down the mouse button while the mouse pointer is over that arrow, more and more of your document appears, line by line, as it moves you closer to its top. (Holding down the mouse button while the pointer is on the bottom arrow moves you closer to the bottom, line by line.)

- Scroll bars that run along the *bottom* of a window can move your view from side to side rather than up and down. They're handy for viewing spreadsheets that extend off the right side of your screen.

- If the scroll bars don't have a little scroll box inside them, then you're already seeing everything on the screen. There's no little elevator to play with. Sniff. Sniff.

- Want to move around in a hurry? Then put the mouse pointer on the little elevator box, hold down the mouse button, and *drag* the little elevator box up or down inside the shaft. For example, if you drag the box up toward the top of its shaft and release it, you can view the top of the document. Dragging it and releasing it down low takes you near the end.

- Windows Me adds another dimension to some scroll bars: the little elevator's *size*. If the elevator is swollen up so big that it's practically filling the scroll bar, the window is currently displaying practically all the information the file has to offer. But if the elevator is a tiny box in a huge scroll bar, you're only viewing a tiny amount of the information contained in the file. Don't be surprised to see the scroll box change size when you add or remove information from a file.

- Clicking or double-clicking the little elevator box itself doesn't do anything, but that doesn't stop most people from trying it anyway.

- If you don't have a mouse, you can't play on the elevator. To view the top of your document, hold down Ctrl and press Home. To see the bottom, hold down Ctrl and press End. Or press the PgUp or PgDn key to move one page at a time.

Undoing what you've just done

Windows Me offers a zillion different ways for you to do the same thing. Here are four ways to access the Undo option, which unspills the milk you've just spilled:

✔ Hold down the Ctrl key and press the Z key. (This little quickie is known as the *shortcut key method*.) The last mistake you made is reversed, sparing you from further shame.

✔ Hold down the Alt key and press the Backspace key. (This other quickie often works when the Ctrl+Z trick fails.)

✔ Click Edit and then click Undo from the menu that falls down. (This approach is known as *wading through the menus*.) The last command you made is undone, saving you from any damage.

✔ Press and release the Alt key, press the letter E (from Edit), and then press the letter U (from Undo). (This *Alt key method* is handy when you don't have a mouse.) Your last bungle is unbungled, reversing any grievous penalties.

Don't feel like you have to learn all four methods. For example, if you can remember the Ctrl+Z key combination, you can forget about the menu method or the Alt key method.

Or, if you don't want to remember *anything,* stick with the menu method. Just pluck the Undo command as it appears on the menu.

Finally, if you don't have a mouse, you'll have to remember the Alt key or Ctrl key business until you remember to buy a mouse.

The taskbar

Windows Me converts your computer monitor's screen into a desktop. But because your newly computerized desktop is probably only 15 inches wide, all your programs and windows cover each other up like memos tossed onto a spike.

To keep track of the action, Windows Me introduces the taskbar. It usually clings to the bottom of your screen and simply lists what windows are currently open. If you've found the Start button, you've found the taskbar — the Start button lives on the taskbar's left or top end.

✔ Whenever you open a window, Windows Me tosses that window's name onto a button on the taskbar. If you open a lot of windows, the taskbar automatically shrinks all its buttons so they'll fit.

✔ To switch from one window to another, just click the desired window's name from its button on the taskbar. Wham! That window shoots to the top of the pile.

✔ Are all those open windows looking too crowded? Click a blank part of the taskbar with your right mouse button and choose the Minimize All Windows option. All your currently open windows turn into buttons on the taskbar.

✔ You can't find your taskbar? Try pointing off the edge of your screen, slowly, trying each of the four sides. If you hit the correct side, some specially configured taskbars will stop goofing around and come back to the screen. But be wary: Windows Me computers can use more than one monitor, and the taskbar can live on *any* of those monitor's edges — and that can lead to a lot of searching. (Ignore the mouse, hold down Control, and press Escape to bring the darn thing out into the open.)

✔ Press your keyboard's *Windows* key — the weird little key on your keyboard's bottom left corner — and your Start button pops into view, no matter where it was hiding.

✔ You can find loads more information about the taskbar in Chapter 10.

Borders

A *border* is that thin edge enclosing a window. Compared with a bar, it's really tiny.

✔ You drag borders from side to side to change a window's size. I discuss how to do that in Chapter 6.

✔ You can't use a mouse to change a window's size if the window doesn't have a border. A few unruly borders keep the window locked at its current size, no matter how much you fiddle.

✔ If you like to trifle in details, you can make a border thicker or thinner through the Windows Me Control Panel, which I discuss in Chapter 9. In fact, laptop owners often thicken their windows' borders to make them a little easier to grab with those awkward trackballs.

✔ Other than that, you won't be using borders much.

The Button Family

Three basic species of buttons flourish throughout the Windows Me environment: command buttons, option buttons, and minimize/maximize buttons. All three species are closely related, and yet they look and act quite differently.

Command buttons

Command buttons may be the simplest to figure out — Microsoft labeled them! Command buttons are most commonly found in *dialog boxes,* which are little pop-up forms that Windows Me makes you fill out before it will work for you.

For example, when you ask Windows Me to open a file, it sends out a form in a dialog box. You have to fill out the form, telling Windows Me what file you're after, where it's located, and other equally cumbersome details.

Table 5-1 identifies some of the more common command buttons that you encounter in Windows Me.

Table 5-1	Common Windows Me Command Buttons	
Command Button	*Habitat*	*Description*
OK	Found in nearly every pop-up dialog box	A click on this button says, "I'm done filling out the form, and I'm ready to move on." Windows Me then reads what you've typed into the form and processes your request. (Pressing the Enter key does the same thing as clicking the OK button.)
Cancel	Found in nearly every pop-up dialog box	If you've somehow loused things up when filling out a form, click the Cancel button. The pop-up box disappears, and everything returns to normal. Whew! (The Esc key does the same thing.)
?	Found in nearly every pop-up dialog box	Stumped? Click this button. Yet another box pops up, this time offering help with your current situation. (The F1 function key does the same thing.)
< Back Next > Finish	Found when you must answer a string of questions as you fill out a form	Boy, would this have come in handy in elementary school! By clicking the Back button, Windows returns you to the previous window so that you can change your answer. Click the Next button to move to the next question; click Finish when you're confident that the form's filled out correctly.

Command Button	Habitat	Description
Setup... Settings... Pizza...	Found less often in pop-up dialog boxes	If you encounter a button with ellipsis dots (. . .) after the word, brace yourself: Selecting that button brings yet another box to the screen. From there, you must choose even more settings, options, or toppings.
Click here to make this your home page set home page	Found sprinkled nearly everywhere	Windows Me adopted much of the Internet Web world, where buttons no longer look like buttons. Just about anything can be a button. The clues? When your mouse pointer turns into a little hand, it's hovering over a button. (Little pictures that waver on the screen are telltale signs, too.)

✔ By selecting a command button, you're telling Windows Me to carry out the command that's written on the button. (Luckily, no command buttons are labeled Explode.)

✔ See how the OK button in Table 5-1 has a slightly darker border than the others? That darker border means that the button is highlighted. Anything in Windows Me that's highlighted takes effect as soon as you press the Enter key; you don't *have* to select it.

✔ Some command buttons have underlined letters that you don't really notice until you stare at them. An underlined letter tells you that you can press that command button by holding down the Alt key while pressing the underlined letter. (That way, you don't have to click or double-click if your mouse is goofing up.)

✔ Instead of scooting your mouse to the Cancel button when you've goofed in a dialog box, just press your Esc key. It does the same thing.

If you've clicked the wrong command button but *haven't yet lifted your finger from the mouse button,* stop! There's still hope. Command buttons take effect only *after* you've lifted your finger from the mouse button. Keep your finger pressed on the button and scoot the mouse pointer away from the button. When the pointer no longer rests on the button, gently lift your finger. Whew! Try *that* trick on any elevator.

Did you stumble across a box that contains a confusing command button or two? Click the question mark in the box's upper-right corner (if there is a question mark, that is). Then, when you click the confusing command button, a helpful comment appears to explain that button's function in life. Also, try merely resting your mouse pointer over the button. Sometimes, Windows takes pity, and sends a helpful caption to explain matters.

Option buttons

Sometimes, Windows Me gets ornery and forces you to select just a single option. For example, you can elect to *eat* your brussels sprouts or *not* eat your brussels sprouts. You can't select both, so Windows Me doesn't let you select both of the options.

Windows Me handles this situation with an *option button.* When you select one option, the little dot hops over to it. If you select the other option, the little dot hops over to it instead. You find option buttons in many dialog boxes. Figure 5-6 shows an example.

Figure 5-6: When you select an option, the black dot hops to it.

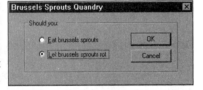

✔ Although Windows Me tempts you with several choices in an option box, it lets you select only one of them. It moves the dot (and little dotted border line) back and forth between the options as your decision wavers. Click the OK button when you've reached a decision. The *dotted* option then takes effect.

✔ If you *can* select more than one option, Windows Me doesn't present you with option buttons. Instead, it offers the more liberal *check boxes,* which are described in the "Check boxes" section later in this chapter.

✔ Option buttons are round. Command buttons, described earlier, are rectangular.

Some old-time computer engineers refer to option buttons as radio buttons, after those push buttons on car radios that switch from station to station, one station at a time.

Minimize/maximize buttons

All the little windows in Windows Me often cover each other up like teenage fans in the front row of a Pearl Jam concert. To restore order, you need to separate the windows by using their minimize/maximize buttons.

These buttons enable you to enlarge the window you want to play with or shrink all the others so they're out of the way. Here's the scoop.

 The minimize button is one of three buttons in the upper-right corner of almost every window. It looks like that little button in the margin next to this paragraph.

A click on the minimize button makes its window disappear, although the program lives on. In fact, its little button still lives on the taskbar along the bottom of your screen. (Click the button to return the window to its normal size.) Keyboard users can press Alt, the spacebar, and then N to minimize a window.

✔ Minimizing a window doesn't destroy its contents; it just transforms the window into a little button on the bar that runs along the bottom of the screen.

✔ To make the button turn back into an on-screen window, click the button on the taskbar along the bottom of your screen. The program reverts to a window in the same size and location as before you shrank it. (Keyboard users can press Alt, the spacebar, and then R.)

✔ Closing a window and minimizing a window are two different things. Closing a window purges the program from the computer's memory. To reopen it, you need to load it off your hard drive again. Turning a window into an icon keeps it handy, loaded into memory, and ready to be used at an instant's notice.

 The maximize button is in the upper-right corner of every window, too. It looks like the one in the margin.

A click on the maximize button makes the window swell up something fierce, taking up as much space on-screen as possible. Keyboard users can press Alt, the spacebar, and then X to maximize their windows.

Don't bother with this Control-menu button stuff

The Control-menu button provides a quick exit from any window: Just give the little ornament a quick double-click. Other than that feature, however, the Control-menu button is pretty useless.

For example, by clicking the Control-menu button once, you get a pull-down menu with a bunch of options. Choose the Move option, and you can move around the window with the keyboard's arrow keys. (But it's much easier to move a window by using the mouse, as you find out in Chapter 6.)

Choosing the Size option lets you change a window's size. (But that's much easier with a mouse, too, as you find out in Chapter 6.)

Don't bother with the menu's Minimize and Maximize options, either. Those two options have their own dedicated buttons, right in the window's other top corner. Click the minimize button (the button with the little line on it) to minimize the window; click the maximize button (the button with the big square on it) to maximize the window. Simple. You don't need to bumble through a menu for the Minimize and Maximize options when minimize and maximize buttons are already staring you in the face.

The Close option is redundant. You can close the window faster by clicking the dedicated Close button — the button with the X on it in the window's far, upper-right corner.

So don't bother messing with the Control-menu button because it's just a waste of time.

(The Control-menu button may come in handy if you lose your laptop's mouse, however. Should this disastrous accident happen to you, press Alt and the spacebar to bring up the Control menu and then press any of the underlined letters to access the function.)

✔ If you're frustrated with all those windows that are overlapping each other, click your current window's maximize button. The window muscles its way to the top, filling the screen like a *real* program.

✔ Immediately after you maximize a window, its little maximize button turns into a *restore button* (described momentarily). The restore button lets you shrink the window back down when you're through giving it the whole playing field.

You don't *have* to click the maximize button to maximize a window. Just double-click its *title bar,* the thick strip along the window's top bearing its name. That double-click does the same thing as clicking the maximize button, and the title bar is much easier to aim for.

 In the upper-right corner of every maximized window is the restore button, which looks like the button in the margin.

After a window is maximized, clicking this button returns the window to the size it was before you maximized it. (Keyboard users can press Alt, the spacebar, and then R.)

> ✔ Restore buttons appear only in windows that fill the entire screen (which is no great loss because you need a restore button only when the window is maximized).

The Dopey Control-Menu Button

Just as all houses have circuit breakers, all windows have *Control-menu buttons*, and the buttons differ on each program. However, the buttons always perch in the top-left corner of a window. (Sharp-eyed readers will notice that the button is actually a miniature icon representing the program.)

That little hood ornament hides a menu full of rather useless options, so ignore all of them but this: Double-click the Control-menu button whenever you want to leave a window in a hurry.

> ✔ Some people never use the Control-menu button at all. They just click the Close button — that button with the X on it in the window's far, upper-right corner.

> ✔ If you click the Control-menu button, a secret hidden menu appears, but it's pretty useless. So ignore it, skip the technical chatter in the nearby sidebar about the Control-menu button, and move along to the more stimulating dialog boxes that follow.

Dialog Box Stuff (Lots of Gibberish)

Sooner or later, you'll have to sit down and tell Windows Me something personal — the name of a file to open, for example, or the name of a file to print. To handle this personal chatter, Windows Me sends out a dialog box.

A *dialog box* is merely another little window. But instead of containing a program, it contains a little form or checklist for you to fill out. These forms can have bunches of different parts, which are discussed in the following sections. Don't bother trying to remember the names of the parts, however. It's more important to figure out how they work.

Text boxes

A *text box* works just like a fill-in-the-blanks test in history class. You can type anything you want into a text box — even numbers. For example, Figure 5-7 shows a dialog box that pops up when you want to search for some words or characters in WordPad.

Figure 5-7:
This dialog box from WordPad contains a text box.

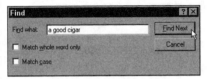

When you type words or characters into this box and press the Enter key, WordPad searches for them. If it finds them, WordPad shows them to you on the page. If it doesn't find them, WordPad sends out a robotic dialog box saying it's finished searching.

- ✔ Two clues let you know whether a text box is *active* — that is, ready for you to start typing stuff into it: The box's current information is highlighted, or a cursor is blinking inside it. In either case, just start typing the new stuff. (The older, highlighted information disappears as the new stuff replaces it.)

- ✔ If the text box *isn't* highlighted or there *isn't* a blinking cursor inside it, it's not ready for you to start typing. To announce your presence, click inside it. Then start typing. Or press Tab until the box becomes highlighted or contains a cursor.

- ✔ If you click inside a text box that already contains words, you must delete the information with the Delete or Backspace key before you can start typing in new information. (Or you can double-click the old information; that way, the incoming text automatically replaces the old text.)

Regular list boxes

Some boxes don't let you type stuff into them. They already contain information. Boxes containing lists of information are called, appropriately enough, *list boxes*. For example, WordPad brings up a list box if you're inspired enough to want to change its *font* — the way the letters look (see Figure 5-8).

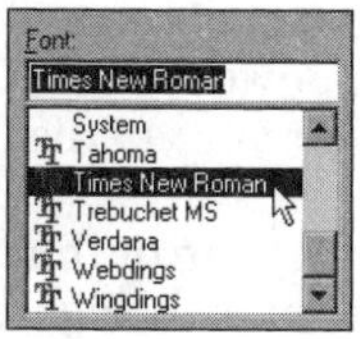

Figure 5-8:
You can
select a font
from the list
box to
change the
way letters
look in
WordPad.

✔ See how the Times New Roman font is highlighted? It's the currently selected font. Press Enter (or click the OK command button), and WordPad uses that font in your current paragraph.

✔ See the scroll bar along the side of the list box? It works just as it does anywhere else: Click the little scroll arrows (or press the up or down arrow) to move the list up or down, and you can see any names that don't fit in the box.

✔ Many list boxes have a text box above them. When you click a name in the list box, that name hops into the text box. Sure, you could type the name into the text box yourself, but it wouldn't be nearly as much fun.

✔ When confronted with a bunch of names in a list box, type the first letter of the name you're after. Windows Me immediately scrolls down the list to the first name beginning with that letter.

TIP

When one just isn't enough

Because Windows Me can display only one pattern on your desktop at a time, you can select only one pattern from the desktop's list box. Other list boxes, like those in Windows Explorer, let you select a bunch of names simultaneously. Here's how:

✔ To select more than one item, hold down the Ctrl key and click each item you want. Each item stays highlighted.

✔ To select a bunch of adjacent items from a list box, click the first item you want. Then hold down Shift and click the last item you

want. Windows Me immediately highlights the first item, last item, and every item in between. Pretty sneaky, huh?

✔ Finally, when grabbing bunches of icons, try using the "rubber band" trick: Point at an area of the screen next to one icon, and, while holding down the mouse button, move the mouse until you've drawn a lasso around all the icons. After you've highlighted the icons you want, let go of the mouse button, and they remain highlighted. Fun!

Drop-down list boxes

List boxes are convenient, but they take up a great deal of room. So, Windows
Me sometimes hides list boxes, just as it hides pull-down menus. Then, if you
click in the right place, the list box appears, ready for your perusal.

So, where's the right place? It's that downward-pointing arrow button, just
like the one shown next to the box beside the Font option in Figure 5-9. (The
mouse pointer is pointing to it.)

Figure 5-9:
Click the
downward-
pointing
arrow next
to the Font
box to see a
drop-down
list box.

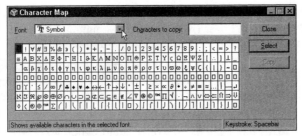

Figure 5-10 shows the drop-down list box, after being clicked by the mouse.

Figure 5-10:
A list box
drops down
to display all
the fonts
that are
available.

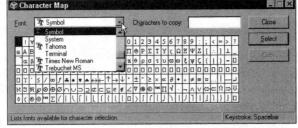

To make a drop-down list box drop down without using a mouse, press the
Tab key until you highlight the box next to the little arrow. Hold down the Alt
key and press the down-arrow key, and the drop-down list starts to dangle.

- Unlike regular list boxes, drop-down list boxes don't have a text box
  above them. That thing that *looks* like a text box just shows the currently selected item from the list; you can't type anything in there.

- To scoot around quickly in a drop-down list box, press the first letter of
  the item you're after. The first item beginning with that letter is instantly
  highlighted. You can press the up- or down-arrow key to see the words
  and phrases nearby.

✔ Another way to scoot around quickly in a drop-down list box is to click the scroll bar to its right. (Scroll bars are discussed earlier in this chapter, if you need a refresher.)

✔ You can choose only *one* item from the list of a drop-down list box.

✔ The program in Figure 5-10 is called Character Map, and Windows Me usually doesn't install that handy little accessory. To slap the hand of Windows Me and make it install the Character Map, use the Control Panel's Add/Remove Program feature, as I describe in Chapter 10.

Check boxes

Sometimes you can choose from a whopping number of options in a dialog box. A check box is next to each option, and if you want that option, you click in the box. If you don't want it, you leave the box blank. (Keyboard users can press the up- or down-arrow key until a check box is highlighted and then press the space bar.) For example, with the check boxes in the dialog box shown in Figure 5-11, you pick and choose how the Windows Me taskbar behaves.

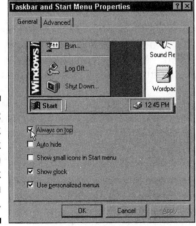

Figure 5-11: A check mark appears in each check box that you choose.

✔ By clicking in a check box, you change its setting. Clicking in an empty square turns on that option. If the square already has a check mark in it, a click turns off that option, removing the check mark.

✔ You can click next to as many check boxes as you want. With radio buttons — those things that look the same but are round — you can select only one option.

✔ To bring up the figure shown in Figure 5-11, right-click on a blank part of your taskbar and choose Properties from the menu that flies up.

Sliding controls

Rich Microsoft programmers, impressed by track lights and sliding light switches in their luxurious new homes, added sliding controls to Windows Me as well. These "virtual" light switches are easy to use and don't wear out nearly as quickly as the real ones do. To slide a control in Windows Me — to adjust the volume level, for example — just drag and drop the sliding lever, like the one shown in Figure 5-12.

Figure 5-12:
To slide a lever, point at it, hold down the mouse button, and move your mouse.

Point at the lever with the mouse and, while holding down the mouse button, move the mouse in the direction you want the sliding lever to move. As you move the mouse, the lever moves, too. When you've moved the lever to a comfortable spot, let go of the mouse button, and Windows Me leaves the lever at its new position. That's it.

✔ Some levers slide to the left and right; others move up and down. None of them move diagonally.

✔ To change the volume in Windows Me, click the little speaker near the clock in the bottom-right corner. A sliding volume control appears, ready to be dragged up or down.

✔ No mouse? Then go buy one. In the meantime, press Tab until a little box appears over the sliding lever; then press your arrow keys in the direction you want the lever to slide.

Just Tell Me How to Open a File!

Enough with the labels and terms. Forget the buttons and bars. How do you load a file into a program? This section gives you the scoop. You follow these steps every time you load a file into a program.

Opening a file is a *file-related* activity, so start by finding the word File in the window's menu bar (see Figure 5-13).

Figure 5-13:
To open a file, you first choose the word File in the window's menu bar.

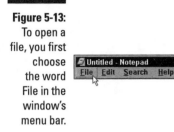

Then simply do the following:

1. **Click File (or press Alt and then F) to knock down that word's hidden little menu.**

   Figure 5-14 shows the File pull-down menu.

Figure 5-14:
When you choose File, the File pull-down menu appears.

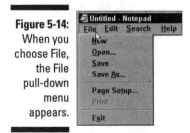

2. **Click Open (or press O) to bring up the Open dialog box.**

   You can predict that Open will call up a dialog box because of the trailing . . . things beside Open on-screen. (Those . . . things are called an *ellipsis,* or *three dots,* depending on the tightness of your English teacher's hair bun.)

   Figure 5-15 shows the Open dialog box that leaps to the front of the screen. In fact, a similar dialog box appears almost any time you mess with the File pull-down menu in any program.

Figure 5-15:
This Open
dialog box
appears
whenever
you open a
file in any
Windows
program.

✔ If you find your filename listed in the first list box (in this case, the one listing the Beer Cheese file), you're in luck. Double-click the file's name, and it automatically jumps into the program. Or hold down Alt and press N, type the file's name, and press Enter. Or click the file's name once and press Enter. Or curse Windows Me for giving you so many options for such a simple procedure.

✔ If you don't find the file's name, it's probably in a different folder, also known as a *directory*. Windows Me often lists places to look along the window's left side, as seen in Figure 5-15. Click History to see names of recently opened files. Click Desktop if the file is located on your desktop. My Documents lets you peek into the My Documents area, a convenient storage space. Head for My Computer to scour the entire computer from the top down, or click My Network Places to scour *other* computers, should you have a network.

✔ Click the little box along the top that is labeled Look in, and Windows Me displays a bunch of other folders to rummage through. Each time you click a different folder, that folder's contents appear in the first list box.

✔ Still can't find the right folder or directory? Perhaps that file is on a different drive. Click one of the other drive icons listed in the Look in box to search in a different drive. Drive icons are those little gray box things; folder icons, well, look like folders.

✔ Could the file be named something strange? Click the Files of type drop-down list box (or hold down Alt and press T) to select a different file type. To see *all* the files in a directory, select the All Files (*.*) option. Then all the files in that directory show up.

✔ Don't know what those little icons along the top are supposed to do? Rest your mouse pointer over the one that has you stumped. After a second or so, the increasingly polite Windows Me brings a box of explanatory information to the screen. For example, rest the mouse pointer over the folder with the explosion in its corner, and Windows Me tells you that clicking that icon creates a new folder.

✔ This stuff is incredibly mind-numbing, of course, if you've never been exposed to directories, drives, folders, wild cards, or other equally painful computer terms. For a more rigorous explanation of this scary file-management stuff, troop to Chapter 11.

✔ If the file is still lost, make Windows find it. Click the Start button's Search button and choose the For Files or Folders option. Type in the name of your file and choose My Computer in the Look in box. (Chapter 7 offers more information about Search because that chapter is dedicated to helping you find lost things in Windows.)

Hey! When Do I Click, and When Do I Double-Click?

That's certainly a legitimate question, but Microsoft only coughs up a vague answer. Microsoft says that you should *click* when you're *selecting* something in Windows Me and you should *double-click* when you're *choosing* something. And even that's not for certain. Huh?

Well, you're *selecting* something when you're *highlighting* it. For example, you may select a check box, an option button, or a filename. You click any of the three to *select* it, and then you look at it to make sure that it looks okay. If you're satisfied with your selection, you click the OK button to complete the job.

To *select* something is to set it up for later use.

When you *choose* something, however, the response is more immediate. Choosing a file immediately loads it into your program. Microsoft's "choose" lingo says, "I'm choosing this file, and I want it now, buster."

You *choose* something you want to have carried out immediately.

✔ All right, this explanation is still vague. So always start off by trying a single-click. If clicking once doesn't do the job, try a double-click. It's usually much safer than double-clicking first and asking questions later.

✔ And even this isn't always true. See, Windows Me can be set up so it chooses files when you perform a single-click *or* a double-click. The software enables you to select a file or program by simply resting your pointer over it and then clicking to prod it into action. That's the way the Internet's World Wide Web works, so Windows Me lets you set it up that way, too.

✔ If you accidentally double-click rather than single-click, it usually doesn't matter. You can usually just close a runaway program with a few clicks. But if something terrible happens, hold down the Ctrl key and press the letter Z. You can usually undo any damage.

✔ Like the single-click method? Then choose Folder Options from the Control Panel and choose this option: Single-click to open an item (point to select). Prefer the traditional double-click way? Then go to the same place and choose the other option: Double-click to open an item (single-click to select).

✔ If Windows Me keeps mistaking your purposeful double-click as two disjointed single-clicks, head for the section in Chapter 9 on tinkering with the Control Panel. Adjusting Windows Me so that it recognizes a double-click when you make one is pretty easy.

When Do I Use the Left Mouse Button, and When Do I Use the Right One?

When somebody tells you to "click" something in Windows Me, it almost always means that you should "click with your left mouse button." That's because most Windows Me users are right-handed, and their index finger hovers over the mouse's left button, making it an easy target.

Windows Me, however, also lets you click your *right* mouse button, and it regards the two actions as completely different.

Pointing at something and clicking the right button often brings up a secret hidden menu with some extra options. Right-click a blank portion of your desktop, for example, and a menu pops up, allowing you to organize your desktop's icons or change the way your display looks. Right-clicking an icon often brings up a hidden menu as well.

Or hold down your right mouse button while dragging an item across the desktop. Windows Me brings up a menu, asking you to choose what you want to do with that item. If you drag the item while holding down your left mouse button, Windows Me doesn't ask; it does whatever it wants.

✔ The right mouse button is designed more for advanced users or people with bad memories. The first crowd likes to feel that it's doing something sneaky; the others prefer Windows to remind them what options are possible.

✔ Confused about something on the screen? Try clicking it with your right mouse button, just for kicks. The result may be unexpectedly helpful.

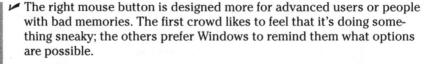

Chapter 6

Moving Windows Around

● ●

In This Chapter

▶ Moving a window to the top of the pile

▶ Moving a window from here to there

▶ Making windows bigger or smaller

▶ Shrinking windows onto the taskbar

▶ Turning taskbar icons back into windows

▶ Switching from window to window

▶ Fiddling with the taskbar

● ●

*A*h, the power of Windows Me. Using separate windows, you can put a spreadsheet, a drawing program, an Internet Web page, and a word processor on-screen *at the same time*.

You can copy a hot-looking graphic from your drawing program and toss it into your memo. You can stick a chunk of your spreadsheet into your memo, too. In the background, the Web can display a constantly running news update. And why not? All four windows can be on-screen *at the same time*.

You have only one problem: With so many windows on-screen at the same time, you can't see anything but a confusing jumble of programs.

This chapter shows how to move those darn windows around on-screen so that you can see at least *one* of them.

Moving a Window to the Top of the Pile

Take a good look at the mixture of windows on-screen. Sometimes you can recognize a tiny portion of the window you're after. If so, you're in luck. Move the mouse pointer until it hovers over that tiny portion of the window and click the mouse button. Shazam! Windows Me immediately brings the clicked-on window to the front of the screen.

That newly enlarged window probably covers up strategic parts of other windows. But at least you'll be able to get some work finished, one window at a time.

- ✔ Windows Me places a lot of windows on-screen simultaneously. But unless you have two heads, you'll probably use just one window at a time, leaving the remaining programs to wait patiently in the background. The window that's on top, ready to be used, is called the *active* window.

- ✔ The active window is the one with the most lively title bar along its top. The active window's title bar is a brighter color than all the others.

- ✔ The last window you click is the active window. All your subsequent keystrokes and mouse movements will affect that window.

- ✔ Some programs can run in the background, even if they're not in the currently active window. Some communications programs can keep talking to other computers in the background, for example, and some spreadsheets can merrily crunch numbers, unconcerned with whether they're the currently active window. Imagine!

Although many windows may be on-screen, you can enter information into only one of them: the active window. To make a window active, click any part of it. It rises to the top, ready to do your bidding. (The Internet and a computer's TV Card can stick information into background windows, but that's not *you* doing it.)

Another way to move to a window is by clicking on its name in the Windows Me taskbar. See "The Way-Cool Taskbar" section, later in this chapter.

Moving a Window from Here to There

Sometimes you want to move a window to a different place on-screen (known in Windows Me parlance as the *desktop*). Maybe part of the window hangs off the edge of the desktop, and you want it centered. Or maybe you want to put two windows on-screen side by side so that you can compare their contents.

In either case, you can move a window by grabbing its *title bar,* that thick bar along its top. Put the mouse pointer over the window's title bar and hold down the mouse button. Now use the title bar as the window's handle. When you move the mouse around, you tug the window along with it.

When you've moved the window to where you want it to stay, release the mouse button to release the window. The window stays put and on top of the pile.

✔ The process of holding down the mouse button while moving the mouse is called *dragging*. When you let go of the mouse button, you're *dropping* what you've dragged.

✔ When placing two windows next to each other on-screen, you usually need to change their sizes as well as their locations. The very next section tells how to change a window's size, but don't forget to read "The Way-Cool Taskbar" section, later in this chapter. It's full of tips and tricks for resizing windows as well as moving them around.

✔ Stuck with a keyboard and no mouse? Press Alt, the spacebar, and M. Then use the arrow keys to move the window around. Press Enter when it's in the right place.

Making a Window Bigger or Smaller

Sometimes, moving the windows around isn't enough. They still cover each other up. Luckily, you don't need any special hardware to make them bigger or smaller. See that thin little border running around the edge of the window? Use the mouse to yank on a window's corner border, and you can change its size.

First, point at the corner with the mouse arrow. When it's positioned over the corner, the arrow turns into a two-headed arrow. Now hold down the mouse button and drag the corner in or out to make the window smaller or bigger. The window's border expands or contracts as you tug on it with the mouse, so you can see what you're doing.

When you're done yanking and the window's border looks about the right size, let go of the mouse button. The window immediately redraws itself, taking the new position.

Here's the procedure, step by step:

1. **Point the mouse pointer at the edge of the corner.**

   It turns into a two-headed arrow, as shown in Figure 6-1.

Figure 6-1:
When the
mouse
points at the
window's
bottom
corner, the
arrow
grows a
second
head, as
seen in the
bottom-right
corner.

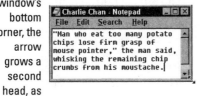

2. **Hold down the mouse button and move the two-headed arrow in or out to make the window bigger or smaller.**

   Figure 6-2 shows how the new outline takes shape when you pull the corner inward to make the window smaller.

Figure 6-2:
As you
move the
mouse, the
window's
border
changes to
reflect its
new shape.

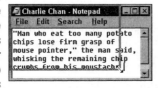

3. **Release the mouse button.**

   The window shapes itself to fit into the border you've just created (see Figure 6-3).

Figure 6-3:
Let go of
the mouse
button, and
the window
fills its
newly
adjusted
border.

That's it!

- This procedure may seem vaguely familiar, because it is. You're just *dragging and dropping* the window's corner to a new size. That *drag-and-drop* concept works throughout Windows Me. For example, you can *drag and drop* a title bar to move an entire window to a new location on-screen.

- You can grab the side border of a window and move it in or out to make it fatter or skinnier. You can grab the top or bottom of a window and move it up or down to make it taller or shorter. But grabbing for a corner is always easiest because then you can make a window fatter, skinnier, taller, or shorter, all with one quick flick of the wrist.

If a window is hanging off the edge of the screen and you can't seem to position it so that all of it fits on-screen, try shrinking it first. Grab a visible corner and drag it toward the window's center. Release the mouse button, and the window shrinks itself to fit in its now smaller border. Then grab the window's title bar and hold down the mouse button. When you drag the title bar back toward the center of the screen, you can see the whole window once again.

Making a Window Fill the Whole Screen

Sooner or later, you get tired of all this New Age, multiwindow mumbo jumbo. Why can't you just put *one* huge window on-screen? Well, you can.

To make any window grow as big as it gets, double-click its *title bar,* that topmost bar along the top of the window. The window leaps up to fill the screen, covering up all the other windows.

To bring the pumped-up window back to normal size, double-click its title bar once again. The window shrinks to its former size, and you can see everything that it was covering up.

- ✔ When a window fills the entire screen, it loses its borders. That means that you can no longer change its size by tugging on its title bar or dragging its borders. Those borders just aren't there anymore.

- ✔ If you're morally opposed to double-clicking a window's title bar to expand it, you can expand it another way. Click the window's *maximize button,* the middle-most of the three little boxes in its top-right corner. The window hastily fills the entire screen. At the same time, the maximize button turns into a *restore* button; click the restore button when you want the window to return to its previous size.

- ✔ Refer to Chapter 5 for more information on the maximize, minimize, and restore buttons.

- ✔ If you don't have a mouse, you can make the window bigger by holding down Alt, pressing the spacebar, and pressing X. But for goodness sake, buy a mouse so that you don't have to try to remember these complicated commands!

- ✔ DOS programs running in on-screen windows don't usually fill the screen. When you double-click their title bars, they get bigger, but Windows Me still keeps 'em relatively small. If you take them out of the window, however, they fill the screen completely and shove Windows Me completely into the background. To take a DOS program out of a window, click the DOS window to make it active and then hold down Alt and press Enter. The DOS program suddenly lunges for the entire screen, and Windows Me disappears. To bring it back, hold Alt and press Enter again.

Shrinking Windows to the Taskbar

Windows spawn windows. You start with one window to write a letter to Mother. You open another window to check her address, for example, and then yet another to see whether you've forgotten any recent birthdays. Before you know it, four more windows are crowded across the desktop.

To combat the clutter, Windows Me provides a simple means of window control: You can transform a window from a screen-cluttering square into a tiny button at the bottom of the screen.

See the three buttons lurking in just about every window's top-right corner? Click the *minimize button* — the button with the little line in it. Whoosh! The window disappears, represented by its little button on the bar running along the bottom of your screen. Click that button, and your window hops back onto the screen, ready for action.

The difference can be dramatic. Figure 6-4 shows a desktop with a bunch of open windows.

Figure 6-5 shows that same desktop after all windows but one have been turned into buttons along the taskbar. Those other windows are still readily available, mind you. Just click a window's button from the taskbar along the bottom of the screen, and that window instantly leaps back to its former place on-screen.

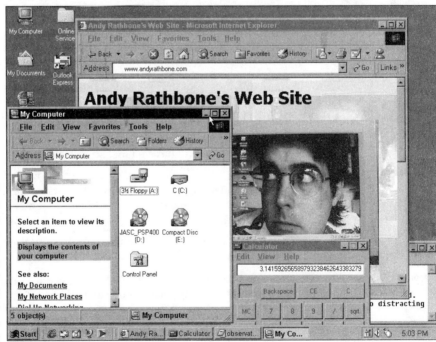

Figure 6-4:
A desktop can be distracting with too many windows open simultaneously.

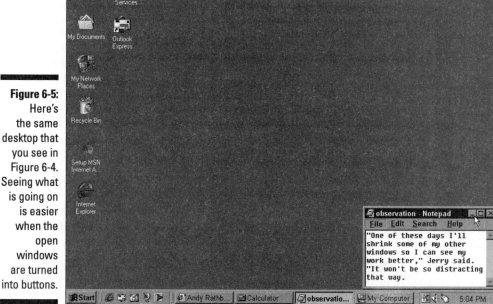

Figure 6-5:
Here's
the same
desktop that
you see in
Figure 6-4.
Seeing what
is going on
is easier
when the
open
windows
are turned
into buttons.

✔ To shrink an open window so that it's out of the way, click the left-most of the three buttons in the window's top-right corner. The window *mini-mizes* itself into a button and lines itself up on the bar along the bottom of the screen.

✔ The buttons on the taskbar all have a label so that you can tell which program each button represents.

✔ When you minimize a window, you neither destroy its contents nor close it. You merely change its shape. It is still loaded into memory, waiting for you to play with it again.

✔ To put the window back where it was, click its button on the taskbar. It hops back up to the same place it was before.

✔ Whenever you load a program by using the Start button or Explorer, that program's name automatically appears on the taskbar. If one of your open windows ever gets lost on your desktop, click its name on the taskbar. The window immediately jumps to the forefront.

✔ Do you want to shrink all your open windows into buttons, and in a hurry? Right-click a blank area of your taskbar and choose Minimize All Windows from the menu that pops up. Slurp. Windows Me sucks all the open windows off the screen, tidying things up quickly.

✔ Keyboard users can press Alt, the spacebar, and N to minimize a window. Holding down Alt and pressing the Tab key brings up a new window for restoring your minimized programs to their former glory. (That fun little tip gets its own section, titled "The Alt+Tab trick," later in this chapter.)

✔ Using the Windows Me Active Desktop option to stick Internet windows onto your desktop as wallpaper? Those Internet windows act like wallpaper, so they don't have minimize buttons. They work more like big, permanent stickers. (To turn the Active Desktop on or off, right-click a blank part of your desktop, choose the Active Desktop option from the pop-up menu, and click the View as Web Page option.)

Turning Taskbar Buttons into Windows

To turn a minimized window at the bottom of the screen back into a useful program in the middle of the screen, just click its name on the taskbar. Pretty simple, huh?

✔ If you prefer wading through menus, just click the shrunken window's button with your *right* mouse button. A Control menu shoots out the top of the button's head. Click the menu's Restore option, and the program leaps back to its former window position.

✔ In addition to using a click, you can use a few other methods to turn icons back into program windows. The very next section describes one way, and "The Way-Cool Taskbar" section, later in this chapter, describes another.

Keeping your icons straight

Don't be confused by a program's icon on your desktop and a program's button on the taskbar along the bottom of your screen. They're two different things. The button at the bottom of the screen stands for a program that has already been loaded into the computer's memory. It's already running, ready for immediate action. The icon on your desktop or in Windows Me Explorer stands for a program that is sitting on the computer's hard drive waiting to be loaded.

If you mistakenly click the icon in the Windows Explorer or desktop rather than the button on the taskbar at the bottom of the screen, you load a second copy of that program. Two versions of the program are loaded: one running as a window, and the other running as a taskbar button waiting to be turned back into a window.

Running two versions can cause confusion — especially if you start entering stuff into both versions of the same program. You won't know which window has the *right* version!

Switching from Window to Window

Sometimes, switching from window to window is easy. If you can see any part of the window you want — a corner, a bar, or a piece of dust — just click it. That's all it takes to bring that window to the front of the screen, ready for action.

You can also just click that window's button on the taskbar along the bottom of your screen. The following sections give a few extra tricks for switching from window to window to window.

The Alt+Tab trick

This trick is so much fun that Microsoft should have plastered it across the front of the Windows Me box instead of hiding it in the middle of the manual.

Hold down Alt and press Tab. A most-welcome box pops up in the center of the screen, naming the last program you've touched (see Figure 6-6).

Figure 6-6:
When you hold down Alt and press Tab, Windows Me displays the name of the last program you used.

Surfer's Baby Backpack - WordPad

If the program you're after is named, rejoice! And remove your finger from the Alt key. The window named in that box leaps to the screen.

If you're looking for a *different* program, keep your finger on the Alt key and press Tab once again. At each press of Tab, Windows Me displays the name of another open program. When you see the one you want, release the Alt key, and then hoot and holler. The program leaps to the screen, ready for your working pleasure.

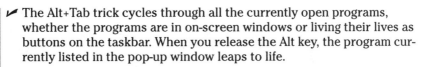

✔ The Alt+Tab trick cycles through all the currently open programs, whether the programs are in on-screen windows or living their lives as buttons on the taskbar. When you release the Alt key, the program currently listed in the pop-up window leaps to life.

✔ The Alt+Tab trick works even if you're running a DOS program with Windows Me lurking in the background. The DOS program disappears while the pop-up box has its moment in the sun. (And the DOS program returns when you're done playing around, too.)

✔ The first time you press Tab, the little pop-up window lists the name of the program you last accessed. If you prefer to cycle through the program names in the opposite direction, hold down Shift *and* Alt while pressing Tab. If you agree that this is a pretty frivolous option, rub your stomach and pat your head at the same time.

The Alt+Esc trick

The concept is getting kind of stale with this one, but here goes: If you hold down Alt and press Esc, Windows Me cycles through all the open programs, but in a slightly less efficient way.

Instead of bringing its name to a big box in the middle of the screen, Windows Me simply highlights the program, whether it's in a window or sitting as a button on the taskbar. Sometimes this method can be handy, but usually it's a little slower.

If Windows Me is currently cycling through a program on the taskbar, the Alt+Esc trick simply highlights the button at the bottom of the screen. That's not much of a visual indicator, and most of the time it won't even catch your eye.

When you see the window you want, release the Alt key. If it's an open window, it becomes the active window. But if you release the Alt key while a button's name is highlighted, you need to take one more step: You need to click the button or press Enter to get the window on-screen.

The Alt+Esc trick is a little slower and a little less handy than the Alt+Tab trick described in the preceding section.

The Way-Cool Taskbar

This section introduces one of the handiest tricks in Windows Me, so pull your chair in a little closer. Windows Me comes with a special program that keeps track of all the open programs. Called the *taskbar,* it always knows what programs are running and where they are. Shown in Figure 6-7, the taskbar normally lives along the bottom of your screen, although Chapter 10 shows how to move it to any edge you want. (*Hint:* Just "drag" it there.)

Figure 6-7:
Always handy, the taskbar lists your currently running programs and lets you bring them to the forefront by clicking on their names.

From the taskbar, you can perform powerful magic on your open windows, as shown in the next few sections.

✔ See how the button for Calculator looks "pushed in" in Figure 6-7? That's because Calculator is the currently active window on the desktop. One of your taskbar's buttons always looks "pushed in" unless you close or minimize all the windows on your desktop.

✔ Don't see the taskbar? Then hold down Ctrl and press Esc. Windows Me instantly brings the taskbar and Start menu to the surface, ready to do your bidding. If the taskbar merely lurks along the edge, grab the visible part with your mouse and drag it toward the center of the screen until the entire taskbar is visible.

Switching to another window

See a window you want to play with listed on the taskbar? Just click its name, and it rises to the surface. Simple. (Especially if you've ever labored under some older versions of Windows.) If the taskbar isn't showing for some reason, pressing Ctrl+Esc calls it to the forefront.

Ending a task

Mad at a program? Then kill it. Click the program's name on the taskbar with your *right* mouse button and then click the word Close from the menu that pops up (or press C). The highlighted program quits, just as if you'd chosen its Exit command from within its own window. The departing program gives you a chance to save any work before it quits and disappears from the screen.

Cascading and tiling windows

Sometimes those windows are scattered *everywhere*. How can you clean up in a hurry? By using the Cascade and Tile commands. Click a blank spot on the taskbar with the *right* mouse button — the spot on or near the clock is usually good — and the cascade and tile commands appear.

The two commands organize your open windows in drastically different ways. Figure 6-8 shows what your screen looks like when you choose the Cascade command.

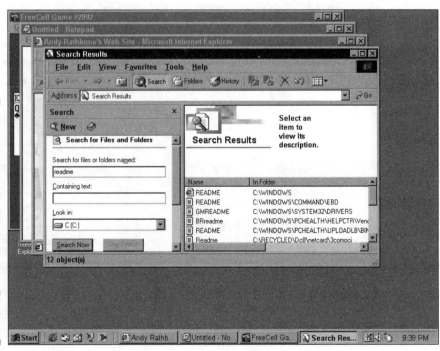

Figure 6-8: The taskbar's Cascade command piles all the open windows neatly across the screen. It's a favorite command of blackjack players.

Talk about neat and orderly! The taskbar grabs all the windows and deals them out like cards across the desktop. When you choose the taskbar's Cascade Windows command, all the open windows are lined up neatly on-screen with their title bars showing.

The Tile Windows Horizontally and Tile Windows Vertically commands rearrange the windows, too, but in a slightly different way (see Figure 6-9). The tile commands arrange all the currently open windows across the screen, giving each one the same amount of space. This arrangement helps you find a window that has been missing for a few hours.

Note: Both the Tile and Cascade commands arrange only open windows. They don't open up any windows currently shrunken into buttons on the taskbar.

If you have only two open windows, the Tile commands arrange them side by side, making it easy for you to compare their contents. The Tile Windows Vertically command places them side by side *vertically,* which makes them useless for comparing text: You can only see the first few words of each sentence. Choose the Tile Windows Horizontally command if you want to see complete sentences.

Figure 6-9:
The taskbar's Tile commands organize the open windows like tiles on the shower floor. You can see them all, but they're often too small to be of much use.

Arranging icons on the desktop

The taskbar can be considered a housekeeper of sorts, but it *only* does windows. It arranges the open windows neatly across the screen, but it doesn't touch any icons living on your desktop.

If the open windows look fine but the desktop's icons look a little shabby, right-click a blank area of your desktop. When the menu pops up, click the Line Up Icons command, and Windows gently moves your icons so they're in a pleasant grid. They're still in roughly the same spot you left them; they're just lined up.

To make Windows rearrange them completely, choose the Arrange Icons command, then select the way you want Windows Me to line up your icons: by Name, Type, Size, or Date. Or, simply choose the Auto Arrange option from the same menu. Then your desktop's icons always stay in neat, orderly rows.

The taskbar is an easily accessible helper. Take advantage of it often when you're having difficulty finding windows or when you want to clean up the desktop so that you can find things.

Finding the taskbar

Is the taskbar missing from the bottom of your screen? Hold down Ctrl and press Esc, and the taskbar instantly appears. If you'd prefer that the taskbar not disappear sometimes, head for Chapter 10. It explains how to customize your taskbar so that it doesn't bail on you.

Chapter 7

I Can't Find It!

Sooner or later, Windows Me gives you that head-scratching feeling. "Golly," you say, as you frantically tug on your mouse cord, "that stuff was *right there* a second ago. Where did it go?"

When Windows Me starts playing hide-and-seek with your information, this chapter tells you where to search and how to make it stop playing foolish games. Then, when you find your Solitaire window, you can get back to work.

Plucking a Lost Window from the Taskbar

Forget about that huge, 1940s rolltop mahogany desk in the resale shop window. The Windows Me peewee desktop can't be any bigger than the size of your monitor (or two monitors, if you add another monitor and video card, as I describe in Chapter 19).

In a way, Windows Me works more like those spike memo holders than like an actual desktop. Every time you open a new window, you're tossing another piece of information onto the spike. The window on top is relatively easy to see, but what's lying directly underneath it?

If you can see a window's ragged edge protruding from any part of the pile, click it. The window magically rushes to the top of the pile. But what if you can't see *any* part of the window at all? How do you know that it's even on the desktop?

You can solve this mystery by calling up your helpful Windows Me detective: the taskbar. The taskbar keeps a master list of everything that's happening on your screen (even the invisible stuff).

Solve this mystery by calling up your helpful Windows Me detective: the taskbar (see Figure 7-1). The taskbar normally sits at the bottom of the screen and keeps a master list of everything that's happening on your desktop (even the invisible stuff).

Figure 7-1:
Press the
Ctrl key and
Esc key to
retrieve
missing
taskbars.

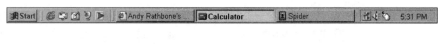

See the list of programs stamped onto buttons on the taskbar? Your missing window is *somewhere* on the list. When you spot it, click its name, and the taskbar instantly tosses your newfound window to the top of the pile.

✔ Most of the time, the taskbar performs admirably in tracking down lost windows. If your window isn't on the list, you've probably closed it. Closing a window, also known as *exiting* a window, takes it off your desktop and out of your computer's memory. To get that window back, you need to open it again, using the services of the Start button (see Chapter 10), the Windows Explorer (see Chapter 11), or the My Computer program (also in Chapter 11).

✔ I lied. Sometimes a window can be running and yet *not* be listed on the taskbar. Some utility programmers figure that people don't *need* to see their programs or their icons. Some screen savers, for example, can be running on your screen and yet not show up on the taskbar. They simply run in the background.

✔ Sometimes you see your missing program listed on the taskbar, and you click its name to dredge it from the depths. But even though the taskbar brings the missing program to the top, you *still* can't find it on your desktop. The program may be hanging off the edge of your desktop, so check out the very next section.

Finding a Window That's Off the Edge of the Screen

Even a window at the top of the pile can be nearly invisible. A window can be moved anywhere on the Windows Me desktop, including off the screen. In fact, you can inadvertently move 99 percent of a window off the screen, leaving just a tiny corner showing (see Figure 7-2). Clicking on the window's name in the taskbar won't be much help in this case, unfortunately. The window's already on top, but it's still too far off the screen to be of any use.

Figure 7-2: FreeCell is almost completely off the bottom-right corner of the screen, making it difficult to locate.

✔ If you can see any part of the rogue window's *title bar* — that thick strip along its top — hold the mouse button down and *drag* the traveler back to the center of the screen.

✔ Sometimes, a window's title bar can be completely off the screen. How can you drag it back into view? Start by clicking on any part of the window that shows. Then hold down your Alt key and press the spacebar. A menu appears from nowhere. Select the word Move, and a mysterious four-headed arrow appears. Press your arrow keys until the window's border moves to a more manageable location and then press Enter. Whew! Don't let it stray that far again!

✔ For an easier way to make Windows Me not only track down all your criminally hidden windows, but also line them up on the screen in *mug shot* fashion, check out the next section.

Tiling and Cascading Windows (The "Deal All the Windows in Front of Me" Approach)

Are you ready to turn Windows Me into a personal card dealer who gathers up all your haphazardly tossed windows and deals them out neatly on the desktop in front of you?

Then turn the taskbar into a card dealer. Click a blank area of your taskbar — near the clock is good — with your *right* mouse button, and a menu pops up. Click the Cascade Windows option, and the taskbar gathers all your open windows and deals them out in front of you, just like in a game of blackjack.

Each window's title bar is neatly exposed, ready to be grabbed and reprimanded with a quick click of the mouse.

Or, click a blank area of the taskbar with your right mouse button and choose Tile Windows Vertically or Tile Windows Horizontally from the pop-up menu. Windows Me *shrinks* all the windows so that they fit on the screen. They're tiny, but hey, at least you can see most of them.

✔ If the missing window doesn't appear in the stack of neatly dealt windows, perhaps it has been minimized. The Cascade Windows command gathers and deals only the open windows; it leaves the minimized windows resting as buttons along the taskbar. The solution? Click the missing window's button on the taskbar *before* cascading the windows across the screen.

✔ The Tile Windows Vertically command arranges the windows vertically, like socks hanging from a clothesline. Tile Windows Horizontally arranges the windows horizontally, like a stack of folded sweatshirts. The difference is the most pronounced when you're tiling only a few windows, however.

✔ You can find more information about the Tile and Cascade commands in Chapter 6. I cover the minimize button in Chapter 5.

Finding Lost Files, Folders, People, or Computers

Windows Me has gotten much better at finding things. And it should; after all, it's the one who's hiding everything. When one of your files, folders, or address book entries — or just about anything else — disappears into the depths of your computer, make Windows Me do the work in getting the darn thing back.

In almost all cases, the Windows Me Search command retrieves your lost goods. To rev it up, click your Start button and choose Search, as shown in Figure 7-3.

Figure 7-3:
The Windows Search command finds files, folders, networked computers, address book entries, and items on the Internet.

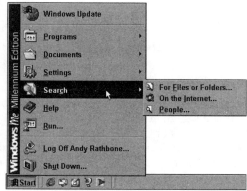

Finding files or folders

The Search window can locate lost files or folders meeting the most minute criteria. Best yet, it can simply search for missing things by their names. For example, suppose that your file called HYDRATOR INSPECTION disappeared over the weekend. To make matters worse, you're not even sure you spelled the words *Hydrator* or *inspection* correctly when saving the file.

What's the solution? Open the Search box from the Start button's Programs area, and choose For Files or Folders. In the Search for Files or Folders Named box, type in any part of the filename you can remember. In this case, type **drat** into the box and click the Search Now button. The Search Results window lists any file or folder with a name that contains *drat,* as shown in Figure 7-4 — quick and simple.

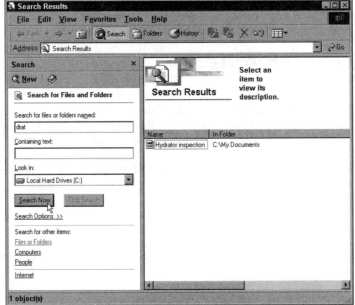

Figure 7-4:
Here, the
Windows
Me Search
program
sniffed out a
file with
drat as part
of its name.

✔ Of course, you don't *have* to keep things quick and simple. For example, the Find program normally searches drive C — your computer's hard drive. If you'd prefer that it search every nook and cranny — all your hard drives and even any floppy disks or CD-ROM drives — click the little downward-pointing arrow near the Look In box. When a menu drops down, click the My Computer setting. That tells the Search program to look *everywhere* on your computer except the Recycle Bin. (Peek inside there yourself.)

✔ Can't remember what you called a file but know the time and date you created it? Click the words Search Options beneath the Search Now button, and click in the Date box. Another box appears, letting you narrow down the search to files that you created only during certain times. (It's especially handy for finding files you know that you created within the past day.)

✔ The Type option lets people search for specific types of files: Bitmap files, faxes, configuration settings, and other more complicated options. To be on the safe side, leave the option set for All Files and Folders, so you know that the Find command is searching through *everything*. The Size option lets you find files of a certain size. Don't bother with the Advanced options. But if you do, make sure that you always leave a check mark in the Advanced option's Search Subfolders option.

Finding snippets of stored information

Help! You remember how much Mr. Jennings *loved* that wine during lunch, so you stealthily typed the wine's name into your computer. Now, at Christmastime, you don't remember the name of the file where you saved the wine's name. You don't remember the date you created the file, either, or even the folder where you stashed the file. In fact, the only thing you remember is how you described the wine's biting bouquet when typing it into your computer: "Like an alligator snap from behind a barge."

Luckily, that description is all Windows Me needs in order to find your file. Click the Start button and choose For Files or Folders from the Search menu, as shown in Figure 7-3. After the Search program pops up, click in the box marked Containing text, and type `barge`, as shown in Figure 7-5.

Figure 7-5:
The Windows Me Search program scours the entire computer for a file containing the word *barge*.

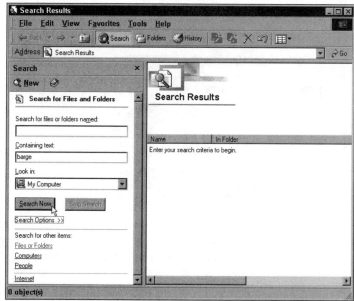

Just like in the preceding section, the Search program searches the computer, looking for files meeting your specifications. This time, however, it searches inside the files themselves, looking for the information you're after.

- ✔ Feel free to limit your search, using any of the tips and examples that I discuss in the preceding section; they apply here as well.

- ✔ CD-ROM discs take a *long* time to search. You can speed things up by telling the Find program to limit its search to hard disks. (Just popping the CD out of the drive is one way to keep the Find program from searching it.)

- ✔ When searching for files containing certain words, type in the words *least* likely to turn up in other files. For example, the word *barge* is more unique than *like, an, snap,* or *behind;* therefore, it's more likely to bring up the file you're searching for. And if *barge* doesn't work, try *alligator.*

Finding people

Looking for that certain someone? The Search command's Find People box will do its best to ferret them out.

Click the Start button, choose Search, and select People. The Find People box appears, as shown in Figure 7-6. It not only looks through your own e-mail Address Book, but also uses several Internet search engines dedicated to finding people.

Figure 7-6:
Windows'
Search
program
locates
missing
people as
well as lost
files.

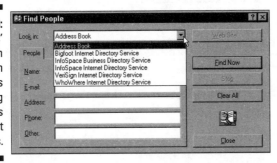

- ✔ If you click the People tab, Windows Me brings up your computer's Address Book. (And, if you've been entering information about your friends into the Address Book — part of Outlook Express — you'll be able to find pertinent information about that particular person.)

✔ You're not limited to searching your own Address Book, however. The Find People window lets you search through five Web sites that specialize in tracking down people and businesses.

✔ The little form that Windows Me makes you fill out is confusing. Instead, choose a search service and click the Web Site button. That takes you straight to the service's Web site, where a less-confusing form awaits. Or skip the Find People program. Instead, go to the Searching the Internet section, described in an upcoming section.

Finding computers

If your computer's connected to other computers, you're on a *network*. That lets you pluck files from other computers — and other computers can do the same from yours.

 The easiest way to find a networked computer is to double-click the desktop's My Network Places icon, as you can see in the margin. That lists all the computers connected to yours on the Network. Double-click on the computer you're after, and start copying or grabbing files.

The Search command does the same thing, but it takes longer. In fact, it's only there for computer nerds who like to do things the hard way. Click the Start button's Search area, choose For Files or Folders, and click the word Computers. After typing the networked computer's name into the Computer Name box, click Search Now.

The networked computer's icon appears in the Search Results box. Yawn.

Searching the Internet

Face it. Windows Me's Internet Explorer comes with too many buttons and boxes. To help out, the Search button tacks a simple form onto Internet Explorer that plows through the Internet to find your particular information.

Click the Start button, choose Search, and select On the Internet to start searching. Click the word More to see all your options. The screen looks like Figure 7-7. Type what words you're after into the Search box and click on the button next to the place Windows Me should search. Here's a rundown of what each option looks for.

Figure 7-7:
Windows
Me's Search
program
scours the
Internet to
retrieve
commonly
sought
information.

Find a Web page: The Search program lists all the Web pages it can find that contain your particular word or words. To examine one of the Web sites, click on its name. (*Tech note:* Search uses the MSN search engine.)

Find a person's address: Wow! Type in a person's name, city, and state, and the Search program digs up his or her street address or e-mail address. If it finds the person, click on his or her name to get the phone number and map to his or her house. (This information comes from www.worldpages.com.)

Find a business: Find the location and phone number of a business. It even finds all the coffee shops in your city. (This information comes from www.infospace.com.)

Previous searches: Choose this one to retrieve information from your previous ten searches — even if you didn't bother to save it.

Find a map: This one's pretty self-explanatory. Type in an address, and Search displays it on a map. After the map appears, feel free to type in a second address for computer-generated driving directions. (This comes from www.expedia.com.)

Look up a word: Forgotten what a quark is? This looks it up faster than you can grab the dictionary. (Search finds this on www.encarta.com.)

Find a picture: Type **butterfly,** for instance, and Search retrieves more than 700 pictures of lepidoptera. (This comes from www.corbis.com.)

Find in Newsgroups: For years, computer folks have chattered on the *Newsgroups,* computerized bulletin boards that I describe in Chapter 13. When you search for a subject here, you'll usually encounter thousands of results. (This is from www.deja.com.)

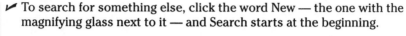

- ✔ To search for something else, click the word New — the one with the magnifying glass next to it — and Search starts at the beginning.

- ✔ If you don't like the default choices used by Search, click Customize to use your own. Substitute AltaVista as your search engine instead of MSN Search, for example.

Chapter 8

That "Cut and Paste" Stuff (Moving Around Words, Pictures, and Sounds)

• •

In This Chapter

▶ Understanding cutting, copying, and pasting

▶ Highlighting what you need

▶ Cutting, copying, deleting, and pasting what you've highlighted

▶ Making the best use of the Clipboard

▶ Putting scraps on the desktop

• •

*U*ntil Windows came along, IBM-compatible computers had a terrible time sharing anything. Their programs were rigid, egotistical things, with no sense of community. Information created by one program couldn't always be shared with another program. Older versions of programs passed down this selfish system to newer versions, enforcing the segregation with *proprietary file formats* and *compatibility tests*.

To counter this bad trip, Windows programmers created a communal workplace where all the programs could groove together peacefully. In the harmonious tribal village of Windows, programs share their information openly in order to make a more beautiful environment for all.

In the Windows co-op, all the windows can beam their vibes to each other freely, without fear of rejection. Work created by one Windows program is accepted totally and lovingly by any other Windows program. Windows programs treat each other equally, even if one program is wearing some pretty freaky threads or, in some gatherings, *no threads at all.*

This chapter shows you how easily you can move those good vibes from one window to another.

Examining the Cut and Paste Concept (And Copy, Too)

Windows Me took a tip from the kindergartners and made *cut and paste* an integral part of all its programs. Information can be electronically *cut* from one window and *pasted* into another window with little fuss and even less mess.

Just about any part of a window is up for grabs. You can highlight an exceptionally well-written paragraph in your word processor, for example, or a spreadsheet chart that tracks the value of your Indian-head pennies. After *highlighting* the desired information, you press a button to *copy* or *cut* it from its window.

At the press of the button, the information heads for a special place in Windows Me called the *Clipboard*. From there, you can paste it into any other open window.

The beauty of Windows Me is that with all those windows on-screen at the same time, you can easily grab bits and pieces from any of them and paste all the parts into a new window.

- Windows programs are designed to work together, so taking information from one window and putting it into another window is easy. Sticking a map onto your party fliers, for example, is *really* easy.

- Cutting and pasting works well for the big stuff, like sticking big charts into memos. But don't overlook it for the small stuff, too. For example, copying someone's name and address from your Address Book program is quicker than typing it by hand at the top of your letter. Or to avoid typographical errors, you can copy an answer from the Windows Me Calculator and paste it into another program.

- When somebody e-mails you a Web address, copy and paste it into Internet Explorer. It's much easier than typing it in by hand, and it is less frustrating because you'll know you didn't make any mistakes.

- When you cut or copy some information, it immediately appears in a special Windows program called the *Clipboard*. From the Clipboard, it can be pasted into other windows. The Clipboard has its own bag of tricks — including the Clipboard Viewer program — so it gets its own section later in this chapter.

- Windows Me doesn't automatically stick the Clipboard Viewer onto every computer during the installation process. If you're among the left out, head for the Control Panel's Add/Remove Programs icon and tell Windows Me to copy the Clipboard Viewer systems tool to your hard drive, a process that I describe in Chapter 9. (**Hint:** Clipboard Viewer is under the Systems Tools section of the Windows Setup tab.)

Highlighting the Important Stuff

Before you can grab information from a window, you have to tell the window exactly what parts you want to grab. The easiest way to tell it is to *highlight* the information with a mouse.

You can highlight a single letter, an entire novel, or anything in between. You can highlight pictures of water lilies. You can even highlight sounds so that you can paste belches into other files.

In most cases, highlighting involves one swift trick with the mouse: Put the mouse arrow or cursor at the beginning of the information you want and hold down the mouse button. Then move the mouse to the end of the information and release the button. That's it! All the stuff lying between where you clicked and released is highlighted. The information usually turns a different color so that you can see what you've grabbed. An example of highlighted text is shown in Figure 8-1.

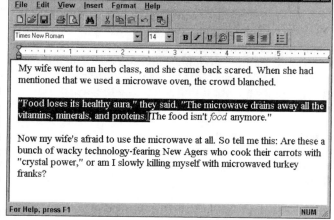

Figure 8-1:
Highlighted
text turns
a different
color
for easy
visibility.

If you're mouseless, use the arrow keys to put the cursor at the beginning of the stuff you want to grab. Then hold down Shift and press the arrow keys until the cursor is at the end of what you want to grab. You see the stuff on-screen become highlighted as you move the arrow keys. This trick works with almost every Windows Me program. (If you're after text, hold down Ctrl, too, and the text is highlighted word by word.)

Some programs have a few shortcuts for highlighting parts of their information:

✔ To highlight a single *word* in Notepad, WordPad, or most text boxes, point at it with the mouse and double-click. The word turns black, meaning that it's highlighted. (In WordPad, you can hold down the button on its second click, and then, by moving the mouse around, you can quickly highlight additional text word by word.)

✔ To highlight a single *line* in WordPad, click next to it in the left margin. Keep holding down the mouse button and move the mouse up or down to highlight additional text line by line.

✔ To highlight a *paragraph* in WordPad, double-click next to it in the left margin. Keep holding down the mouse button on the second click and move the mouse to highlight additional text paragraph by paragraph.

✔ To highlight an entire *document* in WordPad, hold down Ctrl and click anywhere in the left margin. (To highlight the entire document in Notepad, press and release Alt and then press E and then A. So much for consistency between Windows Me programs.)

✔ To highlight a portion of text in just about any Windows Me program, click at the text's beginning, hold down Shift, and click at the end of the desired text. Everything between those two points becomes highlighted.

✔ To highlight part of a picture or drawing while in Paint, click the little tool button with the dotted lines in a square. (The button is called the Select tool, as Windows Me informs you if you rest your mouse pointer over the tool for a second.) After clicking the Select tool, hold down the mouse button and slide the mouse over the desired part of the picture.

After you've highlighted text, you must either cut it or copy it *immediately*. If you do anything else, like absentmindedly click the mouse someplace else in your document, all your highlighted text reverts to normal, just like Cinderella after midnight.

Highlighted something? To cut or copy it immediately, right-click on it. When the menu pops up, choose Cut or Copy, depending on your needs.

Be careful after you highlight a bunch of text. If you press a key — the spacebar, for example — Windows Me almost always replaces your highlighted text with the character that you type — in this case, a space. To reverse that calamity and bring your highlighted text back to life, hold down Alt and press the Backspace key.

Deleting, Cutting, or Copying What You Highlighted

After you highlight some information (which I describe in the preceding section, in case you just entered the classroom), you're ready to start playing with it. You can delete it, cut it, or copy it. All three options differ drastically.

This clever tip bears repeating. After highlighting something, right-click on it. When the menu pops up, choose Cut or Copy, depending on your needs.

Deleting the information

Deleting the information just wipes it out. Zap! It just disappears from the window. To delete highlighted information, just press the Delete or Backspace key.

- ✔ If you've accidentally deleted the wrong thing, panic. Then hold down Ctrl and press the letter Z. Your deletion is graciously undone. Any deleted information pops back up on-screen. Whew!

- ✔ Holding down Alt and pressing Backspace also undoes your last mistake. (Unless you've just said something dumb at a party, in that case, use Ctrl+Z.)

Cutting the information

Cutting the highlighted information wipes it off the screen, just as the Delete command does, but with a big difference: When the information is removed from the window, it is copied to a special Windows Me storage tank called the *Clipboard*.

When you're looking at the screen, cutting and deleting look identical. In fact, the first few times you try to cut something, you feel panicky, thinking that you may have accidentally deleted it instead. (This feeling never really goes away, either.)

To cut highlighted stuff, hold down Shift and press Delete. Whoosh! The highlighted text disappears from the window, scoots through the underground tubes of Windows Me, and waits on the Clipboard for further action.

✔ One way to tell whether your Cut command actually worked is to paste the information back into your document. If it appears, you know that the command worked, and you can cut it out again right away. If it doesn't appear, you know that something has gone dreadfully wrong. (For the Paste command, discussed a little later, hold down Shift and press Insert.)

✔ Microsoft's lawyers kicked butt in the Apple lawsuit, so Windows now uses the same cut keys as the Macintosh. You can hold down Ctrl and press the letter *X* to cut. (Get it? That's an *X,* as in *you're crossing,* or *X-ing, something out.*)

Copying the information

Compared with cutting or deleting, *copying* information is quite anticlimactic. When you cut or delete, the information disappears from the screen. But when you copy information to the Clipboard, the highlighted information just sits there in the window. In fact, it looks as if nothing has happened, so you repeat the Copy command a few times before giving up and just hoping it worked.

To copy highlighted information, hold down Ctrl and press Insert (the 0 on the numeric keypad or Ins on some keyboards). Although nothing seems to happen, that information really does head for the Clipboard.

✔ Feel free to cut and paste files back and forth in My Computer. When you cut a file, however, Windows simply turns its name gray until you paste it. (Making the file disappear would be too scary.) Changed your mind in mid cut? Press Esc to turn the name back to black and cancel the cut.

✔ Windows Me uses the same Copy keys as the Macintosh does. If you don't like the Ctrl+Insert combination, you can hold down Ctrl and press C to copy. This combination is a little easier to remember, actually, because C is the first letter of *copy.*

✔ To copy an image of your entire Windows Me desktop (the *whole screen*) to the Clipboard, press the Print Screen key, which is sometimes labeled PrtScrn or something similar. (Some older keyboards make you hold down Shift simultaneously.) A snapshot of your screen heads for the Clipboard, ready to be pasted someplace else. Computer nerds call this snapshot a *screen shot.* All the pictures of windows in this book are screen shots. (And, no, the information doesn't also head for your printer.)

✔ To copy an image of your currently active window (just one window — nothing surrounding it), hold down Alt while you press Print Screen. The window's picture appears on the Clipboard. (You usually don't have to hold down Shift with this one, even for wacky keyboards. But if Alt+Print Screen doesn't work, hey, try holding down Shift anyway.)

Finding out more about cutting, copying, and deleting

Want to know more about cutting, copying, and deleting? Read on (you really should read this stuff).

✔ Windows Me often puts *toolbars* across the tops of its programs. Figure 8-2 shows the toolbar buttons that stand for cutting, copying, and pasting things.

Figure 8-2:
Clicking
these
toolbar
buttons
cuts, copies,
or pastes
highlighted
information.

Cut
|
Paste
|
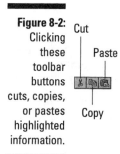
|
Copy

✔ If you prefer to use menus, the Cut, Copy, and Paste commands tumble down when you select the word Edit on any menu bar.

✔ When you're using the Print Screen key trick to copy a window or the entire screen to the Clipboard (see the preceding section), one important component is left out: The mouse arrow is *not* included in the picture, even if it was in plain sight when you took the picture. (Are you asking yourself how all the little arrows got in this book's pictures? Well, I drew most of 'em in by hand!)

✔ Sometimes, figuring out whether the Cut or Copy commands are really working is difficult. To know for sure, keep the Windows Clipboard Viewer showing at the bottom of the screen. Then you can watch the images appear on it when you press the buttons. (The Clipboard Viewer is listed on the Start menu under Accessories, which is listed in the Programs section. Not listed? Head for Chapter 9; you must tell Windows Me to install the Clipboard Viewer program.)

✔ Don't keep screen shots or large graphics on the Clipboard any longer than necessary. They consume a lot of memory that your other programs could be using. To clear off any memory-hogging detritus, copy a single word to the Clipboard, or call up the Clipboard Viewer and press Delete.

Pasting Information into Another Window

After you've cut or copied information to the special Windows Me Clipboard storage tank, it's ready for travel. You can *paste* that information into just about any other window.

Pasting is relatively straightforward compared with highlighting, copying, or cutting: Click the mouse anywhere in the destination window and click in the spot where you want the stuff to appear. Then hold down Shift and press Insert (the 0 key on the numeric keypad). Presto! Anything that's sitting on the Clipboard immediately leaps into that window.

✔ Another way to paste stuff is to hold down Ctrl and press V. That combination does the same thing as Shift+Insert. (It also is the command those funny-looking Macintosh computers use to paste stuff.)

✔ You can also choose the Paste command from a window's menu bar. Select the word Edit and then select the word Paste. But don't select the words Paste Special. That command is for Object Linking and Embedding stuff.

✔ Some programs have toolbars along their tops. Clicking the Paste button, shown in Figure 8-2, pastes the Clipboard's current contents into your document.

✔ The Paste command inserts a *copy* of the information that's sitting on the Clipboard. The information stays on the Clipboard, so you can keep pasting it into other windows if you want. In fact, the Clipboard's contents stay the same until a new Cut or Copy command replaces them with new information.

Using the Clipboard Viewer

Windows Me employs a special program to let you see all the stuff that's being slung around by cutting and copying. Called the *Clipboard Viewer*, it's merely a window that displays anything that has been cut or copied to the Clipboard.

To see the Clipboard Viewer, click the Start button and choose Programs from the menu. Choose Accessories from the new menu, followed by System Tools and, finally, Clipboard Viewer. The Clipboard Viewer displays any information you've cut or copied recently. Figures 8-3, 8-4, and 8-5 show some examples.

Figure 8-3:
This Clipboard contains a recently copied picture.

Figure 8-4:
This Clipboard contains text recently copied from a Windows program.

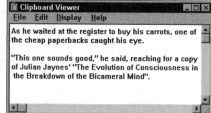

Figure 8-5:
This Clipboard contains a sound copied from the Windows Me Sound Recorder.

✔ Sometimes, the Clipboard Viewer can't show you exactly what you've copied. For example, if you copy a sound from the Windows Me Sound Recorder, you just see a picture of the Sound Recorder's icon. And, at the risk of getting metaphysical, what does a sound look like anyway?

✔ The Clipboard functions automatically and transparently. Unless you make a special effort, you don't even know it's there. (That's why Windows Me tosses in the Clipboard Viewer program — it lets you see what the Clipboard is up to.)

The *Clipboard* is a special area inside memory where Windows Me keeps track of information that's been cut or copied. The *Clipboard Viewer* is a program that lets you see the information that's currently on the Clipboard.

✔ To better track what's being cut and pasted, some people leave the Clipboard Viewer sitting open at the bottom of the screen. Then they can actually *see* what they've cut or copied.

✔ Most of the time, the Clipboard is used just for temporary operations — a quick cut here, a quick paste there, and then on to the next job. But the Clipboard Viewer lets you save the Clipboard's contents for later use. Choose File from the menu bar and then choose Save As from the pull-down menu. Type in a filename and click the OK command button (or just press Enter).

✔ The Clipboard can hold only one thing at a time. Each time you cut or copy something else, you replace the Clipboard's contents with something new. If you want to collect a bunch of *clips* for later pasting, use the Save As option that I describe in the preceding paragraph. The Clipboard also starts up empty each time you start Windows Me.

✔ No Clipboard Viewer on your Start menu? Windows Me doesn't always install it automatically. Head for the Add/Remove Programs section in Chapter 9 for ways to add the Windows accessories that Windows Me left out.

Leaving Scraps on the Desktop Deliberately

The Clipboard is a handy way to copy information from one place to another, but it has a major limitation: Every time you copy something new to the Clipboard, it replaces what was copied there before. What if you want to copy a *bunch* of things from a document?

If you are cutting and pasting over a real desktop, you can leave little scraps lying everywhere, ready for later use. The same *scraps* concept works with Windows Me: You can move information from window to window, using the desktop as a temporary storage area for your scraps of information.

For example, suppose that you have some paragraphs in a WordPad document that you want to copy to some other places. Highlight the first paragraph, drag it out of the WordPad window, and drop it onto the desktop. Poof! A small Scrap icon appears on your desktop. See another interesting paragraph? Drag it onto the desktop as well: Another Scrap icon appears.

Eventually, you'll have copies of your report's best paragraphs sitting in little scraps on your desktop. To move any of the scraps into another document, just drag them into that other document's window and let go.

Any remaining, unused scraps can be dumped into the Recycle Bin or simply left on the desktop, adding a nice, comfortable layer of clutter.

To make a scrap, highlight the information you want to move, usually by running the mouse pointer over it while holding down the mouse button. Then point at the highlighted information and, while holding down the mouse button, point at the desktop. Let go of the mouse button, and a scrap containing that information appears on the desktop.

Note: Not all Windows Me applications support Scraps. In fact, WordPad is probably the only program in the Windows Me box that makes good use of Scraps. Other programs, such as Microsoft Office 2000, let you use scraps, though, so you haven't wasted your time reading about them.

Chapter 9

Customizing Windows Me (Fiddling with the Control Panel)

• •

• •

*I*n a way, working with Windows Me is like remodeling a bathroom. You can spend time on the practical things, like calculating the optimum dimensions for piping or choosing the proper brand of caulking to seal the sink and tub. Or you can spend your time on the more aesthetic options, like adding an oak toilet-paper holder, a granite countertop, or a rattan cover for the tissue box.

Windows Me handles its remodeling through its Control Panel — a window full of icons that customize the program to fit the needs of you and your computer. On the eminently practical side, you can call up the System icon and check the Read-ahead Optimization of your hard drives.

Or stick with the decorating options: Change the color of the title bars to teal, for example, or cover the Windows Me desktop with daisy patterns or pin-stripe wallpaper.

This chapter shows you how to transform Windows Me into that program you've always dreamed of owning someday.

Finding the Control Panel

Just like a house's circuit breaker box, the Control Panel holds the switches that control the Windows Me program's various settings. Flip open the Control Panel, and you can while away an entire workday adjusting all the various Windows Me options.

 To find the Control Panel, double-click your desktop's My Computer icon, shown in the margin. When the My Computer window pops up, double-click the oh-so-important Control Panel icon hidden inside. When the Control Panel window pops up, however, as you can see in Figure 9-1, sometimes its switches aren't all visible. Windows Me hides the ones that it doesn't think you need.

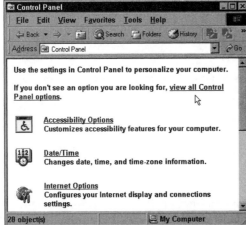

Figure 9-1:
To see *all* of the Control Panel's settings, click where it says View All Control Panel Options.

To see them all, click where it says view all Control Panel options. Voila! Bunches of icons appear, as you can see in Figure 9-2. In fact, you may need to make the window larger to see them all. (Hit Chapter 6 for window-sizing tips.)

Figure 9-2:
Click any of
the Control
Panel's
icons to
change the
settings
for that
particular
subject.

Everybody's Control Panel looks different because different people can afford different computer toys. For example, the keyboards on some Gateway computers let you control the volume of your DVD player. So, their Control Panels include an icon to change that keyboard's special settings. Some laptop owners use high-tech "infrared" ports to beam information to other laptops. Their Control Panel has a Wireless Link icon. Table 9-1 explains the icons you may come across in your copy of Windows Me.

I discuss the most important options in more glowing detail later in this chapter.

✔ Don't worry about that overwhelming display of options in the Control Panel; chances are, you'll use very few of them. And don't worry if your Control Panel doesn't look identical to the one in this book. Renegade programs often toss their own icons onto the Control Panel.

✔ If the Control Panel's icons don't look as big as the ones in Figure 9-2, choose Large Icons from the View menu. (Or right-click in a blank part of the Control Panel window and choose Large Icons from the View menu that pops up.)

✔ Prefer accessing Control Panel through the Start button? Click the Start button, choose Settings, and select Control Panel from the menu.

✔ For an easy way to see what each icon does, rest your mouse pointer over a mysterious icon — without clicking. After a few seconds, a reminder appears, explaining the icon's function.

✔ Many of the Control Panel's menus can be reached *without* calling up the Control Panel. Double-click the taskbar's little clock to summon the Date/Time menu, for example; right-click a blank part of the desktop and choose Properties to bring up the Display's menu.

Table 9-1	Deciphering the Control Panel Icons	
The Icon	*What It Does*	*Chances You'll Use It*
Accessibility Options	Microsoft performed admirably in making Windows Me accessible to everybody. These options help make the monitor easier to read, add special sonic signals, and the customize Windows program's controls to work more easily with people with physical limitations.	If you need any of these options, you'll know.
Add New Hardware	Installed that new [insert name of expensive computer gadget here]? Head for this area to summon the Hardware Installation Wizard. The Wizard, a helpful piece of "advice counselor" software, handles the messy chores of introducing Windows Me to new computer parts.	Run this whenever you install new computer parts into your computer.
Add/Remove Programs	Double-click here to make Windows Me install new software or remove software you no longer want. This icon also tells Windows Me to install any software it left out when it installed itself. Finally, use this to create a "Startup Disk" to keep on hand for helping fix your computer if it crashes.	Use this whenever you install or delete software.
Automatic Updates	When set up through here, Windows Me automatically connects to Microsoft's Web site and downloads updates and fixes for potential problems.	Leave this set on the Notify option; then forget about it.

The Icon	What It Does	Chances You'll Use It
Date/Time	This area lets you change your computer's date, time, and time zone settings.	Used to reset the clock, or when moving to a new time zone. (That lets Windows Me automatically adjust the clock for daylight savings time.)
Desktop Themes	A haven for decorators, this contains bunches of precreated wallpaper, colors, fonts, and screen savers to spruce up Windows Me with cool themes. (Windows Me normally keeps this off your computer — except when you add it through the Add/Remove Programs icon.)	Best used as a fun time-waster to put off upcoming projects.
Dial-Up Networking	This icon is your computer's connection to other computers or to the Internet.	Only used once: when first typing in the settings for your Internet Service Provider.
Display	Double-click the Display icon to change your screen's wallpaper, colors, resolution, screen saver, and other display-oriented settings. (Double-click a blank part of your desktop to summon the same menu.)	Used often. This icon lets you fine-tune what you'll be staring at all day: your monitor settings.
Find Fast	Added only by Microsoft Outlook, FindFast is an expensive collection of programs, including Word and Excel, that automatically indexes your Outlook documents so you can find them more quickly.	If you've installed Office onto Windows Me, use FindFast to locate missing Word documents and Excel spreadsheets.
	This changes the way Windows displays its folders on the screen and how they behave.	Usually used once or twice, then ignored.
Fonts	Windows Me comes with basic fonts like Arial and `Courier`. If you head back to the software store and buy more, like *Cascade Script*, install them by double-clicking this icon. (***Nerdly Note:*** This icon is actually a shortcut to the real Fonts setting area. Chapters 3 and 10 cover shortcuts.)	Most programs install and maintain their fonts automatically. ***Tip:*** Double-click any font listed here to see what it looks like.

(continued)

Table 9-1 *(continued)*

The Icon	*What It Does*	*Chances You'll Use It*
Gaming Options	Windows Me usually spots newly installed joysticks and gamepads and installs them automatically. Double-click here for help with problems. Also, here's where you calibrate and test your joystick if you're losing.	Avid game players tweak this for every new game.
[internet icon]	When you're ready to join the Internet and surf the World Wide Web, this icon's waiting for you. It opens a Pandora's box of buttons that let you customize the way Windows Me talks through the Internet. (Chapter 13 shows how to point and click your way through the Internet.)	Rarely, except when setting everything up for the first time. After your Internet access is set up, everything's pretty low-maintenance.
Keyboard	This changes how long the keyboard takes to repeat a letter when you hold down a key. Yawn. Or, if you pack up the computer and move to Sweden, double-click here to switch to the Swedish language format (or anything from Afrikaans to Ukrainian). Finally, here's where you tell Windows Me whether you've upgraded from an older 83- or 84-key keyboard to a newer 101- or 102-key keyboard — the ones with the numeric keypads.	Rarely. Check out the settings if your keyboard's giving you problems, though. Specifically, make sure that your Language settings correspond to your particular country.
Mail	Another goody added by Microsoft Outlook, it lets you configure your mail accounts.	Rarely used; most mail programs take you here automatically as part of their setup process.
Modems	Before you can talk to other computers over the phone lines, you need a modem. Double-click here, and Windows Me tries to figure out what sort of modem you have so that it can boss it around. These menus also let you adjust modem settings.	Rarely. Windows usually detects and installs new modems automatically.

The Icon	What It Does	Chances You'll Use It
Mouse	Make that mouse scoot faster across the screen, change it from right-handed to left-handed, fine-tune your double-click, choose between brands, and change all sorts of mouse-related behaviors.	Rarely. Dirty mouseballs and rollers — not software settings — cause most mouse problems. But check this out for fun.
Multi-function Keyboard	Added by Gateway computers with special keyboards with special, built-in buttons.	Gateway computer owners can change volume levels, control DVDs, get e-mail, and more — all with their cool Multifunction Keyboards. (No, I don't own stock in Gateway, and some other companies offer similar keyboards.)
My Network Places	Here's how you link computers together with special cables in your home or office so they talk to each other, sharing files or a printer. Setting everything up, unfortunately, is a pretty gruesome project.	Networking — even the home networking bundled with Windows Me — is too complicated for this book. (But it's just right for this book's sequel, my *MORE Microsoft Windows Me For Dummies* book from IDG Books Worldwide, Inc.)
ODBC Data Sources (32bit)	I've never used it, actually. But I'm sure that it does something useful.	Look at this only to see how confusing computers can be. Then leave it alone.
Passwords	This works with the Users icon to help manage passwords when more than one person uses the same PC.	If a PC's multiple users want to customize the computer's colors and settings for their own use, they each create their own password here.
PC Card (PCMCIA)	The size of a thick credit card, these slip into a laptop and commonly house modems, network connections, digital memory cards, and other ultraportable computer goodies.	Most often seen in laptops, but an increasing number of desktoppers attach a PC Card port to read Compact Flash cards from their digital cameras and palmtops.

(continued)

Table 9-1 *(continued)*

The Icon	What It Does	Chances You'll Use It
Power Options	Windows Me is very power-conscious on new computers and laptops. Use this to automatically turn off the monitor — or the entire computer — when you haven't used it for awhile. Choose your Power scheme setting at the top, and Windows sets the rest of the schemes for you.	Used frequently by laptoppers. Other people make Windows Me turn off their monitors after 30 minutes of inactivity.
Printers	Come here to tell Windows Me about your new printer, adjust the settings on your old printer, or choose which printer (or fax card) you want Windows Me to use. *Technical Note:* This isn't really an icon; it's a shortcut that leads to the Printer setup program.	As often as you buy printers — or permanently change settings on your printer. (Right-click a printer icon and choose Properties to change its settings.)
Regional Settings	This changes the way Windows Me displays and sorts numbers, international currency, the date, and the time. (If you've simply changed time zones, just double-click the date/time display on the bottom-right corner of the taskbar, a process described later in this chapter.)	Used mostly by laptoppers with Frequent Flyer cards.
Scanners and Cameras	Windows Me makes an effort to handle those troublesome scanners and digital cameras. If Windows doesn't automatically find your scanner or digital camera, try installing those devices here.	Use this to check the connections to the digital cameras and scanners that connect through your serial port.
Scheduled Tasks	The Task Scheduler keeps Windows Me running smoothly, because it automatically performs maintenance at certain times.	Ignore it. Windows Me automatically sets things up to run at the right times.

The Icon	What It Does	Chances You'll Use It
Sounds and Multimedia	The most fun! Make Windows Me play different sounds for different events. Try out some of the preset settings in the Schemes menu. Sound card owners drop by here to tweak their gear settings, adjust play-back/record volumes, fiddle with MIDI instruments, and play with other goodies, like video capture cards, as well as their CD and DVD players.	Used mostly at homes or small offices where the boss doesn't mind computers that make exploding sounds when they crash.
	Like racecar mechanics, computer gurus can fiddle around in here for hours. Don't play in here unless a nearby computer guru can serve as Safety Patrol. This is scary stuff.	This area's usage increases with the level of the user's experience.
Taskbar and Start Menu	Customize your Start button menu, alphabetize its contents, and fiddle with your taskbar.	Most people head here to either alphabetize their Start menu or turn off the "personalized" menus that leave off some options.
Telephony	Part of the Modem area, it lets you enter your area code and other telephone information.	Never; you'll already have filled this out during your Modem installation.
Users	Windows can get "personal" with a family of users. When Joe types in his password, for example, Windows replaces Jen's "X-Files" wallpaper with "Packers" photos and assigns football sounds to Joe's mouse clicks.	Creates a personal "feel" when a single computer is used by more than one person.
Wireless Link	Used mostly for James Bond types with fancy laptops or palmtops that shoot information to each other or to high-tech printers.	Useful for palmtops and laptops, but rarely for desktop PCs.

Customizing the Display

The most-often-used part of the Control Panel is probably the Display icon, which looks like the icon in the margin.

Double-click on the Control Panel's Display icon to change the Windows wallpaper, screen saver, and other visual aspects of the Windows Me desktop. When the Display Properties window pops up, as shown in Figure 9-3, it shows a preview of any background file that you click.

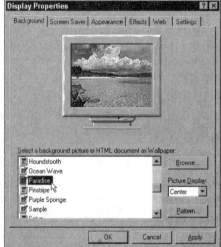

Figure 9-3:
Choose one of the pictures listed on the Background tab to use it as wallpaper.

Unlike several other switches in the Control Panel, the Display icon doesn't control anything too dangerous. Feel free to fiddle around with all the settings (except the ones that talk about the Internet or the Web). You can't cause any major harm. If you do want to play, however, be sure that you write down any original settings. Then you can always return your display to normal if something looks odd.

You don't have to root through the Start button and the Control Panel to get to the Display icon's contents. Instead, just click a blank part of your desktop with your right mouse button. When the menu pops up out of nowhere, click Properties. That bypasses the Control Panel and takes you straight to the Display settings area.

The next few sections describe how to customize different parts of your display after you double-click the Control Panel's Display icon.

The display's background

When Windows Me first installs itself, it paints a boring monotone background across the screen and then starts sprinkling windows and icons over it. However, Microsoft snuck more exciting backgrounds, known as *wallpaper,* onto your hard drive, just waiting to be installed. You can choose a pinstripe pattern that matches your suit. Or you can create your own wallpaper in Paint, the Windows Me graphics program, and hang your new wallpaper yourself. If you have a digital camera, you can add your own wallpaper to reflect your personality (see Figure 9-4).

To change the wallpaper, double-click the Display icon from the Control Panel. (Or, click a blank spot of your desktop with your right mouse button and choose Properties from the menu that appears from nowhere.)

When the rather large dialog box appears, click one of the filenames listed in the window. Click any name for a preview as to how your selection would look as wallpaper (refer to Figure 9-3).

Figure 9-4: Use pictures from your digital camera for Windows wallpaper, the backdrop beneath all the windows and icons.

To scroll up or down the list of potential wallpaper files, click the little arrows on the bar to the right of the names. If you aren't using a mouse, select an item by using the arrow keys to highlight the item you want and then pressing Enter. In a long list, you can find a certain name more quickly by pressing the name's first letter.

Apply button to make Windows Me display it on your desktop. Like the way your new wallpaper looks on-screen? Click OK. The dialog box disappears, and you are back at your desktop (with the new wallpaper displayed proudly in the background).

> ✔ Wallpaper images can be *tiled* repeatedly across the screen, *centered* in the middle, or *stretched* to fill the entire screen. Small pictures should be tiled; larger pictures should be centered or stretched, whichever looks best. Set your preference by selecting it from the Picture Display box.

> ✔ Wallpaper files are merely bitmaps, or files created in Windows Me Paint. (Bitmap files end with the letters BMP.) Anything you create in Windows Me Paint can be used as wallpaper. In fact, you can even use Paint to alter the wallpaper that Microsoft provides with Windows Me.

> ✔ Windows Me also lets you use a Web site from the Internet in the form of an HTML file on your desktop. They're fun, but they can get in the way. If you accidentally click an item on the Web page while aiming for a desktop icon, Internet Explorer rises to the forefront to display your Web page.

> ✔ Windows Me lists only wallpaper that's stored directly in the Windows folder. If you create some potential wallpaper in Paint, you have to move the file to the Windows folder before it shows up in the Desktop dialog box's master list; or, you have to choose the file by clicking on the Browse button. If this concept seems strange, foreign, confusing, or all three, check out Chapter 11 for more information about folders and moving files between them.

> ✔ Small files that are *tiled* across the screen take up much less memory than large files that are *centered* on-screen. If Windows Me seems slow or if it sends you furtive messages saying that it's running out of memory, try tiling some smaller bits of wallpaper.

> ✔ Patterns, accessed through the Pattern button, are a poor-man's wallpaper. They're only one color, and they don't vary much. If Windows Me keeps complaining about needing more memory, however, dump your wallpaper and switch to patterns. They don't eat up nearly as much memory.

> ✔ Did you happen to spot an eye-catching picture while Web surfing with Internet Explorer? Click that Web site's picture with your right mouse button and select the Set as Wallpaper option. Sneaky Microsoft copies that picture to your desktop and leaves it on the screen as your new wallpaper. (Just keep the image on your own desktop; don't try to sell it or give it away, or you may run afoul of copyright laws.)

The display's screen saver

In the dinosaur days of computing, computer monitors were permanently damaged when an oft-used program burned its image onto the screen. The program's faint outlines showed up even when the monitor was turned off.

To prevent this *burn-in,* people installed a *screen saver* to jump in when a computer hadn't been used for a while. The screen saver would either blank the screen or fill it with wavy lines to keep the program's display from etching itself into the screen.

Today's monitors don't really have this problem, but people use screen savers anyway — mainly because they look cool.

✔ Windows comes with several screen savers built in, although none of them is activated at first. To set one up, click the Screen Saver tab along the top of the Display Properties dialog box (see Figure 9-3). Then click the downward-pointing arrow in the Screen Saver box. Finally, select the screen saver you want.

✔ Immediately after choosing a screen saver, click the Preview command button to see what the screen saver looks like. Wiggle the mouse or press the spacebar to come back to Windows Me.

✔ Fiddlers can click Settings for more options — changing colors or animation speed, for instance.

✔ Click in the Password Protected box to set a password; then when the screen saver kicks in, you won't be able to see the screen again until you type in the password.

✔ Click the up or down arrows next to the Wait box to tell the screen saver when to kick in. If you set the option to 5, for example, Windows Me waits until you haven't touched the mouse or keyboard for five minutes before letting the screen saver out of its cage.

✔ Windows Me comes with more screen savers than it initially installs. To make Windows Me install *all* its screen savers, use the Control Panel's Add/Remove Programs icon, which I describe later in this chapter, click the Windows Setup tab, double-click Accessories, and look for the Screen Savers option.

✔ If your monitor's fairly new, click the Settings button at the bottom of the Screen Saver page. Here, you can tell Windows Me to turn off your monitor when you haven't used it for a while. That way, you never have to remember to turn off your monitor. (Monitors don't like to be left turned on.) Feel free to turn your hard disk off after an hour or so, too, to save wear, tear, and energy.

The display's appearance (getting better colors)

Feeling blue? You can make Windows Me appear in any color you want by clicking on the tab marked Appearance, found along the top of the Display menu.

The Appearance dialog box opens, enabling you to choose between several Microsoft-designed color schemes or to create your own. (Tell your boss that a more pleasant color scheme will enhance your productivity.) Figure 9-5 shows the Appearance tab of the Display Properties dialog box.

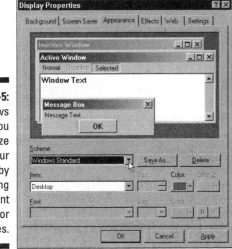

Figure 9-5:
Windows
Me lets you
personalize
your
computer by
choosing
different
color
schemes.

To choose among previously designed color schemes, click the arrow next to the box beneath Scheme. After the list drops down, click the name of the scheme you want to try out. Each time you select a new color scheme, the sample window shows you how the colors will look.

If you want to change one of the color schemes slightly, go for it: Click the box beneath Item to see a list of areas you can fiddle with. For example, to change the font Windows Me uses for icon titles, select Icon from the list and select a different font from the ones listed in the Font box.

And, if you want even more choices, you can mix your own colors by choosing Other from the Color menu and clicking on the Define Custom Colors command button.

Feel free to play around with the colors by trying out different schemes or designing your own combinations. Playing with the colors is an easy way to see what names Windows Me uses for its different components. It's also a fun way to work with dialog boxes. But if you goof something awful and all the letters suddenly disappear, click the Cancel button — fast. (It's the middle of the three buttons along the bottom.) Letters disappear when they've been changed to the same color as their background.

- Color schemes don't refer to color alone; they can change the appearance of Windows Me in other ways. For example, the Icon Spacing (Horizontal) setting determines how closely your icons sit next to each other. The Scrollbar setting determines the width of the scroll bars and their elevatorlike buttons that you click to move around in a document.

- Created an outstanding new color scheme? Click the Save As button and type in a new name for your creation. If you ever grow weary of your creative new color scheme, you can always return to the Windows Me original colors by selecting Windows Standard.

- Windows Me continues to display your newly chosen colors until you head back to the Appearance menu and change them again.

- The Appearance menu is pretty boring after you've checked out the Desktop Themes program, also found on the Control Panel. Desktop Themes, discussed later in this chapter, decorates your computer to match your hobbies and interests, from deep-sea diving to plowing fields. (I'm not kidding — check it out!)

- Is all this talk of "dialog boxes," "command buttons," and "funny arrow things" getting you down? Head to Chapter 5 for a field guide to figuring out Windows Me menus.

The weird "Effects" and Web tabs

Sharp-eyed Windows Me users will notice two odd tabs when they ogle the Display Properties window: Effects and Web. The Effects tab doesn't really do much; if your normal desktop icons (like My Computer, Network Neighborhood, and the Recycle Bin) suddenly look funny, head back here and click the Default Icon button to restore order.

The Web tab lets you inject Web pages or pieces of them into your desktop in a process

called Active Desktop, which I describe later in this chapter. It's fun for awhile; then it's simply distracting. Using an open Web page for your desktop is like leaving a spreadout newspaper on your desk and trying to work. Most people keep their Internet content in their browsers where it belongs.

Display settings (playing with new video modes)

Just as Windows Me can print to hundreds of different brands of printers, it can accommodate zillions of different monitors, too. It can even display different *video modes* on the same monitor.

For example, Windows Me can display different numbers of colors on the screen, or it can shrink the size of everything, packing more information onto the screen. The number of colors and the size of the information on-screen comprise a *video mode,* or *video resolution.*

Some Windows Me programs only work in a specific video mode, and those programs casually ask you to switch to that mode. Huh?

Here's what's happening: Monitors plug into a special place on the back of the computer. That special place is an outlet on a *video card* — the gizmo that translates your computer's language into something you can *see* on the monitor. That card handles all the video-mode switches. By making the card switch between modes, you can send more or fewer colors to your monitor or pack more or less information onto the screen.

To make a video card switch to a different video mode, click the Settings tab, one of the six tabs along the top of the Control Panel's Display menu, shown back in Figure 9-3. (Can't find the Display menu? Click a blank part of your desktop by using the right mouse button and choose Properties from the menu that springs up.)

Two monitors . . . *at the same time!*

Plug a second video card into your computer, plug in a second monitor, and Windows Me will probably be able to spread its display across both monitors — or even three, if you install another card and monitor.

It sounds frivolous, but this new feature can be kind of handy, actually. For instance, you can run your Internet browser on one monitor while keeping your desktop handy for other work. Or, you can spread your work out, making it easy to cut and paste between bunches of open windows.

A few words of caution, however: This two-monitor stuff is new, so not all programs can handle it. Also, TV Viewer cards can only display TV shows on the *primary monitor* — your first monitor. The TV show simply disappears if you try dragging its window to the second monitor.

As you can see in Figure 9-6, the Settings menu lets you select the video mode that you want Windows Me to display on-screen. (Click the arrow next to the Colors box to change the number of colors Windows Me is currently displaying; click in the Screen Area box to change the current resolution.) Windows Me gives you a chance to back out if you choose a video mode your computer can't handle, thank goodness.

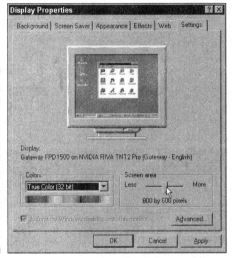

Figure 9-6:
The Settings area lets you change the amount of information Windows squeezes onto your monitor.

✔ Monitors and cards can display Windows Me in different *resolutions*. The higher the resolution, the more information Windows Me can pack onto the screen (and the smaller the windows become, too). Windows Me refers to resolution as *Desktop area*. For more information about this monitor/card/resolution stuff, troop over to Chapter 2 and read the section about computer parts that I told you to ignore.

✔ To switch to a higher resolution, use your mouse to slide the little bar in the Screen Area box. Then watch how the screen changes. The more you slide the bar to the right, the more information Windows Me can pack onto the screen. Unfortunately, the information also gets smaller. Click the Apply button after you select a new resolution to see it in action.

✔ When Windows Me switches to the new resolution, it usually gives you 15 seconds to click a button saying that you approve of the change. If your card or monitor can't handle the new resolution, you won't be able to see the button on-screen. Then, because you didn't click the button, Windows Me automatically changes back to the original resolution. Whew!

✔ Depending on how you're set up, Windows Me sometimes prefers to restart your computer when changing the amount of colors or resolution. To determine how Windows Me handles your video changes, click the Advanced button on the bottom of the Settings screen.

✔ Want to change the number of colors Windows Me can throw onto the screen? Click the little arrow in the Colors box. After the list drops down, select the number of colors you want.

✔ New video cards usually come with a disk that contains special information called a *driver.* If Windows Me doesn't recognize your breed of video card, it may ask you to insert this disk when you're changing video modes.

✔ If you'll be looking at pictures taken with a digital camera, you'll probably want Windows Me to display as many colors as possible. High Color, or 16-bit mode, will display a total of 65,000 colors; True Color, or 24-bit mode, slaps up to 16 million colors on the monitor. Switch back to fewer colors when you're done, however, if Windows Me starts running too slowly.

✔ Windows Me works well with two or more monitors simultaneously and can display different video resolutions on each monitor. You need a separate PCI video card to power each monitor, however. See the nearby "Two monitors . . . *at the same time!*" sidebar for more information.

✔ If Windows Me acts goofy with your video card or monitor — or you've recently installed new ones — head for the "Adding New Hardware" section, later in this chapter. Windows Me probably needs to be formally introduced to your new equipment before it will talk to it.

Folder Options and the Active Desktop

Some people store their folders in a fireproof MacMahon Bros. file cabinet and spread them across a finely polished mahogany desk for viewing; others pick them up off the floor and hope the papers don't fall out.

To accommodate different working styles, Windows Me offers several ways of viewing your folders. The Active Desktop option makes Windows look and act like a Web page from the Internet. Another makes it resemble the "classic" style that it's used for years. Yet another incorporates features from both schools.

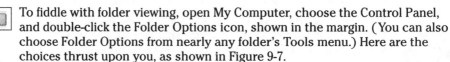 To fiddle with folder viewing, open My Computer, choose the Control Panel, and double-click the Folder Options icon, shown in the margin. (You can also choose Folder Options from nearly any folder's Tools menu.) Here are the choices thrust upon you, as shown in Figure 9-7.

 Fiddling with Folder Options isn't particularly dangerous, but they can make Windows Me behave mighty strange. If something terribly weird happens, here's how to make it return to less troublesome times. Open the Folder Options icon in Control Panel and click the Restore Defaults button, also seen in Figure 9-7. Order is restored; your folders and desktop now behave the way they did when Windows Me was first installed.

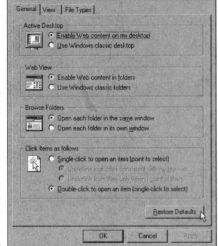

Active Desktop

What the heck is Active Desktop? Normally, your desktop simply displays wallpaper that stays put. Active Desktop replaces your wallpaper with things that are *active*. Many are connected to the Internet and update themselves automatically.

An Active Desktop item can be a stock ticker at the bottom of your screen, constantly displaying stock prices. It can turn your desktop into a weather map, displaying temperatures around the country. Many people write their own Active Desktop items, available for downloading on the Internet. (Search for "Active Desktop" at www.alltheweb.com for a sampling of the available desktop goodies.)

Your favorite Web page can be selected for an Active Desktop item. Instead of seeing your desktop, you see your favorite Web page spread across your monitor, with all your normal icons spread across it.

Before jumping into Active Desktop, think about it for awhile: Do you want the Internet to spread across your desktop, or would you prefer that it stay neatly enclosed in your Web browser, Internet Explorer? I discuss these two options in the next section.

Enable Web content on my desktop

Choose this option to turn on the Active Desktop. Once turned on, Active Desktop lets you embed Web pages, pictures, or special applications (such as Internet stock tickers) into your desktop. Figure 9-8 shows Windows Me with its Active Desktop turned on, and little Web page goodies, from Amazon booksellers to the Microsoft Investor stock ticker, sprinkled across the desktop.

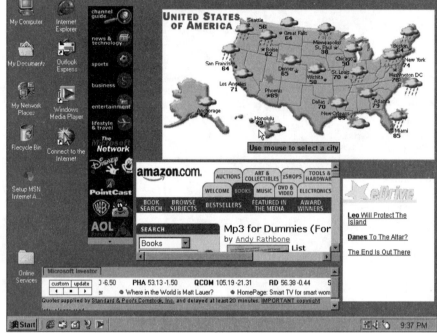

Figure 9-8:
When
turned on,
the Active
Desktop lets
you embed
bits of the
Internet
into your
desktop.

If Figure 9-8 had the Active Desktop turned off, all that Webby stuff would disappear, leaving only the wallpaper in the background.

The Active Desktop is designed for Internet-savvy users. It's tough enough pointing and clicking at the correct icon. When your desktop uses a Web page as a backdrop, you may accidentally click the wrong item and find yourself on the Internet when you don't want to.

Whenever you right-click a blank portion of your desktop and choose any of the settings from the Active Desktop option, Windows Me turns on the Active Desktop — even if you don't specifically ask it to. To turn it off, open the Control Panel's Folder Options icon and click the Restore Defaults button.

Classic style

After you install Windows Me, it subscribes to the "classic desktop" look that makes Windows Me look and act like Windows 98 and Windows 95. Wallpaper, not active Web pages, covers your desktop. That makes everything simpler and more soothing to the soul. (If a computer could ever be considered soothing to the soul, that is.)

Web view

The Active Desktop options control how much of the Internet appears on your desktop. The Web View section, by contrast, controls how much of the Internet's "style" is used when presenting folders. Compared with the Active Desktop, it's quite innocuous — even quite handy. I describe the two choices next.

Enable Web content in folders

Turn this option on, because it's quite handy. When you click an icon containing a graphic or a Web page, the folder shows a little preview in the left side, as shown in Figure 9-9. You use the other options much less frequently.

Figure 9-9: When you click a Web link or a file storing a picture, the folder places a preview of the file's contents on its left side.

The other options take more effort. To find them, open a folder, click View from the menu bar, and choose Customize this folder. There, you can edit an HTML template (difficult stuff), add wallpaper to the folder, and add a descriptive comment for easily identifying what's inside the folder.

Use Windows classic folders

Choose this, and your folders will merely display icons. They won't show icon previews, as shown in Figure 9-9.

Browse folders

Unless folders sit directly on your desktop, they usually live inside another folder, waiting to be opened. That leaves a big question: When you open a folder, do you want it to leap onto your screen in its own window? Or do you want that new folder's contents to simply replace the existing folder on your screen? Each method has its advantages, as I describe next. Neither one is correct. Try it both ways and choose the one you prefer.

Open each folder in the same window

Choose this option to make your newly opened folders replace the folder they lived in. It keeps everything neat and tidy, especially when you're looking for a folder that's buried deep inside layers of other folders: Although you may click your way through a half-dozen folders, you'll only have a single folder open on the screen.

Here's a tricky tip: Even with this option selected, you can still make a new folder pop up in its own window, leaving its "parent" folder in place. Hold Ctrl while double-clicking the folder. The old folder remains on the screen, and the folder you chose will open up in its own window. That lets you see two folders on the screen, making it easy to copy files back and forth.

Open each folder in its own window

This selection offers the alternative. It makes each newly opened folder leap onto the screen in its own window, leaving the old one in its place. This makes it easy to see which folder this new one heralded from, but it leaves a cluttered desktop.

If you open a folder, discover it's the wrong one, and want to go back to the previous folder, here's a quick way to return: Press the Backspace key. Yes, it sounds scary at first, but it doesn't delete anything — it just puts the folder back where it was.

Click items as follows

Here's the same single-click versus double-click question that boils down to this: Do you want to start programs and open folders by simply clicking them or clicking them twice in rapid succession (the ol' double-click)?

Single-click to open an item (point to select)

If you choose the single-click option, you'll find yet two more options: The first one underlines your icon's titles, just like on a Web page. The other option underlines your icon's titles only when you point at them. Decisions, decisions!

Double-click to open an item (single-click to select)

Choose this one, and you double-click an icon to make it leap to life, just like older versions of Windows. That's the way Windows Me comes installed — and I prefer it. It makes it easier to keep track of when I'm on the Internet and when I'm on Windows (although Microsoft keeps trying to turn them into the same thing).

View and File Types

These two options, the last two tabs in the Folder Options window, contain some mighty confusing stuff. Luckily, you can pretty much ignore them.

Clicking the View tab presents advanced options for advanced users. By clicking various options, users can see a file's path in the title bar, for instance, or view system files and their files' extensions. The File Types tab shows what extensions belong to which programs. Windows keeps track of this stuff, so there's little reason for you to.

Don't worry if some of these Windows Me options seem rather confusing or pointless. They are.

✔ This stuff is for people who *really* like to fiddle with their computers; chances are, you can avoid it unless your computer forces you to make one of these Internet decisions.

✔ If you've been comfortable with Windows 98 or Windows 95, always choose the "classic" styles. If you're comfortable with the Internet, try the Web-page style. But only choose the Custom settings — and the Active Desktop — if you like to fiddle around with your computer and try new things.

Adding Fun Desktop Themes and Effects

A millionaire's wallpaper, Desktop Themes decorate your display with dazzling sights and sounds. Feeling spacey? Click the Space option to add a gaseous nebula and space station to your wallpaper. Your fonts look 60s-era computerized, and the screen saver makes the space station spin and astronauts float around in the background.

Desktop Themes come with a fatal flaw, however. They don't include a way to revert to your regular desktop. After you install a theme, you're stuck in Theme land, and you can only switch from one theme to another. So, when you first double-click your Desktop Themes icon and your current desktop appears in the preview window, heed this warning:

Immediately after double-clicking the Desktop Themes icon, click the Save As button. When the Save Theme window appears, type My Regular Desktop in the File Name box. Finally, click the Save button. To switch back to your regular desktop, choose My Regular Desktop from Microsoft's list of Desktop Themes.

✔ Don't see the Desktop Themes option on the Control Panel? Double-click the Control Panel's Add/Remove Programs icon, click the Windows Setup tab, and click Desktop Themes from the Components menu. Click the OK button, and Windows Me will install the Desktop Themes. (It may ask for your original Windows Me CD, however.)

✔ If you didn't save your original desktop, it's not too late to remove a Desktop Theme. It just takes longer. First, remove Desktop Themes by using the Add/Remove Programs icon (the opposite of the tip above). Click the Control Panel's Display icon and choose your wallpaper. While in the Display Properties window, click the Effects tab. Click each icon and choose Default Icon, one at a time. Click the Appearance tab, choose Windows Standard, and choose OK. Finally, if your mouse pointer looks weird, click the Control Panel's Mouse icon and choose the Pointers Tab. Wade through the error messages and choose (None) under Scheme. Click OK, and you should be okay.

Viewing Your Computer's Fonts

Sure, you see the names of the fonts in your word-processing program. But how can you tell what they *look* like before choosing one? To find out, choose the Control Panel's Fonts icon.

From there, you see what fonts come with Windows Me, you install additional fonts, and you delete the ugly ones you don't like anymore.

To be on the safe side, don't delete any fonts that come with Windows Me; only delete fonts that you've installed yourself. Windows programs often borrow Windows Me fonts for menus. If you delete those fonts, your menus mysteriously vanish. And for goodness sake, don't delete any fonts beginning with the letters **MS.** (Don't delete the fonts that have red lettering in their icons, either.)

Double-click any font icon to see what that particular font looks like. For example, if you double-click the icon marked *Impact* font, Windows Me brings up an eye chart displaying how that font would look on the printed page, as shown in Figure 9-10. (Click the Print button to see what it really looks like on the printed page.)

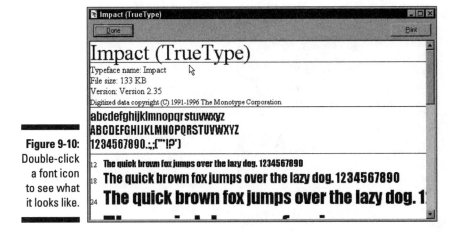

Figure 9-10:
Double-click
a font icon
to see what
it looks like.

> ✔ Icons marked with the letters "TT" are TrueType fonts, so they'll always
>   look better than the fonts marked with the letter "A."
>
> ✔ *Note:* You'll probably never need to fiddle with the Fonts icon. Just know
>   that it's there in case you ever want to view your fonts.

Making Windows Me Recognize Your Double-Click

Clicking twice with a mouse button is called a double-click; most users do a
lot of double-clicking in Windows Me. But sometimes you can't click fast
enough to satisfy Windows Me. It thinks that your double-clicks are just two
single clicks. If you have this problem, head for the Control Panel's Mouse
icon.

Double-clicking the Mouse icon brings up the settings for your mouse, as
shown in Figure 9-11. Because different computers come with different
brands of mice, the following instructions may not work for you, but you can
generally access the same types of options for any mouse. Try pressing F1 for
help if an option seems confusing.

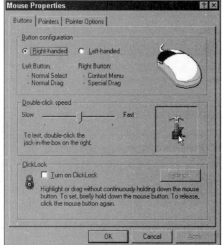

Figure 9-11:
Double-click
in the test
area box to
check your
current
double-click
settings.

To check the double-click speed, double-click the box with the little spinning handle. Each time Windows Me recognizes your double-click, a little puppet with water-buffalo horns pops out of the Jack in the Box. Double-click again, and the puppet disappears.

Slide the scroll box toward the words Fast or Slow until Windows Me successfully recognizes your double-click efforts. Click the OK button when you're through, and you're back in business.

 Can't double-click the Mouse icon quickly enough for Windows Me to open the darn thing up? Just click once, and poke the Enter key with your finger. Or click once with the right button and choose Open from the menu that shoots out of the Mouse icon's head. Yep, there are a lot of ways to do the same thing in Windows Me.

 If you're left-handed, click in the little circle marked Left-handed, shown along the top of Figure 9-11, and click the Apply button. Then you can hold the mouse in your left hand and still click with your index finger.

 For a psychedelic experience, click the tab marked Pointer Options along the window's top and then click in the box marked Show pointer trails. Windows Me makes *ghost arrows* follow the mouse pointer. Laptop users can spot the arrow more easily when ghosts follow it. The more you slide the little box toward the long side of the bar, the longer your trail of mouse ghosts grows.

✔ The mouse arrow doesn't have to move at the same speed as the mouse. To make the arrow *zip* across the screen with just a tiny push, click the Pointer Options tab along the top. Then, in the Pointer speed box, slide the little box toward the side of the scroll bar marked Fast. To slow down the mouse, allowing for more precise pointing, slide the box toward the Slow side.

✔ Some brands of mice come with fancier features and their own different settings page. The Microsoft IntelliMouse, described in the mouse section of Chapter 2, lets you control on-screen action by spinning a wheel embedded in the poor mouse's neck. Laptop users with touch-pads and trackballs will find their adjustment areas here, too.

✔ Mouse acting up something fierce? Pointer darting around obstinately like an excited dachshund on a walk? Maybe you need to clean your mouse, a simple maintenance task described in Chapter 14.

Setting the Computer's Time and Date

Many computer users don't bother to set the computer's clock. They just look at their wristwatches to see when it's time to stop working. But they're missing out on an important computing feature: Computers always stamp new files with the current date and time. If the computer doesn't know the correct date, it stamps files with the *wrong* date. Then how can you find the files you created yesterday? Last week?

Also, Windows Me sometimes does some funny things to the computer's internal clock, so you may want to reset the date and time if you notice that the computer is living in the past (or prematurely jumping to the future).

 To reset the computer's time or date, choose the Control Panel's Date/Time icon.

A double-click on the Date/Time icon brings a little calendar to the screen, as shown in Figure 9-12. To change the date, click the correct date as listed on the on-screen calendar. If the date's off by a month or more, click the little arrow next to the currently listed month. A list drops down, letting you choose a different month. To change the year or the hour, click the number you want to change and then click the up or down arrows to make the number bigger or smaller. When the number is correct, click the OK button for Windows Me to make the changes.

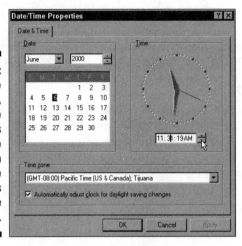

Figure 9-12:
To change
the time,
click the
numbers
beneath the
clock; then
click the
little arrows
next to the
numbers.

✔ Moved to a new time zone? Click the Time Zone tab along the top of the window. Click the downward-pointing arrow next to the currently listed time zone. A *long* list of countries and locations appears; click the one where you're currently hanging your hat.

✔ Windows Me has a Search program, which I describe in Chapter 7, that can locate files by the time and date they were created, modified, or last accessed — but *only* if you keep your computer's date and time set correctly.

✔ Most computers have an internal clock that automatically keeps track of the time and date. Nevertheless, those clocks aren't always reliable, especially among laptops with "power-saving" features. Check your $2,000 computer's clock against your $20 wristwatch every few weeks to make sure that the computer is on the mark.

For an even quicker way to change your computer's time or date, double-click the little clock Windows Me puts on the taskbar that lives along the edge of the screen. Windows Me brings up the Date/Time menu, just as if you'd waded through the Control Panel and double-clicked the Date/Time icon.

Fiddling with the Printer

Most of the time, the printer will work fine. Especially after you turn it *on* and try printing again. In fact, most people will never need to read this section.

Occasionally, however, you may need to tweak some printer settings. You may need to install a new printer or remove an old one that you sell (so it won't keep cluttering up the list of printers). Either way, start by choosing the Control Panel's Printers icon.

The Printers dialog box surfaces, as shown in Figure 9-13.

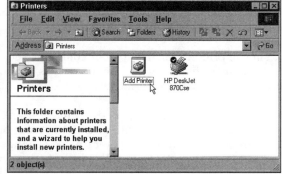

Figure 9-13: Double-clicking the Add Printer icon tells Windows about your new printer.

 Is the My Computer window open? Double-click the Printers icon hiding in there. That step takes you to the same Printers dialog box as the Control Panel does. (Or, choose Printers from the Start button's Settings menu.)

If you're installing a new printer, grab the Windows Me compact disc or floppy disks that came in the box; you'll probably need them during the installation.

1. **To add a new printer, double-click the Control Panel's Printer icon and click the Add Printer icon.**

   Magic! A Windows Me Wizard appears, ready to set up your new printer.

2. **Click the Next button and then follow the Wizard's instructions.**

   For example, click whether your printer is physically connected to your computer, or if it's shared with other computers over a network.

3. **Click the Next button and follow the Wizard's instructions.**

   The Add Printer Wizard box lists the names of printer manufacturers on the left; click the name of your printer's manufacturer, and the right side of the box lists the models of printers that that manufacturer makes.

4. **Double-click your printer's name when you see it listed. Windows Me asks you to stick the appropriate setup disks into a drive, and the drive makes some grinding noises.**

   After a moment, you see the new printer listed in the box.

5. **Click the new printer's icon and choose the Set As Default Printer option from the window's File menu.**

   That's it. If you're like most people, your printer will work like a charm. If it doesn't, you may have to wade through the technical stuff in the side-bar (in this chapter) about printer ports and such.

If you have more than one printer attached to your computer, select your most-oft-used printer as the *default* printer. That choice tells Windows Me to assume that it's printing to that oft-used printer.

✔ To remove a printer you no longer use, choose Printers from the Start menu's Settings menu. Click its name with your right mouse button, and then click Delete from the menu. That printer's name no longer appears as an option when you try to print from a Windows Me-based program.

✔ You can change printer options from within many programs. Choose Files in a program's menu bar and then choose Print Setup. From there, you can often access the same box of printer options as you find in the Control Panel.

✔ Some printers offer a variety of options. For example, you can print from different paper trays or print at different resolutions. To play with these options, double-click the Control Panel's Printer icon and right-click your printer's icon. When the menu pops up, choose Properties to change things like paper sizes, fonts, and types of graphics.

✔ If your printer isn't listed in the Windows Me master list, you may have to contact the printer's manufacturer for a *driver*. When it comes in the mail or is downloaded through the Internet, repeat the process for adding a printer, but click the Have Disk button. Windows Me asks you to stick in the manufacturer's disk so that it can copy the *driver* onto the hard disk. (For more information, check out the section "Adding New Hardware" later in this chapter.)

✔ Check out your printer's installation guide. Some manufacturers prefer you to use their own software and steer clear of the Printer Wizard.

✔ Working with printers can be more complicated than trying to retrieve a stray hamster from inside the kitchen cupboards. Feel free to use any of the Help buttons in the dialog boxes. Chances are, they'll offer some helpful advice, and some are actually customized for your particular brand of printer. Too bad they can't catch hamsters.

Printer ports and configuration nonsense

Windows Me shoots information to printers through *ports* (little metal outlets on the computer's rump). Most printers connect to a port called *LPT1:*, or the first *line printer port.*

Always select this option first. If it works, skip the rest of this technical chatter. You've already found success!

Some people, however, insist on plugging printers into a second printer port, or *LPT2:*. (If you meet one of these people, ask them why.) Still other people buy those weird-and-very-rare *serial* printers, which plug into *serial ports* (also known as *COM ports*). Others plug into the relatively new *USB* port.

Different brands of printers work with Windows Me in different ways, but here are a few tips. To connect a printer to a different port, click the printer's icon with your right mouse button and choose Properties from the pop-up menu. Click

the tab marked Details, and you can select the port you want. Look to see what port you're plugging the printer into, and select that port from the menu. (Computer ports are rarely labeled, so you'll probably have to bribe a computer guru to help you out. Start tossing Chee(tos around your chair and desk; computer gurus are attracted by the smell. No Chee(tos? Head to Chapter 2 for port pictures.)

If you're connecting a printer to a serial port, you need to do one more little chore: Configure the serial port. Click the Port Settings box, found on that same Details tab page, and make sure that the following numbers and characters appear, in this order: 9600, 8, N, 1, Xon/Xoff.

The printer should be all set. If not, call over a computer guru. At least you have to go through all this printer hassle only once — unless you buy another printer.

Sounds and Multimedia

The term *multimedia* means mixing two or more mediums — usually combining sound and pictures. A plain old television, for example, could be called a *multimedia tool,* especially if you're trying to impress somebody.

Windows Me can mix sound and pictures if you have a *sound card:* a gizmo costing less than $100 that slips inside the computer and hooks up to a pair of speakers or a stereo.

Macintosh computers have had sound for years. And for years, Mac owners have been able to *assign sounds to system events.* In lay language, that means having the computer make a professional baseball player's spitting sound when it ejects a floppy disk.

In Windows Me, you can't assign sounds to the floppy drives, but you can assign noises to other *events* by double-clicking the Control Panel's Sounds and Multimedia icon.

The Sounds and Multimedia Properties dialog box appears (see Figure 9-14). Windows Me automatically plays sounds for several system events. An event can be anything as simple as when a menu pops up or when Windows Me first starts up in the morning.

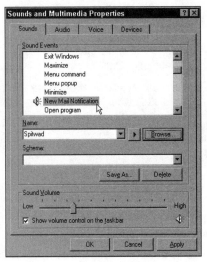

Figure 9-14: Windows Me plays back different sounds when different things happen on your computer.

Windows Me lists the events on the top of the box and lists the possible sounds directly below them in the box called Name. To assign a sound, click the event first and then click the sound you want to hear for that event. In Figure 9-14, for example, Windows Me is set up to make a spitting sound whenever a new piece of electronic mail comes in over the wire.

✔ Are you satisfied with your new choices of sounds? Click in the box marked Save As and change the words Windows Default to something else, like My Own Sounds. That way, you can still change back to the more polite Windows Default sounds when you don't want houseguests to hear your computer spit. (You can change back to My Own Sounds after they've left.)

✔ For some automatic sound schemes, choose the Desktop Themes icon from the Control Panel. It assigns lots of cutesy sounds automatically to different Windows setups. It's really fun until it becomes annoying.

✔ To take advantage of this multimedia feature, your computer needs a sound card. Stuck with an old computer? Buy and install a sound card, and then tell Windows Me about your new card by clicking the Control Panel's Add New Hardware icon, described later in this chapter.

✔ To hear a sound before you assign it, click its name and then click the Preview button (the little black triangle next to the speaker).

✔ You can record your own sounds through most sound cards. You can probably pick up a cheap microphone at Radio Shack; some sound cards don't include one. Be forewarned: Sound consumes a *lot* of disk space, so stick with short recordings — short and sweet B.B. King guitar riffs, for example, or the sound of a doorbell ringing.

✔ Windows only lets you assign files stored in its WAV format. You can't use MP3 files, MIDI files, or any other cool sound formats.

✔ Sound card not working right? You may have to muddle through the different settings, described in the nearby dreary technical sidebar "Multimedia setup problems."

Multimedia setup problems

Multimedia gadgetry inevitably brings a multitude of setup problems. There are simply too many file formats and program settings for an easy ride. Although Windows Me does an excellent job of setting up your computer's hardware automatically, the Control Panel's Sounds and Multimedia Properties icon lets techno-fiddlers change some of the settings. Because different computers use different parts, the settings listed under the Multimedia icon vary, but here's a general look at what they can do:

Sounds: As described elsewhere in this chapter, this area lets you assign different sounds to different events.

Audio: This page controls your sound card's volume settings as well as its recording quality. The better the quality of the recording, the more hard disk space your recordings consume. Some sound cards include a mixer for setting the volumes from a variety of different sources:

CDs, microphones, synthesized sounds, and others. **Tip:** A quick way to adjust the computer's volume is to double-click the little speaker in the corner of the taskbar. (If you don't see that taskbar's little speaker control, click the box next to the words, Show Volume Control on the Taskbar.)

Voice: Want to sing along to some tunes? Here's where you see if your sound card can play music and record your voice at the same time. Be sure to click the Voice Test button before trying anything else.

Devices: Here, Windows Me lists all the multimedia devices attached to your computer (as well as a few devices you may want to add to your computer in the future). By clicking on a device and clicking on the Properties button near the bottom, you can turn a device on or off. You'll rarely use this. Sound and video mavens like to see what codes they have installed.

Adding New Hardware

When you wolf down a sandwich for lunch, you know what you ate. After all, you picked it out at the deli counter, chewed it, swallowed it, and wiped the breadcrumbs away from the corner of your mouth.

But when you add a new part to your computer, it's turned off — Windows Me is asleep. And when you turn the computer back on and Windows Me returns to life, it may not notice the surgical handiwork.

Here's the good news, however: If you simply tell Windows Me to *look* for the new part, it will probably find it. In fact, Windows Me will not only spot the new part, but it will introduce itself and start a warm and friendly working relationship using the right settings.

 The Control Panel's Add New Hardware icon handles the process of introducing Windows Me to anything you've recently attached to your computer.

Here's how to tell Windows Me to look for any new computer parts you may have stuffed inside or plugged into your computer:

1. **Double-click the Control Panel's Add New Hardware icon and click the Next button.**

   The Windows Me Hardware Installation Wizard pops out of a hat, ready to introduce Windows Me to whatever part you've stuffed inside your computer.

2. **Click the Next button.**

   Windows Me looks for any recognizable "Plug and Play" devices installed in your computer.

Here's where things start getting a little different. Did Windows Me find anything new? If so, click the newly installed part's name from the list, click the Finish button, and follow the rest of the Wizard's instructions.

If the Wizard didn't find anything, though, click the Yes button, telling Windows to search for devices that aren't Plug and Play-compatible. If it finds the device, rejoice — and click the device's name for Windows to install it.

If Windows still can't locate your newly installed part, however, you need to contact the manufacturer of your new part and ask for a *Windows Me driver*.

> ✔ Adding a new modem? Then Windows Me will want to know your current country and area code, as well as whether you dial a special number (such as a 9) to reach an outside line. If you want to change this stuff later, double-click the Control Panel's Modem icon, which brings you to the same page that the Add New Hardware icon does.

> ✔ Sometimes Windows Me detects a newly inserted part as soon as you turn on your computer. It occasionally recruits a Wizard to help you set it up.
>
> ✔ Windows Me is pretty good about identifying various gadgets that people have stuffed inside it, especially if your computer is Plug and Play-compatible and you're installing a Plug and Play part. You can find more information about Plug and Play in Chapter 3.

Adding and Removing Programs

 By adding an Add/Remove Programs icon to the Control Panel, Windows Me is trying to trick you into thinking that it's easier than ever to install a program. Nope.

Here's how the installation programs work if you're lucky. When you get a new program, look for a disk marked Install or Installation, and stick the disk into any disk drive that it fits. If the program came on a compact disc, put the disc into your compact disc drive.

Next, double-click the Control Panel's Add/Remove Programs icon, click the Install button, and click Next from the next screen. Windows Me searches all your disk drives for a disk containing an installation program; if it finds an installation program, it runs it, effectively installing the program. If it doesn't find one, it just gives up.

> ✔ Programs that live on compact discs often install themselves automatically: Just put them in your disc drive and shut the door.

> ✔ If the Add/Remove Programs icon doesn't automatically install your new program, all isn't lost. Make a new folder somewhere on your hard drive and copy all the files from the program's disk to the new folder. Then, to load the program, double-click the program's icon (it's usually named Setup) from within that folder. Chapter 11 is filled with tips on creating folders, copying files, and sticking new programs on the Start menu.
>
> ✔ The Add/Remove Programs icon can *uninstall* programs, too. It brings up a list of installed programs; click the unwanted program's name, click the Add/Remove button, and Windows will scrape the program from your computer's innards.

> ✔ *Always* use the Add/Remove Programs icon to uninstall your unwanted programs. Simply deleting their folders won't do the trick. In fact, it confuses your computer, and you might see strange error messages.

✔ The Windows Setup tab at the top of the Add/Remove Programs screen lets you add or remove some of the programs that came with Windows Me: programs for laptop users, extra wallpaper and sounds, network utilities, games, The Microsoft Network online service, and a few other goodies. To add one of the programs, click in its check box. To remove one that you've installed, click in its check box. (Its check mark disappears, as does the program, when you click the Apply button.)

✔ Most programs that you buy at software stores come with installation programs, so Windows Me can install them without too much trouble. Some of the smaller shareware programs found on online services don't come with installation programs, unfortunately, so you'll have to install them yourself.

✔ Can't find the Welcome program — a tutorial for new Windows Me users that's mentioned when Windows Me first loads itself? From the Start button, click Programs and choose Help from the menu. When the Help and Support window appears, click the words Tours and Tutorials from the top of the window. It lists more than 20 tours; yours is on the very top.

✔ For safety's sake, make a Startup Disk — a disk that can still start up your computer if something dreadful happens. Put a blank floppy — or a floppy with destructible information — in drive A and click the StartUp Disk tab from the top of the Add/Remove Programs program. Click the Create Disk button and follow the instructions.

Icons Covered Elsewhere

Windows overlaps itself in many areas, and that includes the Control Panel. Many of Control Panel's icons are merely shortcuts to programs that live elsewhere. Here's where the book describes those icons in more detail.

✔ Automatic Updates lets you schedule how often the Windows Update program runs. The Windows Update program lives on your Start menu, so it's covered in Chapter 10. Don't mess with Automatic Updates unless your computer keeps giving you strange messages about updates not found. Then, open the icon and choose the Turn Off Automatic Updating option. You can simply click the Start Menu's Windows Update program every once in awhile.

✔ Dial-Up Networking is where you enter your phone number and connection information for connecting to the Internet. The Internet Connection Wizard, covered in Chapter 12, automatically runs this program, so it's included there.

✔ The Modem icon lets you configure your modem. Normally, you don't need to touch it after it's set up by Dial-Up Networking (which is covered as part of the Internet Connection Wizard in Chapter 12).

 ✔ The Mouse icon lets you adjust your mouse-click properties. It's fairly easy to figure out. If you need more mouse information, head for Chapter 3.

 ✔ If your computer goes to sleep on you and never wakes up, open the Power Options icon, choose Always On in the Power Schemes area, and make sure Never is listed under System stand by.

 ✔ Scanners and Cameras only lists scanners and cameras that connect through your computer's serial port. If Windows can't find them through the Add Hardware icon, try clicking this icon.

 ✔ Scheduled Tasks is covered in Chapter 12, because it also appears on the Start menu.

 ✔ Taskbar and Start Menu is covered in Chapter 10 — an entire chapter devoted to the Start Button, Taskbar, and Desktop.

Icons You Should Avoid

Unless you have a very pressing reason, avoid these icons in the Control Panel: Network, ODBC Data Sources (32bit), Passwords, Regional Settings, System, Telephony, and Users.

 ✔ The Network icon controls how Windows Me talks to other computers through your office's network — those cables meandering from PC to PC. Talk to your network administrator before playing with this icon "just to see what it does." If you plan to use Windows Me's Home Networking, check out *MORE Microsoft Windows Me For Dummies;* I don't have enough pages left in this book.

 ✔ The Regional Settings icon changes the keyboard layout to the one used by people in other countries. It doesn't make the Windows Me dialog boxes appear in German (although you can order the German version of Windows Me from Microsoft). Instead, a foreign keyboard layout makes certain keys produce foreign characters. It also changes the way currency appears and stuff like that.

 ✔ The information listed in the System icon turns on network hounds and techno-nerds. It's out of the realm of this book. Check out Brian Livingston's *Windows Me Secrets* (IDG Books Worldwide, Inc.) for that sort of advanced-level stuff.

✔ The Passwords icon is kind of like the switch in fancy cars that can remember different seat- and mirror-adjustment settings for up to four different drivers. By assigning different passwords to different computer users, Windows Me can switch to a customized desktop setting for each person who logs in.

✔ Nobody really knows what the ODBC Data Sources (32bit) icon does.

✔ Finally, the Telephony and Users icons are for people who enjoy fiddling with their computers — not for people who just want to get their work done and go home.

Part III
Using Windows Me Applications (And Surfing the Web, Should the Mood Strike)

The 5th Wave   By Rich Tennant

"IT'S A MEMO FROM SOFTWARE DOCUMENTATION. IT'S EITHER AN EXPLANATION OF HOW THE NEW SATELLITE COMMUNICATIONS NETWORK FUNCTIONS, OR DIRECTIONS FOR REPLACING BATTERIES IN THE SMOKE DETECTORS."

In this part . . .

Did you know that

- ✔ Rubber bands last longer when refrigerated?
- ✔ A human's eyelashes generally fall off after 5 months?
- ✔ Windows Me comes with a bunch of free programs that aren't even mentioned on the outside of the box?

This part takes a look at all the stuff you're getting for nothing. Well, for the price on your sales receipt, anyway.

Chapter 10

The Windows Me Desktop, Start Button, and Taskbar

. . . .

In This Chapter

▶ Using the desktop

▶ Making shortcuts

▶ Deleting files, folders, programs, and icons

▶ Retrieving deleted items from the Recycle Bin

▶ Discovering the Start button's reason to live

▶ Putting programs on the Start button menu

▶ Making programs start automatically with Windows

▶ Using the taskbar

▶ Controlling Print Manager

. . . .

*I*n the old days of computing, pale technoweenies typed disgustingly long strings of code words into computers to make the computers do something — anything.

With Windows Me, computers reach the age of modern convenience. To start a program, simply click a button. There's a slight complication, however: The buttons no longer *look* like buttons. In fact, some of the buttons are hidden, revealed only by the push of yet another button (if you're lucky enough to stumble upon the right place to push).

To make matters worse, some of the buttons fall off and land on your desktop. (Don't worry, they're *supposed* to do that.)

This chapter covers the three main Windows Me buttonmongers: the desktop, the taskbar, and that mother of all buttons — the Start button.

Rolling Objects along the Windows Me Desktop

Normally, nobody would think of mounting a desktop sideways. Keeping the pencils from rolling off a normal desk is hard enough.

But in Windows Me, your computer monitor's screen is known as the Windows *desktop,* and it's the area where all your work takes place. When working with Windows Me, you'll be creating files and folders right on your new electronic desktop and arranging those files and folders across the screen.

For example, do you need to write a letter asking the neighbor to return the circular saw she borrowed? Here's how to put the desktop's functions to immediate use.

Point at just about any Windows Me item and click your right mouse button to see a menu listing the things you're allowed to do with that item.

1. **Click an uncovered area of your desktop with your right mouse button.**

   A menu pops up, as shown in Figure 10-1.

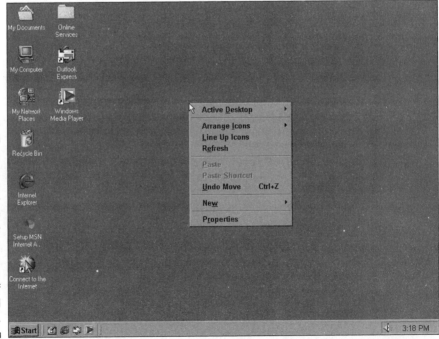

Figure 10-1:
Clicking an empty area of your desktop with your right mouse button brings up a list of helpful options.

2. Point at the word New and click WordPad Document from the menu that appears.

Because you're creating something new — a new letter — you should point at the word New. Windows Me lists the new things you can create on the desktop. Choose WordPad Document, as shown in Figure 10-2.

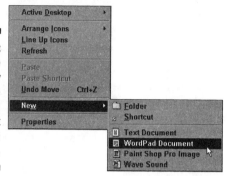

Figure 10-2:
Point at the word New and choose WordPad Document from the menu.

As your computer fills up with programs, your menu choices change, too. In fact, if you install Microsoft Word, it sometimes kicks WordPad off the menu completely. If you don't see WordPad on the menu, choose Run from the Start menu, type WordPad into the Run box, and press Enter. WordPad opens automatically, ready for action. Now run ahead to Step 5.

3. Type a title for your letter and press Enter.

When an icon for a WordPad document appears on the desktop, Windows Me doesn't want you to lose it. So, the first step is to give it a name of up to 255 characters. As soon as you start typing, your new title replaces the old name of New WordPad Document, as shown in Figure 10-3. (Occasionally, Windows Me frets about your choice of name; if so, try a different name or skip ahead to Chapter 11 to see why Windows is so finicky about names.)

Figure 10-3:
Start typing to create the icon's new name.

4. Double-click your newly created WordPad icon to open it.

Double-clicking the new icon calls up WordPad, the word processor, so you can write the letter requesting the return of your circular saw.

5. Write your letter.

Remember, word processors automatically wrap your sentences to the next line for you; don't hit the Enter key when you're nearing the right side of the page. (I address WordPad's letter-writing intuitiveness more fully in Chapter 12.)

6. Click Save from the WordPad File menu to save the letter.

If you created the file by right-clicking the desktop, you've already named the file, and Windows will save it without further ado. If you opened WordPad through the Start menu's Run command, now's the time to choose a name for the file.

7. Head back to the WordPad File menu and choose Print to send the letter to the printer.

8. Close the file by clicking on the X in its upper-right corner; then store the file by dragging its icon to a folder. Or to delete it, drag the file to the Recycle Bin.

After you finish writing and printing the letter, you need to decide what to do with the file. You can simply leave its icon on your desk, but that clutters things up. Instead, drag and drop the letter into the My Documents folder that's conveniently located on your desktop. (Dragging and dropping is covered in Chapter 3.)

If you want to save the letter in your own folder inside My Documents, open the My Documents folder and click inside it with your right mouse button. When the menu appears, click New and choose Folder from the New menu that pops up. Windows Me tosses a new folder into the My Documents folder, ready for you to rename and drag your letter inside.

If you want to delete the letter, drag the icon to your Recycle Bin, which I describe in the next section.

✔ Windows Me is designed for you to work right on top of the desktop. From the desktop, you can create new things like files, folders, sounds, and graphics — just about anything. After working with your new file or folder, you can store it or delete it.

✔ You can store your favorite files and folders in the My Documents folder, or leave them right on the desktop. Or, to be more organized, create new folders in the My Documents folder to store your newly created files.

✔ Are you confused about what something is supposed to do? Click it with your right mouse button, or simply rest the pointer over the confusing spot. Windows Me often tosses up a menu that lists just about everything you can do with that particular object. This trick works on many icons found on your desktop or throughout your programs.

✔ Is your desktop looking rather cluttered? Make Windows Me line up the icons in orderly rows: Click the desktop with the right mouse button and choose Line Up Icons from the menu that appears.

Using the Recycle Bin

Recycle Bin

The Recycle Bin, that little oval wastebasket on your desktop, is supposed to work like a *real* Recycle Bin. Seen in the margin, it's something you can fish the Sunday paper out of if somebody pitched the comics section before you had a chance to read it.

If you want to get rid of something in Windows Me — a file or folder, for example — simply drag it to the Recycle Bin. Point at the file or folder's icon with the mouse and, while holding down the left mouse button, point at the Recycle Bin. Let go of the mouse button, and your detritus disappears. Windows Me stuffs it into the Recycle Bin.

But if you want to bypass that cute metaphor, there's another way to delete stuff: Click your unwanted file or folder's icon with the right mouse button and choose Delete from the menu that pops up. Windows Me asks cautiously if you're *sure* that you want to delete the icon. If you click the Yes button, Windows Me dumps the icon into the Recycle Bin, just as if you'd dragged it there. Whoosh!

So if you like to drag and drop, feel free to drag your garbage to the Recycle Bin and let go. If you prefer the menus, click with your right mouse button and choose Delete. Or, if you like alternative lifestyles, click the unwanted icon with your left button and push your keyboard's Delete key. All three methods toss the file into the Recycle Bin, where it can be salvaged later or, eventually, purged for good.

Terribly boring desktop trivia

That's right — Windows Me considers the desktop to be a mammoth folder. That mammoth folder opens across your screen when you start Windows Me, and it closes up when you shut down Windows Me with the Start button's Shut Down command.

The Desktop folder hides inside your Windows folder. But if you want to see inside and poke it with a sharp stick, here's how to find it:

1. **Open Windows Explorer.**

2. **Go to your Windows folder and look for the Desktop folder.**

You can delete unwanted items from here as well as from your actual desktop. Also, any item dumped into this folder will appear upon your desktop, usually along the left side.

✔ Want to retrieve something you've deleted? Double-click the Recycle Bin icon, and a window appears, listing deleted items. See the name of your accidentally deleted icon? Click it with your right mouse button and choose Restore to send it back to the folder where it was deleted. Or drag it to the desktop or any other folder: Point at the icon's name and, while holding down the left mouse button, point at its desired location. Let go of the mouse button, and the Recycle Bin coughs up the deleted item, good as new.

✔ Sometimes, the Recycle Bin can get pretty full. If you're searching fruitlessly for a file you've recently deleted, tell the Recycle Bin to sort the filenames in the order in which they were deleted. Click View, point at Arrange Icons, and choose by Delete Date from the menu that pops out. Recycle Bin now lists the most recently deleted files at the bottom.

✔ The Recycle Bin icon changes from an empty wastepaper basket to a full one as soon as it's holding a deleted file. You may have to squint a little to notice the pieces of paper sticking out of the trashcan's top.

✔ A Recycle Bin can eat up 10 percent (or more) of your hard disk space. To free up some space, cut down on the amount of room it reserves for saving your deleted files. Click the Recycle Bin with your right mouse button and choose Properties from its menu. Normally, Recycle Bin waits until your deleted files consume 10 percent of your hard drive before it begins purging your oldest deleted files. If you want the Recycle Bin to hang on to more deleted files, increase the percentage. If you're a sure-fingered clicker who seldom makes mistakes, decrease the percentage.

Making a shortcut

Some people like to organize their desktop, putting a pencil sharpener on one corner and a box of Kleenex on the other corner. Other people like their Kleenex box in the top desk drawer. Microsoft knew that one desktop design could never please everybody, so Windows Me lets people customize their desktops to suit individual tastes and needs.

For example, you may find yourself frequently copying files to a floppy disk in drive A. Normally, to perform that operation, you open the My Computer icon and drag your files to the drive A icon living in there. But there's a quicker way, and it's called a Windows Me *shortcut*. A shortcut is simply a push button — an icon — that stands for something else.

For example, here's how to put a shortcut for drive A on your desktop:

1. **Double-click the desktop's My Computer icon.**

   The My Computer folder opens up, showing the icons for your disk drives as well as folders for your Control Panel and Printer. (My Computer gets more coverage in Chapter 11.)

2. **With your right mouse button, drag the drive A icon to the desktop.**

   Point at the drive A icon and, while holding down your right mouse button, point at the desktop, as shown in Figure 10-4. Let go of your mouse button.

3. **Choose Create Shortcut(s) Here from the menu.**

   Windows Me puts an icon for drive A on your desktop, but it looks a little different from the drive A icon you dragged. Because it's only a shortcut — not the original icon — it has a little arrow in its corner, as seen in the margin.

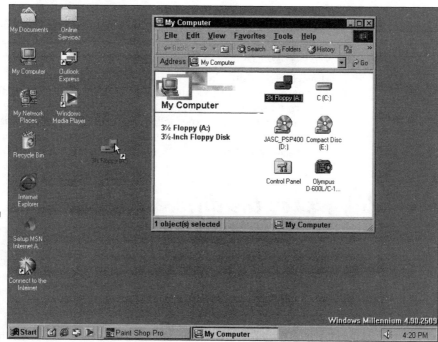

Figure 10-4: Dragging the drive A icon to the desktop creates a shortcut.

That's it. Now you won't need to root through the My Computer or Explorer folders and programs to access drive A. The drive A shortcut on your desktop works just as well as the *real* drive A icon found in My Computer and Explorer. To copy or move files to your A drive, just drag them to the newly created shortcut.

✔ Feel free to create desktop shortcuts for your most commonly accessed programs, files, or disk drives. Shortcuts are a quick way to make Windows Me easier to use.

✔ If your newly dragged icon doesn't have an arrow in its bottom corner, don't let go of the mouse! You might not be making a shortcut. Instead, you've probably dragged the *real* program to your desktop, and other programs may not be able to find it. Press the Esc button with your free hand, and Windows stops what you were doing. (You probably mistakenly held down the *left* mouse button instead of the correct button — the *right* button.)

✔ Have you grown tired of a shortcut? Feel free to delete it. Deleting a shortcut has no effect on the original file, folder, or program that it represents.

✔ You can make as many shortcuts as you'd like. You can even make several shortcuts for the same thing. For example, you can put a shortcut for drive A in *all* your folders.

✔ Windows Me shortcuts aren't very good at keeping track of moving files. If you create a shortcut to a file or program and then move that file or program to a different folder, the shortcut won't be able to find that file or program anymore. Windows will panic and try searching for it, but it may not be able to find it. Shortcuts, by contrast, can be moved anywhere without problems.

Uh, what's the difference between a shortcut and an icon?

An icon for a file, folder, or program looks pretty much like a shortcut, except the shortcut has an arrow wedged in its lower reaches. And double-clicking on a shortcut and double-clicking on an icon do pretty much the same thing: start a program or load a file or folder.

But a shortcut is only a servant of sorts. When you double-click the shortcut, it runs over to the program, file, or folder that the shortcut represents and kick-starts that program, file, or folder into action.

You could do the same thing yourself by rummaging through your computer's folders, finding the program, file, or folder you're after, and personally double-clicking on its icon to bring it to life. But it's often more convenient to create a shortcut so that you don't have to rummage so much.

> ✔ If you delete a shortcut — the icon with the little arrow — you're not doing any real harm. You're just firing the servant that fetched things for you, probably creating more work for yourself in the process.
>
> ✔ If you accidentally delete a shortcut, you can pull it out of the Recycle Bin, just like anything else that's deleted in Windows Me.

The Start Button's Reason to Live

The Start button lives on your taskbar, and it's always ready for action. By using the Start button, you can start programs, adjust the Windows Me settings, find help for sticky situations, or, thankfully, shut down Windows Me and get away from the computer for a while.

The little Start button is so eager to please, in fact, that it starts shooting out menus full of options as soon as you click it. Just click the button once, and the first layer of menus pops out, as shown in Figure 10-5.

Figure 10-5:
Click the taskbar's Start button to see a list of options.

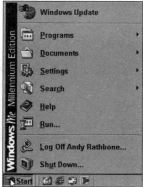

The explosive Table 10-1 shows what the different parts of the Start button do when you point at them.

Table 10-1	The Start Button
This Part	*Does This When You Point at It*
Windows Update	After joining the Internet and registering Windows Me, you can let somebody else play mechanic. Click here, and Windows Me automatically bellies up to a special Microsoft Web site, analyzes itself, and installs any updated software that may help it run better.
Programs	Probably the most-used spot. Point here, and a second menu appears, listing available programs and folders containing related programs.
Documents	Point here to see the names of the last 15 files you've played with. Spot one you want to open again? Click its name to reopen it. *Warning:* Some programs shirk their responsibility and don't list their files here.
Settings	Allows access to the Control Panel and Printer settings, as well as ways to customize the Start button menus and taskbar.
Search	Lost a program or file? Head here to make Windows Me search for it.
	Clicking here brings up the Windows Me Help menu.
Run...	Used mostly by old-school, "stick-shift" computer users, it lets you start a program by typing the program's name and location.
Log Off Andy Rathbone...	Click here if you're nice enough to log off and let somebody else use your computer.
Shut Down...	Click here to either shut down and restart Windows or shut it down for the day.
Start	Clicking the Start button makes the Start menu shoot out of the button's head.

✔ The Start button menu changes as you add programs to your computer. That change means that the Start button menu on your friend's computer probably offers slightly different menus than the ones on your own computer.

✔ See the little arrows on the menu next to the words Programs, Documents, Settings, and Search? The arrows mean that when you point at those words, another menu pops up, offering more-detailed options.

✔ Need to open a file yet another time? Before you spend time clicking your way through folders, see if it's listed under the Start button's Documents area. You can often find your past 15 documents listed there, ready to be opened with a click. Plus, clicking there gives you quick access to your My Documents and My Pictures folders.

Starting a program from the Start button

This one's easy. Click the Start button and when the menu pops out of the button's head, point at the word Programs. Yet another menu pops up, this one listing the names of programs or folders full of programs.

If you see your program listed, click the name. Wham! Windows Me kicks that program to the screen. If you don't see your program listed, try pointing at the tiny folders listed on the menu. New menus fly out of those folders, listing even more programs.

When you spot your program's name, just click it. In fact, you don't have to click until you see the program's name: The Start button opens and closes all the menus automatically, depending on where the mouse arrow is pointing at the time.

✔ Still don't see your program listed by name? Then head for Chapter 7 and find the section on finding lost files and folders. You can tell Windows Me to find your program for you.

✔ There's another way to load a program that's not listed — if you know where the program's living on your hard drive. Choose Run from the Start button menu, type the program's name, and press Enter. If Windows Me finds the program, it runs it. If it can't find the program, though, click the Browse button. Shazam! Yet another box appears, this time listing programs by name. Pick your way through the dialog box until you see your program; then double-click its name and click the OK button to load it.

✔ If you don't know how to *pick your way through* this particular dialog box, head to the section of Chapter 5 on opening a file. (This particular dialog box rears its head every time you load or save a file or open a program.)

Adding a program to the Start button

The Windows Me Start button works great — until you're hankering for something that's not listed on the menu. How do you add things to the Start button's menu?

If you're installing a Windows program that comes with its own installation program, breathe a sigh of relief. Those programs automatically put themselves on the Start button menu. But what if your program comes from a simpler household and doesn't have an installation program? Well, it means more work for you, as described here:

1. **Install the program.**

   Install the program, whether you acquired it from the Internet, a compact disc, or a floppy disk. (Double-click the Control Panel's Add/Remove Programs icon to install a program, a process described in Chapter 9.) Hit Chapter 11 if you're a little sketchy about creating folders and copying files.

2. **Click the Start button and then point at Settings.**

   A menu shoots out from the right side of the Start menu.

3. **Click Taskbar & Start Menu and then click the Advanced tab.**

   The tab lurks along the top, on the right side. You can also access the Taskbar and Start Menu through its icon on the Control Panel.

4. **Click the Add button and choose Browse.**

   A new box pops up, as shown in Figure 10-6.

Figure 10-6: Double-click a folder, and the Browse box lists the programs living inside that folder.

Click the folder where the program and its files live. (The installation program usually mentions where it is copying the program's files.)

Hint: If you can't find the program's folder, click the icon of the little folder with the arrow inside, up near the top. That click tells Windows Me to work its way up the folder listings, eventually showing you a list of your computer's disk drives. After you reach that point, click your way back down through the proper folders until you reach your program's folder.

5. Double-click the icon of the program you want to add.

The program's filename appears in the Command line box. (By double-clicking the program's name, you were able to avoid typing the name yourself.)

6. Click the Next button and then click the folder where you want your program to appear on the Start menu. Click the Next button again.

For example, if you want your new program to appear under the Programs heading, simply click the Programs folder. To place it in a new folder, click the New Folder button.

7. Type the name that you want to see on the menu for that program and then click the Finish button.

Most people just type the program's name. (Just as many people have nicknames, most program's filenames are different from their *real* names. For example, you'd probably want to change WP — the filename — to WordPerfect — the program's real name.)

8. Click the OK button at the bottom of the box.

That click gets rid of the Taskbar Properties box and *really* finishes the job. Now, when you click the Start button, you see your new program listed on the menu.

✔ Windows Me lets you add programs to the Start menu in several ways. The one I just listed is probably the easiest one to follow step by step.

✔ To get rid of unwanted menu items, follow these steps but click the Remove button rather than the Add button in Step 4.

✔ Just like your Windows Me desktop, the Start menu is really just a plain old folder. Right-click the Start button and choose Explore to see it. The folder is a directory called Start Menu, and it lives in the folder where Windows Me is installed, usually Windows on your C: drive. Any program shortcuts that you put in the Start Menu folder appear as items on the Start menu. Also, to rearrange the items on the menu, rearrange the folders in the Start Menu folder.

A quicker but dirtier way to add programs to the Start menu

There's a quicker way to add a program to the Start menu, but it's not as versatile. The steps listed in this chapter let you add a program's icon anyplace on the menu. But if you simply want the program's icon on the menu *now,* and you don't care about location, try this:

Open the My Computer or Explorer program and find the folder containing your program. Then drag the program's icon over to the Start button and let go: To drag, point at the program and, while holding down the mouse button, point at the Start button. When the icon hovers over the Start button, let go of the mouse button.

Now, when you click the Start button, you see your newly installed program's icon at the very top.

Shutting down Windows Me

Although the big argument used to be about saturated and unsaturated fats, today's generation has found a new source of disagreement: Should a computer be left on all the time or turned off at the end of the day? Both camps have decent arguments, and there's no real answer (except that you should always turn off your monitor when you won't be using it for a half hour or so).

However, if you decide to turn off your computer, don't just head for the off switch. First, you need to tell Windows Me about your plans.

To do that, click the Shut Down command from the Start menu and then click the Shut Down button from the box that appears. Finally, click the Yes button; that click tells Windows Me to put away all your programs and to make sure that you've saved all your important files.

After Windows Me has prepared the computer to be turned off, a message on the screen says that it's okay to reach for the Big Switch.

Windows Me's Shut Down menu offers several options now, as you can see by the following list:

Shut down: Click here, and Windows Me saves your work, prepares your computer to be shut off, and tells you when it's okay to turn off the power. Use this option when you're done computing for the day.

Restart: Here, Windows saves your work and prepares your computer to be shut off. However, it then restarts your computer. Use this option when installing new software, changing settings, or trying to stop Windows Me from doing something awfully weird.

Standby: Save your work before choosing this one; it doesn't save your work automatically. Instead, it lets your computer doze for a bit to save power, but it wakes up at the touch of a button.

Hibernate: Only offered on some computers, this works much like Shut down. It saves your work and turns off your computer. However, when turned on again, your computer presents your desktop just as you left it: Open programs and windows appear in the same place.

✔ The Hibernate command takes all of your currently open information and writes it to the hard drive in one big chunk. Then, to re-create your desktop, it reads that big chunk and places it back on your desktop. It's not as safe as shutting down your computer.

✔ If Windows Me is acting weird — or if Windows Me tells you to shut down and restart your computer — click the Shut Down command from the Start menu. However, choose the Restart option from the box. Windows Me saves all your files, shuts itself down, and comes back to life, ready for more work.

✔ Don't ever turn off your computer unless you've first used the Shut Down command from the Start button. Windows Me needs to prepare itself for the shutdown, or it may accidentally eat some of your important information.

Making Windows Start Programs Automatically

Many people sit down at a computer, turn it on, and go through the same mechanical process of loading their oft-used programs. Believe it or not, Windows Me can automate this computerized task.

The solution is the StartUp folder, found lurking in the Start button's Programs menu. When Windows Me wakes up, it peeks inside that StartUp folder. If it finds a shortcut lurking, it grabs that shortcut's program and tosses it onto the screen.

Here's how to determine which programs wake up along with Windows Me and which ones get to sleep in a little.

1. **Click the Start button with your *right* mouse button and choose the Open option.**

   Your My Computer program comes to the screen to display the goodies in your Start menu.

2. **Double-click the folder named Programs.**

   You see shortcuts and folders for all the programs currently listed in your Start button's Programs area.

3. **Double-click the folder named StartUp to open it onto your screen.**

4. **Drag and drop any programs you want to start automatically into the StartUp window.**

   Windows Me automatically turns those program's icons into shortcuts. And whenever you start Windows Me from scratch, those programs load up right along with it.

- Do you find yourself using the StartUp area a lot? Make a shortcut that points straight toward it and leave the shortcut on your desktop. Drag and drop programs into the StartUp shortcut, and that program's shortcut will appear in the StartUp area, ready to load itself whenever your computer starts up.

- You decide which programs start up when Windows Me does by dragging and dropping files and shortcuts in and out of the StartUp folder.

- Don't want Windows Me to automatically start one of those programs in the StartUp folder? Then wait until you see the Windows Me logo on-screen and hold down the Shift key. Keep holding down Shift until Windows Me finishes loading and let go — the StartUp programs will stay seated.

The Taskbar

Put a second or third window onto the Windows Me desktop, and you'll immediately see the Big Problem: Windows and programs tend to cover each other up, making them difficult to locate.

The solution is the taskbar. Shown in Figure 10-7, the taskbar is that little bar running along the bottom edge of your screen.

Figure 10-7:
The taskbar lists the names of all your currently running programs and open folders.

The taskbar keeps track of all the open folders and currently running programs by listing their names. And, luckily, the taskbar is almost always visible, no matter how cluttered your desktop becomes.

- ✔ When you want to bring a program, file, or folder to the forefront of the screen, click its name on the taskbar.

- ✔ If the taskbar's Start menu *does* manage to disappear, press Ctrl+Esc; that action usually brings the Start menu to the surface.

- ✔ If you can only see part of the taskbar — it's hanging off the edge of the screen, for example — point at the edge you can see. When the mouse pointer turns into a two-headed arrow, hold down your mouse button and move the mouse to drag the taskbar back into view.

- ✔ If the taskbar looks too bloated, try the same trick. Point at its edge until the mouse pointer turns into a two-headed arrow and then drag the taskbar's edge inward until it's the right size.

Clicking the taskbar's sensitive areas

Like a crafty card player, the taskbar comes with a few tips and tricks. For one thing, it has the Start button. With a click on the Start button, you can launch programs, change settings, find programs, get help, and order takeout food. (Well, forget the food, but you can do all the things mentioned in the Start button section earlier in this chapter.)

The Start button is only one of the taskbar's tricks; some others are listed in Figure 10-8.

Clicking the Start button brings up the Start menu, described earlier in this chapter. Also, hold the mouse pointer over the clock, and Windows Me shows the current day and date. Or if you want to change the time or date, a double-click on the clock summons the Windows Me time/date change program.

If you have a sound card, click the little speaker to bring up the volume control, as shown in Figure 10-9. Slide the volume knob up for louder sound; slide it down for peace and quiet. (Or click the Mute box to turn the sound off completely.)

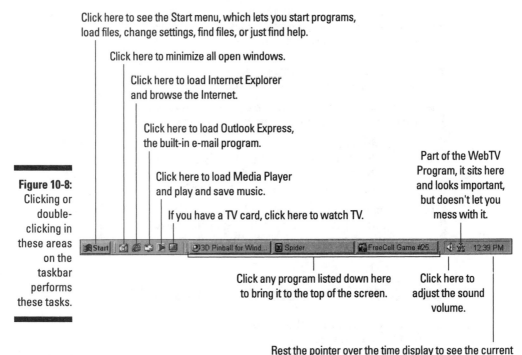

Click here to see the Start menu, which lets you start programs,
load files, change settings, find files, or just find help.

Click here to minimize all open windows.

Click here to load Internet Explorer
and browse the Internet.

Click here to load Outlook Express,
the built-in e-mail program.

Click here to load Media Player
and play and save music.

If you have a TV card, click here to watch TV.

Part of the WebTV
Program, it sits here
and looks important,
but doesn't let you
mess with it.

Figure 10-8:
Clicking or
double-
clicking in
these areas
on the
taskbar
performs
these tasks.

Click any program listed down here
to bring it to the top of the screen.

Click here to
adjust the sound
volume.

Rest the pointer over the time display to see the current
day and date. Double-click to reset the time or date.

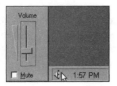

Figure 10-9:
Clicking the
little
speaker lets
you adjust
the sound
card's
volume.

Double-click the little speaker to bring up a more advanced mixer program,
as shown in Figure 10-10, if your sound card offers that feature. Mixers let you
adjust volume levels for your microphone, line inputs, CD players, and other
features.

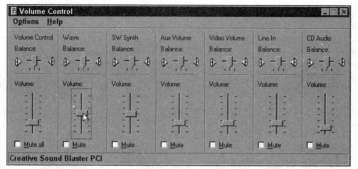

Figure 10-10:
Double-clicking the little speaker brings up a mixer program for the sound card.

✔ Other icons often appear next to the clock, depending on what Windows Me is up to. If you're printing, for example, you see a little printer down there. Laptops sometimes show a battery power-level gauge. As with all the other icons, if you double-click the printer or battery gauge, Windows Me brings up information about the printer's or battery's status.

✔ Want to minimize all your desktop's open windows in a hurry? Click a blank part of the taskbar with your right mouse button and choose the Minimize All Windows option from the pop-up menu. All the programs keep running, but they're now minimized to icons along the taskbar. To bring them back to the screen, just click their names from the taskbar.

✔ For an even faster way to minimize all your desktop's open windows, click the little icon down by the Start button. As you can see in Figure 10-8, it's a square with blue-tipped corners, a white rectangle in the center, and a little pencil thing resting on top of it all.

✔ To organize your open windows, click a blank part of the taskbar with your right mouse button and choose one of the tile commands. Windows Me scoops up all your open windows and lays them back down in neat, orderly squares.

Customizing the taskbar

Although Windows Me starts the taskbar along the bottom of the screen, it doesn't have to stay there. If you prefer that your taskbar hang from the top of your screen like a bat, just drag it there. Point at a blank spot of the taskbar and, while holding down your mouse button, point at the top of the screen. Let go of the mouse button, and the taskbar dangles from the roof, as shown in Figure 10-11.

Figure 10-11:
You can
move the
taskbar to
any side of
the screen
by dragging
it there.

Do you prefer the taskbar along one side? Drag it there, as shown in
Figure 10-12. (The buttons become more difficult to read, however.)

If the taskbar is starting to look too crowded, you can make it wider by dragging the top side and dragging its edge upward, as shown in Figure 10-13.

✔ To change other taskbar options, click a bare taskbar area with your
right mouse button and choose Properties from the pop-up menu. From
there, you can make the taskbar always stay on top of the current pile of
windows, make the taskbar automatically hide itself, hide the clock, and
shrink the Start menu icons. Whenever you click an option button, a
handy on-screen picture previews the change. If the change looks good,
click the OK button to save it.

✔ If you're using two or more monitors with your computer, go wild! You
can drag the taskbar to the edge of any of your monitors. It can dangle
from the top, line the bottom, or stick to the side of any monitor
attached to your computer.

✔ Feel free to experiment with the taskbar, changing its size and position
until it looks right for you. It won't break.

Figure 10-12:
The taskbar's buttons become harder to read when placed along the side.

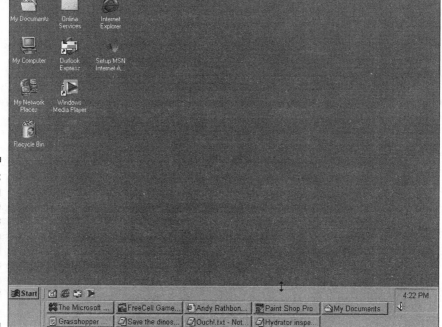

Figure 10-13:
Dragging the taskbar's edge upward gives icons more room to display their titles.

Oh, no! The Taskbar looks really weird now!

The taskbar doesn't always resemble the famil-iar entitiy in Figure 10-8. Microsoft lets you cus-tomize it even further, often beyond the point of recognition. To experience this weirdness — or to turn it off, if it's happened to you — right-click on a blank area of the taskbar and click the Toolbars option. A menu pops up, offering sev-eral options, each described below.

✔ **Links:** This fills the taskbar with links to Internet Web pages. (They're the same ones listed in the Links area of Internet Explorer's Favorites menu. Ho hum.)

✔ **Address:** Choose this, and your taskbar con-tains a place for quickly typing in Web sites. Click its little Go button, and Internet Explorer appears with the Web page inside.

✔ **Desktop:** A weird one, this places the icons from your desktop onto your taskbar.

✔ **Quick Launch:** *Choose this one to go back to normal.* That's the way your taskbar is supposed to look. It keeps those little icons by your Start button: Internet Explorer, Outlook Express, Media Player, and the "shrink everything from the desktop" icon.

✔ **New Toolbar:** This lets you place any folder's contents onto your taskbar.

Most people don't choose any of these options except Quick Launch, so feel free to do the same unless you like to fiddle with your com-puter's settings.

Controlling the Printer

Many of the Windows Me features work in the background. You know that they're there *only* when something is wrong and weird messages start flying around. The Windows Me print program is one of those programs.

When you choose the Print command in a program, you may see the little Windows Me printer icon appear at the bottom corner of your screen. When your printer stops spitting out pages, the little printer icon disappears.

Your printer can print only one thing at a time. If you try to print a second memo before the first one is finished, Windows Me jumps in to help. It inter-cepts all the requests and lines them up in order, just like a harried diner cook.

To check up on what is being sent to the printer, double-click the taskbar's little printer icon and you see the print program in all its glory, as shown in Figure 10-14.

Figure 10-14:
After telling
a program
to print a file
or two,
double-click
the little
printer icon
along the
right edge of
the taskbar
to see a
list of files
waiting to
be printed.

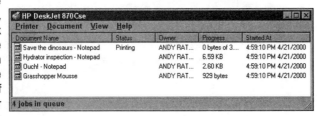

Figure 10-14:
After telling a program to print a file or two, double-click the little printer icon along the right edge of the taskbar to see a list of files waiting to be printed.

✔ When the printer is through with Save the dinosaurs, it moves to the second file in the lineup, which, in this case, is Hydrator inspection.

✔ Changing the order of the files as they're about to be printed is easy. For example, to scoot Ouch! ahead of Hydrator inspection, click its name and hold down the mouse button. Then *drag* the file up so that it cuts in front of Hydrator inspection. Release the button, and the Print Manager changes the printing order. (The printing order is called a *queue,* pronounced *Q.*)

✔ To cancel a print job, click the filename you don't like with your right mouse button and then choose Cancel Printing from the menu that pops up.

✔ If the boss is walking by the printer while you're printing your party flier, choose Document from the menu and select Pause Printing from the menu that drops down. The printer stops. After the boss is out of sight, click Pause Printing again to continue.

✔ If you're on a network (shudder), you may not be able to change the order in which files are being printed. You may not even be able to pause a file.

✔ If your printer is not hooked up, Windows Me will probably try to send your file to the printer anyway. When it doesn't get a response, it sends you a message that your printer isn't ready. Plug the printer in, turn it on, and try again. Or hit Chapter 14 for more printer troubleshooting tips.

Chapter 11

Those Scary Windows Explorer and My Computer Programs

● ●

In This Chapter

▶ Finding out why file managers are so scary

▶ Looking at folders

▶ Loading a program or file

▶ Deleting and undeleting files

▶ Copying and moving files

▶ Copying to a disk

▶ Getting information about files

▶ Finding files that aren't shown

▶ Working with files on a network

▶ Formatting new floppy disks

● ●

*T*he Windows Explorer program is where people wake up from the easy-to-use computing dream, clutching a pillow in horror. These people bought a computer to simplify their work — to banish that awful filing cabinet with squeaky drawers.

But open Windows Me Explorer, and that filing cabinet reappears. Folders, dozens of them, appear. And where did that file go? The My Computer program is a little more visually appealing, but it's still awkward.

This chapter explains how to use the Windows Explorer and My Computer programs, and, along the way, it dishes out a big enough dose of Windows file management for you to get your work done. Here, you'll find out the wacky Windows way to create folders, put files inside, and move everything around with a mere mouse.

Why Is Windows Explorer So Scary?

Windows Explorer combines two wildly different worlds: A heavy file cabinet and Windows software. It's as if somebody tried to combine an automobile with a bathtub. Everybody's confused when the door opens and water pours out.

To see what the fuss is about, click a folder with your right mouse button and, when the little menu pops out, choose the Explore option.

Everybody organizes his or her computer differently. Some people don't organize their computers at all. So, your Windows Explorer window probably looks a little different from the one shown in Figure 11-1.

Like Windows Explorer, the My Computer program, as shown in Figure 11-2, lets you sling files around, but in a slightly different way. The My Computer program is a big panel of buttons — sort of an extension of your desktop — and Windows Explorer is a big panel of filenames with buttons on the right. In fact, some people like the Windows Explorer *text-based* system of names better than the My Computer *picture-based* system. (It's that right-brained versus left-brained stuff.)

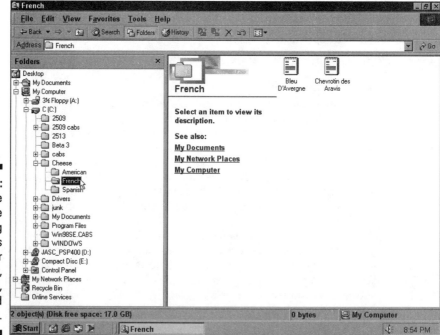

Figure 11-1: Some people prefer using Windows Explorer to print, copy, move, rename, and delete files.

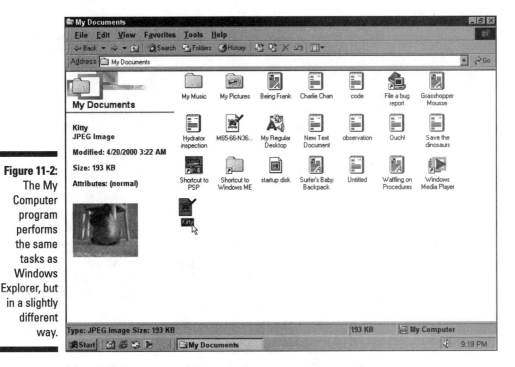

Figure 11-2:
The My Computer program performs the same tasks as Windows Explorer, but in a slightly different way.

✔ Although they both end in the word Explorer, the *Windows Explorer* program is completely different from the *Internet Explorer* program. Windows Explorer lets you fiddle with the files stored inside your computer. Internet Explorer, on the other hand, lets you connect to other computers through the phone lines, swapping information through the Internet and the World Wide Web.

✔ In a way, learning how to deal with files is like learning how to play the piano: Neither is intuitively obvious, and you hit some bad notes with both. Don't be frustrated if you don't seem to be getting the hang of it. Liberace would have hated file management at first, too.

Getting the Lowdown on Folders

This stuff is really boring, but if you don't read it, you'll be just as lost as your files.

A *folder* is a workplace on a disk. Hard drives are divided into many folders to separate your many projects. You can work with a spreadsheet, for example, without having all the word-processing files get in the way.

Any type of disk can have folders, but hard drives need folders the most because they need a way to organize their thousands of files. By dividing a hard drive into little folder compartments, you can more easily see where everything sits.

The Windows Explorer and My Computer programs enable you to probe into different folders and peek at the files you've stuffed inside each one. It's a pretty good organizational scheme, actually. Socks never fall behind a folder and jam the drawer.

Folders used to be called *directories* and *subdirectories*. But some people were getting used to that, so the industry switched to the term *folders*.

- You can place folders inside other folders to add deeper levels of organization, like adding drawer partitions to sort your socks by color. Each sock color partition is a smaller, organizing folder of the larger sock-drawer folder.

- Of course, you can ignore folders and keep all your files right on the Windows Me desktop. That's like tossing everything into the backseat of the car and pawing around to find your tissue box a month later. Stuff that you've organized is a lot easier to find.

- If you're eager to create a folder or two (and it's pretty easy), page ahead to this chapter's "Creating a Folder" section.

- Windows creates several folders when it installs itself on your computer. It created a folder to hold its internal engine parts and a folder to hold programs. Windows creates a My Documents folder in which to place your work. And it creates My Pictures and My Music folders inside the My Documents folders to keep your pictures and music separate from your other stuff.

- Just as manila folders come from trees, computer folders use a *tree metaphor,* shown in Figure 11-3, as they branch out from one main folder to several smaller folders.

Figure 11-3: The structure of folders inside your computer is tree-like, with main folders branching out to smaller folders.

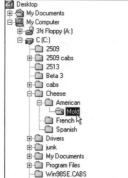

What's all this path stuff?

Sometimes, Windows Me can't find a file, even if it's sitting right there on the hard drive. You have to tell Windows where the file lives. And to do that, you need to know that file's *path*.

A path is like the file's address. When heading for your house, a letter moves to your country, state, city, street, and finally, hopefully, your apartment or house number. A computer path does the same thing. It starts with the letter of the disk drive and ends with the name of the file. In between, the path lists all the folders the computer must travel through to reach the file.

For example, look at the Mold folder in Figure 11-3. For Windows Me to find a file stored there, it starts from the C:\ folder, travels through the Cheese folder, and then goes through the American folder. Only then does it reach the Mold folder.

Take a deep breath. Exhale. Quack like a duck, if you like. Now, the C in C:\ stands for disk drive C.

(In the path, a disk drive letter is always followed by a colon.) The disk drive letter and colon make up the first part of the path. All the other folders are inside the big C: folder, so they're listed after the C: part. Windows separates these nested folders with something called a *backslash,* or \ . The name of the actual file — let's say Sporangium — comes last.

`C:\Cheese\American\Mold\Sporangium` is what you get when you put it all together, and that's the official path of the Sporangium file in the Mold folder.

This stuff can be tricky, so here it is again: The letter for the drive comes first, followed by a colon and a backslash. Then come the names of all the folders, separated by backslashes. Last comes the name of the file (with no backslash after it).

When you click folders, Windows Me puts together the path for you. Thankfully.

Peering into Your Drives and Folders

Knowing all this folder stuff can impress the people at the computer store. But what counts is knowing how to use the Windows Explorer and My Computer programs to get to a file you want. Never fear. Just read on.

Seeing the files on a disk drive

Like everything else in Windows Me, disk drives are represented by buttons, or icons:

Those disk drive buttons live in both the Windows Explorer and My Computer programs (although the ones in Windows Explorer are usually smaller). See the icon labeled *Floppy?* The icon is a picture of a floppy disk and its disk drive. You see a compact disc floating above drives D: and E: to show that they're compact disc drives. Hard drives don't have anything hovering over them except a nagging suspicion that they'll fail horribly at the worst moment.

- ✔ If you're kinda sketchy on those disk drive things, you probably skipped Chapter 2. Trot back there for a refresher.

- ✔ Double-click a drive icon in My Computer, and a window comes up to display the drive's contents. For example, put a disk in drive A and double-click the My Computer's drive A icon. A new window leaps up, showing what files and folders live on the disk in drive A.

- ✔ Click a drive icon in Windows Explorer, and you see the drive contents on the right side of the window.

- ✔ A second window comes in handy when you want to move or copy files from one folder or drive to another, as discussed in the "Copying or Moving a File" section of this chapter.

- ✔ The first icon stands for the floppy drive, drive A. If you click a floppy drive icon when no disk is in the drive, Windows Me stops you gently, suggesting that you insert a disk before proceeding further.

- ✔ Spot an icon called My Network Places? That's a little doorway for peering into other computers linked to your computer — if there are any. You find more network stuff near the end of this chapter.

Seeing what's inside folders

Because folders are really little storage compartments, Windows Me uses a picture of a little folder to stand for each separate place for storing files.

To see what's inside a folder, either in My Computer or on the desktop, just double-click that folder's picture. A new window pops up, showing that folder's contents.

Opening a folder works differently in Windows Explorer. To launch Windows Explorer, right-click on any folder and choose Explorer. Windows Explorer appears, showing folder icons lined up along the left side of a window. One folder, the one you're currently exploring, has a little box around its name.

The files living inside that particular folder appear on the right side of the window. The arrangement looks somewhat like Figure 11-4.

To peek inside a folder while in Windows Explorer, click its name on the left side of the window. You see two things: That folder's next level of folders (if it has one) appears beneath it on the left side of the window, and that folder's filenames spill out into the right side of the window.

Figure 11-4:
When you
click a
folder on the
left side of
Windows
Explorer,
that folder's
contents
appear on
the right
side of the
window.

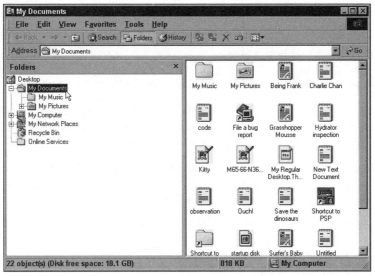

✔ As you keep climbing farther out on a branch and more folders appear, you're moving toward further levels of organization. If you climb back inward, you reach files and folders that have less in common.

✔ Yeah, this stuff is really confusing, but keep one thing in mind: Don't be afraid to double-click, or even single-click, a folder just to see what happens. Clicking folders just changes your viewpoint; nothing dreadful happens, and no tax receipts fall onto the floor. You're just opening and closing file cabinet drawers, harmlessly peeking into folders along the way.

✔ To climb farther out on the branches of folders, keep double-clicking new folders as they appear.

✔ To move back up the branches in Windows Explorer, double-click a folder closer to the left side of the window. Any folders to the right and beneath that folder are now hidden from view.

✔ How do you know which folders contain other folders inside them? Look for the secret symbol by each folder: A plus sign means more folders lurk inside. A minus sign means all that folder's contents are already spilled out for viewing. (Figure 11-4 shows both plus and minus signs next to folders.)

✔ Sometimes, a folder contains too many files to fit in the window. To see more files, click that window's scroll bars. What's a scroll bar? Time to whip out your field guide, Chapter 5.

While in Windows Explorer, move the mouse pointer over the bar separating a folder on the left from its filenames on the right. After the pointer turns into a mutant two-headed arrow, hold down the mouse button. Then move the bar to the left to give the filenames more room, or to the right to give the folders on the left more room. Let go of the mouse button when the split is adjusted correctly, and the window reshapes itself to the new dimensions.

Using a Microsoft IntelliMouse, the kind with the little wheel embedded in the mouse's neck? Point at the list of folders in Explorer and spin the little wheel; the list moves up or down as you spin the wheel.

Can't find a file or folder? Instead of rummaging through folders, check out the Search command that I describe in Chapter 7. It's the fastest way to find files and folders that were "there just a moment ago."

Loading a Program or File

A *file* is a collection of information on a disk. Files come in two basic types: program files and data files.

Program files contain instructions that tell the computer to do something: balance the national budget or dial up the Internet and look at pictures of exotic monkeys.

Data files contain information created with a program, as opposed to computer instructions. If you write a letter to the grocer complaining about his soggy apricots, you're creating a data file.

To open either kind of file in Windows Me, double-click its name. Double-clicking a program file's name brings the program to life on the screen, no matter where the program's name is listed throughout Windows. Double-clicking a data file tells Windows Me to load the file *and* the program that created it. Then it brings both the file and the program to the screen at the same time.

✔ Depending on how your computer is configured, sometimes a single-click does the trick: Point at the file or program to highlight it and then click it to bring it to life. (If that doesn't bring it to life, try a double-click.)

✔ Windows Me sticks little icons next to filenames so that you know whether they're program or data files. In fact, even folders get their own icons so that you won't confuse them with files. Chapter 20, at the tail end of the book, provides a handy reference for figuring out which icon is which.

✔ Because of some bizarre New School of Computing mandate, any data file that Windows recognizes is called a *document.* A document doesn't have to contain words; it can have pictures of worms or sounds of hungry animals.

Don't bother reading this hidden technical stuff

Sometimes, programs store information in a data file. They may need to store information about the way the computer is set up, for example. To keep people from thinking that those files are trash and deleting them, the program hides those files.

You can view the names of these hidden files and folders, however, if you want to play voyeur. Open the Control Panel and choose Folder Options. Select the View tab from along the menu's top and click the Show Hidden Files and Folders button under the Hidden Files and Folders option.

Click the OK button, and the formerly hidden files appear alongside the other filenames. Be sure not to delete them, however: The programs that created them will gag, possibly damaging other files. In fact, click the View tab's Restore Defaults button to hide that stuff again and return the settings to normal.

If the program or folder you're after is already highlighted, just give the Enter key a satisfying little pound with your index finger. That not only opens the program or folder, but it also shows you how many different ways Windows Me lets you do things (which means that you don't need to worry about knowing them all).

Deleting and Undeleting Files and Folders

Sooner or later, you'll want to delete a file that's not important anymore — yesterday's lottery picks, for example, or something you've stumbled on that's too embarrassing to save any longer. But then, hey, suddenly you realize that you've made a mistake and deleted the wrong file. Not to worry: The Windows Me Recycle Bin can probably resurrect that deleted file if you're quick enough — and your file wasn't on a floppy disk.

Getting rid of a file or folder

To permanently remove a file from the hard drive, click its name. Then press Delete. This surprisingly simple trick works for files and even folders. Prefer your mouse? Then right-click the file and choose Delete from the pop-up menu.

The Delete key deletes entire folders, as well as any folders inside them. Make sure that you've selected the right file before you press Delete.

✔ After you choose Delete, Windows tosses a box in your face, asking whether you're sure. If you are, click the Yes button.

✔ Be extra sure that you know what you're doing when deleting any file that has pictures of little "gears" in its icon. These files are sometimes sensitive hidden files, and the computer wants you to leave them alone. (Other than that, they're not particularly exciting, despite the action-oriented gears.)

✔ As soon as you find out how to delete files, you'll want to read the very next section, "How to undelete a file."

Deleting a shortcut from the desktop, My Computer, or Windows Explorer just deletes a button that loads a program. You can always put the button back on. Deleting an icon that doesn't have the little shortcut arrow removes that *file* from the hard disk and puts it into the Recycle Bin, where it eventually disappears.

How to undelete a file

Sooner or later, your finger will push the Delete key at the wrong time, and you'll delete the wrong file. A slip of the finger, the wrong nudge of a mouse, or, if you're in southern California, a small earthquake at the wrong time can make a file disappear. Zap!

Scream! After the tremors subside, double-click the Recycle Bin, and the Recycle Bin box drops down from the heavens, as shown in Figure 11-5.

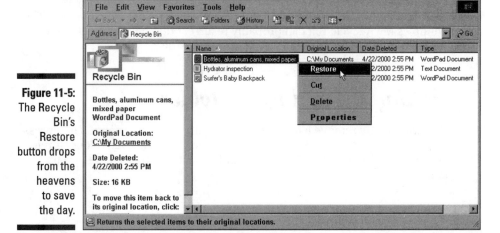

Figure 11-5:
The Recycle
Bin's
Restore
button drops
from the
heavens
to save
the day.

To restore the file to its former place among the living, right-click it and choose Restore. The file appears in the place where you deleted it.

You can also drag deleted files out of the Recycle Bin box: Use the mouse to point at the name of the file you want to retrieve and, while holding down the mouse button, point at the desktop. Then let go of the mouse button. Windows Me moves the once-deleted file out of the Recycle Bin and places the newly revived file onto your desktop.

✔ When undeleting shortcuts and documents, feel free to drag them out of the Recycle Bin. But when undeleting anything else, use the Restore method.

✔ After you restore your file, it's as good as new. Feel free to store it in any other file for safekeeping.

✔ Don't expect the Recycle Bin to contain anything deleted from your floppy disks or computer networks. They're gone for good. (Software stores sell Windows programs for undeleting files from floppy disks.)

✔ The Recycle Bin normally holds about 10 percent of your hard drive's space. For example, if your hard drive is 8GB, the Recycle Bin holds onto 800MB of deleted files. After it reaches that limit, it starts deleting the oldest files to make room for the incoming deleted files. (And the old ones are gone for good, too.)

Copying or Moving a File

To copy or move files to different folders on your hard drive, use your mouse to *drag* them there. For example, here's how to move a file to a different folder on your hard drive. In this case, we're moving the Traveler file from the Home folder to the Morocco folder.

1. **Move the mouse pointer until it hovers over the file you want to move, and then press and hold down the mouse button.**

2. **While holding down the mouse button, use the mouse to point at the folder to which you'd like to move the file.**

   The trick is to hold down the mouse button the whole time. When you move the mouse, its arrow drags the file along with it. For example, Figure 11-6 shows how Windows Explorer looks when I drag the Traveler file from the Home folder to my Morocco folder on my C drive. (The contents of the Home folder are on the right; you can tell that we're viewing the Home folder's contents because the Home folder icon is open and Windows Explorer says Home at its top.)

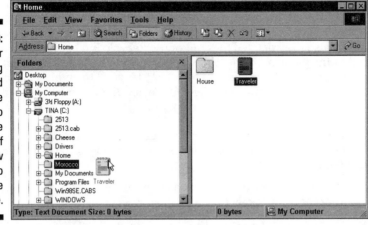

Figure 11-6:
The Traveler
file is being
dragged
to the
Morocco
folder on the
left side of
the window
in order to
move the
file there.

3. Release the mouse button.

When the mouse arrow hovers over the place to which you want to move the file, take your finger off the mouse button.

Moving a file by dragging its name is pretty easy, actually. The hard part often comes when you try to put the file and its destination on-screen at the same time. You often need to use both Windows Explorer and My Computer to put two windows on-screen. After you can see the file and its destination, start dragging.

Both Windows Explorer and My Computer do something awfully dumb to confuse people, however: When you drag a file from one folder to another on the same drive, you *move* the file. When you drag a file from one folder to another on a different drive, you *copy* that file.

I swear I didn't make up these rules. And the process gets more complicated: You can click the file and hold down the Shift key to reverse the rules. Table 11-1 can help you keep these oafish oddities from getting too far out of control.

Table 11-1	Moving Files Around
To Do This . . .	*. . . Do This*
Copy a file to another location on the same disk drive	Hold down the Ctrl key and drag it.
Copy a file to a different disk drive	Drag it there.
Move a file to another location on the same disk drive	Drag it there.

To Do This . . .	. . . Do This
Move a file to a different disk drive	Hold down the Shift key and drag it there.
Make a shortcut while dragging a file	Hold down Ctrl+Shift and drag it there.
Remember these obtuse commands	Refer to the handy Cheat Sheet at the front of this book.

Here's an easy way to remember this stuff when this book's not handy: Always drag icons while holding down the *right* mouse button. Windows Me is then gracious enough to give you a menu of options when you position the icon, and you can choose among moving, copying, or creating a shortcut.

✔ To copy or move files to a floppy disk, drag those files to the icon for that floppy disk, which you should find along the top of the Windows Explorer window.

✔ When you drag a file someplace in Windows Me, look at the icon attached to the mouse pointer. If the document icon has a *plus sign* in it, you're *copying* the file. If the document icon is *blank,* you're *moving* the file. Depending on where you are dragging the file, pressing Ctrl or Shift toggles the plus sign on or off, making it easier to see whether you're currently copying or moving the file.

✔ After you run a program's installation program to put the program on your hard drive, don't ever move the program around. An installation program often wedges a program into Windows pretty handily; if you move the program, it may not work anymore, and you'll have to reinstall it.

Selecting More Than One File or Folder

Windows Me lets you grab an armful of files and folders at one swipe; you don't always have to piddle around, dragging one item at a time.

To pluck several files and folders from a list, hold down the Ctrl key when you click the names. Each name stays highlighted when you click the next name.

To gather several files or folders sitting next to each other, click the first one. Then hold down the Shift key as you click the last one. Those two items are highlighted, along with every file and folder between them.

Windows Me lets you *lasso* files and folders as well. Point slightly above the first file or folder you want; then, while holding down the mouse button, point at the last file or folder. The mouse creates an invisible lasso to surround your files. Let go of the mouse button, and the invisible lasso, er, disappears, leaving all the surrounded files highlighted.

✔ You can drag these armfuls of files in the same way as you drag one.

✔ You can delete these armfuls, too.

✔ You can't rename an armful of files all at once. To rename them, you have to go back to piddling around with one file at a time.

✔ To quickly select all the files in a folder, press Ctrl+A. But here's some more: To grab all but a few files, press Ctrl+A and, while still holding down Ctrl, click on the ones you don't want.

Renaming a File or Folder

Sick of a file or folder's name? Then change it. Just click the offending icon with your right mouse button and choose Rename from the menu that pops up.

The old filename gets highlighted and then disappears when you start typing the file or folder's new name. Press Enter or click the desktop when you're through, and you're off.

Or you can click the file or folder's name to select it, wait a second, and click the file's name again. Windows Me highlights the old name, ready to replace it with your incoming text. (This doesn't work if you've chosen to launch files and programs with a single-click rather than a double-click.)

✔ If you rename a file, only its name changes. The contents are still the same, it's still the same size, and it's still in the same place.

✔ You can't rename groups of files. The files spit in your face if you even try.

✔ Renaming a folder can confuse Windows, however, which often grows accustomed to folder names in the way they're first set up. Don't rename folders that contain programs.

Some icons, like the one for the Recycle Bin, won't let you rename them. How do you know which icons don't let users meddle with their names? Right-click their icons. If you don't see the word *Rename* on the menu, you won't be able to rename the file. Handy button, that right mouse button.

Using Legal Folder Names and Filenames

Windows is pretty picky about what you can and can't name a file or folder. If you stick to plain old letters and numbers, you're fine. But don't try to stick any of the following characters in there:

```
: / \ * | < > ? "
```

If you use any of those characters, Windows Me bounces an error message to the screen, and you have to try again.

These names are illegal:

```
1/2 of my Homework
JOB:2
ONE<TWO
He's no "Gentleman"
```

These names are legal:

```
Half of my Term Paper
JOB2
Two is Bigger than One
A #@$%) Scoundrel
```

✔ As long as you remember the characters that you can and can't use for naming files, you'll probably be okay.

✔ Using a digital camera? Don't use any of those forbidden characters in the file's name, or Windows will freak out when you try to import it into the My Pictures folder.

✔ Like their predecessors, Windows Me programs *brand* files with their own three-letter extensions so that Windows Me knows which program created what file. Normally, Windows Me hides the extensions so that they're not confusing. But if you happen to spot filenames like SAVVY.DOC, README.TXT, and SPONGE.BMP across the hard disk, you'll know that the extensions have been added by the Windows Me programs WordPad, Notepad, and Paint, respectively. Windows Me normally keeps the extensions hidden from view, so you just look at the file's icon for heritage clues.

If you really want to see a filename's extension, choose Folder Options from the folder's Tools menu (or the Control Panel) and then click the tab marked View. Finally, click the little box next to the line that says Hide File Extensions for Known File Types. That removes the check mark; when you click the Apply button, files reveal their extensions. (Click the box again or click the Restore Defaults button to hide the extensions.)

You may see a filename with a weird tilde thing in it, such as `WIGWAM~1.TXT`. That's the special way that Windows Me deals with long filenames. Most older programs expect files to have only eight characters; when there's a conflict, Windows Me whittles down a long filename so that those older programs can use them. When the program's finished, the shorter, weird filename is the file's new name.

Copying a Complete Floppy Disk

To copy files from one disk to another, drag 'em over there, as described a few pages back. To copy an entire floppy disk, however, use the Copy Disk command.

What's the difference? When you're copying files, you're dragging specific filenames. But when you're copying a disk, the Copy Disk command duplicates the disk exactly: It even copies the empty parts! (That's why it takes longer than just dragging the files over.)

The Copy Disk command has two main limitations:

- ✔ It can copy only floppy disks that are the same *size* or *capacity*. Just as you can't pour a full can of beer into a shot glass, you can't copy one disk's information onto another disk unless they hold the same amount of data.
- ✔ It only copies removable disks — floppies, Zip drives, Syquest, and things with even more esoteric names.

Here's how to make a copy of a floppy disk or other removable disk:

1. **Put your floppy disk in your disk drive.**

2. **Double-click the My Computer icon.**

3. **Click your floppy disk's icon with your right mouse button.**

4. **Choose Copy Disk from the pop-up menu.**

    A box appears, letting you confirm which disk and disk drive you want to use for your copy.

5. **Click the Start button to begin making the copy and follow the helpful directions.**

- ✔ All this *capacity* and *size* stuff about disks and drives is slowly digested in Chapter 2.
- ✔ The Copy Disk command can be handy for making backup copies of your favorite programs.

✔ The Copy Disk command completely overwrites the disk that it's copying information to. Don't use a disk containing anything particularly important.

✔ In fact, you should always use the Copy Disk command when making backup copies of programs. Sometimes, programs hide secret files onto their floppies; by making a complete copy of the disk with the Copy Disk command, you can be sure that the entire disk gets copied, hidden files and all.

Creating a Folder

To store new information in a file cabinet, you grab a manila folder, scrawl a name across the top, and start stuffing it with information.

To store new information in Windows Me — a new batch of letters to the hospital billing department, for example — you create a new folder, think up a name for the new folder, and start moving or copying files into it.

New, more organized folders make finding information easier, too. For example, you can clean up a crowded Letters folder by dividing it into two folders: Business Letters and Personal Letters.

Here's how to use Windows Explorer to create a new folder — a folder called Business Letters — that lives in a Letters folder that already exists:

1. **On the left side of the Windows Explorer window, click in the area in which you want the new folder to appear.**

   Click the Letters folder, as shown in Figure 11-7, because you want the Business folder to appear in the Letters folder. (No Letters folder? Then create one by clicking on your C drive and right-clicking in its contents displayed on the right side of Explorer. Choose New, select Folder, type `Letters`, and press the Enter key.)

   Click the Letters folder, and its current contents spill out into the right side of Windows Explorer.

2. **Click the right side of Windows Explorer with your right mouse button and choose New; when the menu appears, choose Folder.**

   The My Computer window lets you create a folder when you right-click in any window; Windows Explorer lets you create a folder only when you right-click within its right-hand side. A box pops up for you to type in a new name for your new folder.

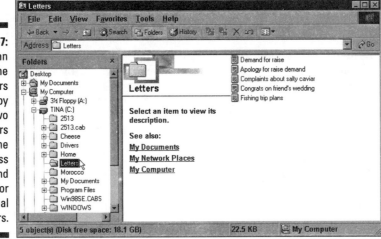

Figure 11-7:
You can organize the Letters folder by creating two new folders inside it: one for business letters and one for personal letters.

3. Type the new folder's name and press Enter.

In this case, type Business Letters. Windows Me can sometimes be picky about names you give to folders and files. For the rules, check out the "Using Legal Folder Names and Filenames" section, earlier in this chapter.

After you type the folder's name and press Enter, the new Business Letters folder is complete, ready for you to start moving your business letter files there. For impeccable organization, follow the same steps to create a Personal Letters folder and move your personal files there, using the "dragging" process, as shown in Figure 11-8 (and explained in the "Copying or Moving a File" section in this chapter).

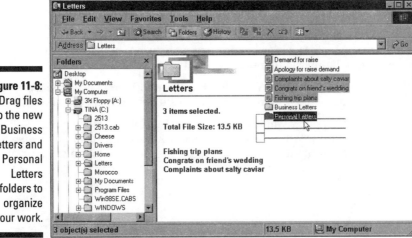

Figure 11-8:
Drag files into the new Business Letters and Personal Letters folders to organize your work.

✔ Want to install a new Windows program that doesn't come with an installation program? Create a new folder for it and copy its files there. Then head to Chapter 10 to see how to put the new program's name in the Start menu for easy clicking.

✔ To move files into a new folder, drag them there. Just follow the directions in the "Copying or Moving a File" section in this chapter.

✔ When copying or moving lots of files, select them all at the same time before dragging them. You can chew on this stuff in the "Selecting More Than One File or Folder" section, earlier in this chapter.

✔ Here's a really quick way to create a new folder inside another folder. Right-click inside the existing folder, choose New, and select Folder from the menu that pops up. That right mouse button is very handy. Don't be afraid to give it a try to see what options it offers.

✔ Just as with naming files, you can use only certain characters when naming folders. (Stick with plain old letters and numbers, and you'll be fine.)

✔ Wondering why the icons are so tiny in Figure 11-8? That's because Windows can display files in several different ways. I describe that in the very next section.

Seeing More Information about Files and Folders

Whenever you create a file or folder, Windows Me scrawls a bunch of secret hidden information on it: its size, the date you created it, and even more trivial stuff. To see what Windows Me is calling the files and folders behind your back, select View from the folder's menu bar and then choose Details from the menu. Instead of seeing large icons with names beneath them, you see bunches of details, as seen in Figure 11-9.

 In fact, you can simply click the itty-bitty downward-pointing arrow next to the right-most button on the toolbar, which lives atop most folders. A drop-down menu appears, listing options for arranging icons, as shown in the margin. (Clicking those options merely changes the way Windows Me displays the icons — it doesn't do any permanent damage.)

✔ Is the toolbar not living on top of your window? Put it there by choosing Standard Buttons from the View menu's Toolbars option. That little bar of buttons now appears atop your window like a mantel over a fireplace.

✔ If you can't remember what those little toolbar buttons do, rest your mouse pointer over a button and pretend it's lost. Windows Me displays a helpful box summing up the button's mission, and, occasionally places a further explanation along the bottom of the window.

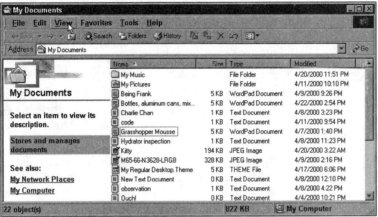

Figure 11-9:
To see more
details
about
a folder's
contents,
choose
Details from
the folder's
View menu.

✔ Although some of the additional file information is handy, it can consume a lot of space, limiting the number of files you can see in the
window. Displaying only the filename is often a better idea. Then, if you
want to see more information about a file or folder, try the following tip.

✔ While on the right side of Explorer, hold down the Alt key and double-
click a file or folder to see its size, creation date, and other exciting computer information.

✔ With the Alt+double-click trick (described in the preceding paragraph),
you can change a file's attributes as well. Attributes are too boring to be
discussed further, so duck beneath the technical stuff coming up in the
nearby sidebar "Who cares about this stuff, anyway?"

At first, Windows Me displays filenames sorted alphabetically by name in its
Windows Explorer and My Computer windows. But, by right-clicking in a folder
and choosing the different sorting methods in the Arrange Icons menu, you display them in a different order. Windows puts the biggest ones at the top of the
list, for example, when you choose Sort by Size. Or you can choose Sort by
Type to keep files created by the same application next to each other. Or you
can choose Sort by Date to keep the most recent files at the top of the list.

When the excitement of sorting wears off, try clicking the little buttons at
the top of each column — size, for instance. That sorts the contents
appropriately — the largest files at the top, for instance.

Dragging, Dropping, and Running

You can drag files around in Windows Me to move them or copy them. But
there's more: You can drag them outside of the Windows Explorer or My
Computer window and drop them into other windows to load them into other
files and programs, as shown in Figure 11-10.

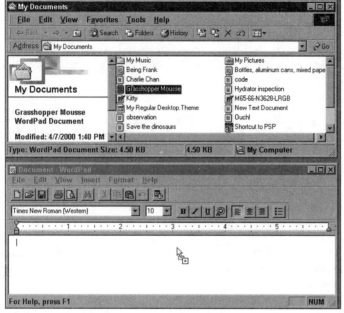

Figure 11-10: The mouse pointer changes shape as you drag the Grasshopper Mousse into the WordPad window.

For example, drag the Grasshopper Mousse into the WordPad window and let go of the mouse button. WordPad loads the Grasshopper Mousse file, just as if you'd double-clicked it in the first place.

This feature brings up all sorts of fun ideas. If you have a sound card, you can listen to music files by dropping them into the Media Player windows. You can drop text files into Notepad to load them quickly. Or you can drop WordPad files into WordPad.

- ✔ Okay, the first thing everybody wants to know is what happens if you drag a sound file into WordPad? Or a WordPad file into Notepad? Or any other combination of files that don't match? Well, Windows Me either embeds one file into the other or sends you a box saying that it got indigestion. Just click OK, and things return to normal. No harm done, either way.

- ✔ The second question everybody asks is: Why bother dragging files around? You can just double-click a file's name to load it. That's true. But this way is more fun and often faster.

- ✔ You've never dragged and dropped before? Chapter 3 contains complete instructions.

> ✔ Some folks will want to know if they can load files by dropping them onto taskbar icons along the screen's bottom. Nope. Windows Me lets you drop things only into *open* windows. But if you drag the object over to the taskbar icon that you're interested in and let the mouse pointer hover over it for awhile, the icon blossoms into an open window, ready to receive the object.

How Do I Make the Network Work?

Windows Me can connect to bunches of other computers through a home network, and, luckily, that makes it pretty easy to grab files from other people's computers. At least it's pretty easy if somebody else has already set up the network. But after the network's running, you'll be running right alongside it. There isn't much new to learn.

 See the My Network Places icon on your computer's desktop (and shown in the margin)? That icon is the key to all the computers currently connected to your computer.

Double-click that icon, and a window appears, as shown in Figure 11-11. Your windows naturally differ because you have different computers. (And the computers probably have different names, too.)

Double-click the icon of the computer that you want to peek inside, and a new window appears showing that computer's contents.

> ✔ When viewing another computer's files, everything works just like it was on your own computer. Feel free to point and click inside the other computer's folders. To copy files back and forth, just drag and drop them to and from your computer's window to the other computer's window.

> ✔ You can only access the computers that your network administrator has given you access to. Don't get carried away; you're not really getting away with anything.

> ✔ When you use a network to delete something from another networked computer — or somebody uses the Network to delete a file from *your* computer — it's gone. It doesn't go into the Recycle Bin. Be careful, especially because the network administrator can usually tell who deleted the file.

> ✔ Windows Me comes with a special Home Networking process to connect your computers with cables. In fact, after you connect them, they can share a single modem. This works great for people with speedy cable modems or DSL modems. Unfortunately, it's too complicated for this book, but I readily handle it in the book's sequel, *MORE Microsoft Windows Me For Dummies.*

Who cares about this stuff, anyway?

Windows Me gives each file four special switches called *attributes.* The computer looks at the way those switches are set before it fiddles with a file.

Read Only: Choosing this attribute allows the file to be read, but not deleted or changed in any way.

Archive: The computer sets this attribute when a file has changed since the last time it was backed up with the Windows Me Backup program.

Hidden: Setting this attribute makes the file invisible during normal operations.

System: Files required by a computer's operating system have this attribute set.

The Properties box makes it easy — perhaps too easy — to change these attributes. In most cases, you should leave them alone. They're just mentioned here so that you'll know what computer nerds mean when they tell cranky people, "Boy, somebody must have set your attribute wrong when you got out of bed this morning."

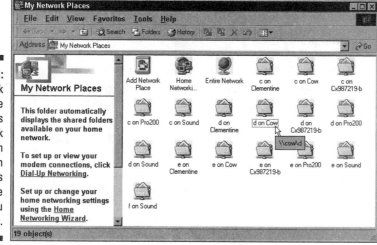

Figure 11-11: Double-click the desktop's My Network Places icon to see which computers on the network you can access.

Making My Computer and Windows Explorer List Missing Files

Sometimes, Windows Me snoozes and doesn't keep track of what's *really* on the disk. Oh, it does pretty well with the hard drive, and it works pretty well if you're just running Windows programs. But it can't tell when you stick in a new floppy disk.

If you ever think that the Windows Explorer or My Computer window is holding out on you, tell it to *refresh,* or take a second look at what's on the floppy disk or hard drive. You can click View from the menu bar and choose Refresh from the pull-down menu, but a quicker way is to press the F5 key. (It's a function key along the top or left side of the keyboard.) Either way, the programs take a second look at what they're supposed to be showing and update their lists, if necessary.

Press the F5 key whenever you stick in a different floppy disk and want to see what files are stored on it. Windows Me then updates the screen to show the *new* floppy's files, not the files from the first disk.

Formatting a New Floppy Disk

Some new floppy disks don't work straight out of the box; your computer burps out an error message if you even try to use them fresh. Floppy disks must be formatted, and unless you paid extra for a box of *preformatted* floppy disks, you must format them yourself. The My Computer program handles this particularly boring chore quite easily. It's still boring, though, as you'll discover when repeating the process 10 or 12 times — once for each disk in the box.

Here's the procedure:

1. **Place the new disk into drive A or drive B.**

2. **In either Windows Explorer or the My Computer window, click the drive's icon with your right mouse button and choose Format from the menu.**

3. **If you're formatting a *high-capacity* disk in drive A, select the Full setting under Format type and select Start in the top-right corner.**

   Almost all disks are 1.44MB these days, so choose that option if you're not sure. Your disk drive whirs for several minutes, before announcing it's finished.

4. **Click the Close button when Windows Me is through.**

   Then remove the floppy disk and return to Step 1 until you've formatted the entire box.

   ✔ You can format disks in your drive B by clicking the drive B: icon with your right mouse button. Likewise, you can change a disk's capacity by clicking the little arrow in the Capacity box.

   ✔ Don't get your hopes up: The Quick (Erase) option won't speed things up unless your disk has already been formatted once before.

   ✔ In fact, if Windows Me ever goes on vacation, you should have an emergency disk. The Add/Remove Programs icon in the Windows Me Control Panel makes one for you. (The straight-faced Windows calls it a *Startup Disk.*)

Chapter 12

The Free Programs!

*W*indows Me, the fanciest version of Windows yet, comes with oodles of free programs. It makes customers happy and makes the Justice Department members flap their long black robes.

Free software is usually as nice as a free lunch. Windows' problem lies with its menu. Sure, some of its freebie programs control important parts of your computer. But more than 50 additional programs merely buff and polish the details. This extraordinarily long chapter explains which freebie programs are worthwhile, and which ones you can safely ignore.

Remember, Windows Me doesn't automatically install *all* its possible freebie programs — that would eat up gobs of your hard drive space. It typically installs the most popular ones.

This chapter describes all the programs that come bundled with Windows. Chances are, you won't find all these programs on your copy of Windows. But if you do, check out the end of this chapter for the "My Version of Windows Me Doesn't Have the Right Programs!" section.

Accessories

By far, the bulk of the Windows Me freebie programs are dumped under the generic menu label "Accessories." Here are programs that make Windows Me easier to see and hear; they let your computer talk to other computers and the Internet, and they entertain you during slow days. Finally, they let you fiddle with Windows' innards during even slower days.

The rest of this section tackles the programs found on the Accessories menu, accessed through the Start button's Programs button.

Accessibility

The Accessibility Wizard creates a customized, easy-to-read version of Windows. It lets you choose your ideal size for fonts, menus, icons, and window borders, making them easier to click. The Wizard enables sounds to accompany certain on-screen actions if you're having difficulty seeing the screen.

Another program, Microsoft Magnifier (shown in Figure 12-1), enlarges the mouse pointer's current location, making small buttons and boxes easier to spot.

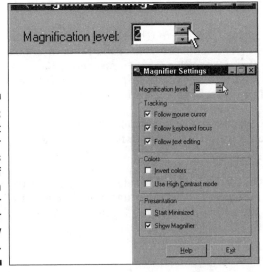

Figure 12-1: Microsoft Magnifier enlarges portions of the screen near your cursor for easy viewing.

Having trouble viewing the screen? Let the Accessibility Wizard and Microsoft Magnifier set up the menus so you can view them easily.

Finally, the On-screen Keyboard program draws a keyboard right onto the desktop. Point and click at the letters with the mouse, and you'll never have to type. (Works well for people with broken keyboards.)

Communications

Much of this stuff applies to the tech-heads, so don't spend too much time here. If you're trying to connect to the Internet, however, head for the "Internet Connection Wizard" a few paragraphs ahead. It walks you through the process, waving the wand as necessary.

Dial-Up Networking

This controls how your computer talks to another computer over the phone lines. Dial-up networking locates your computer's modem, remembers your area code, and finds out the other computer's phone number, location, and any code words. Don't bother with it. The Internet Connection Wizard, which I describe shortly, already incorporates this area as it gently guides you through the Internet setup process, waving its wand along the way.

Direct Cable Connection

Direct Cable Connection swaps information over cables plugged between two PCs. The program's pretty easy, actually. The hard part is buying the right cables. You need a Parallel File Transfer cable — hopefully rated either ECP or EPP — to connect between the parallel ports of both computers. (Serial File Transfer cables are much slower.) Follow the program's directions, and you've created a sort of mini-network.

Calling other computers with HyperTerminal

An old-school modem program, HyperTerminal, works only with *text-based* online services, which are quickly disappearing, such as CompuServe's old formats and computer bulletin boards. It doesn't work with graphics-based bulletin boards, such as those on America Online and the newer portions of CompuServe. And no, you can't use HyperTerminal for looking at cool pictures on the World Wide Web.

Only the most advanced computer users will use HyperTerminal.

Home Networking Wizard

Have you finally bought a second computer for your household? A third? This program shows how to link 'em all together to share information or even a single modem or printer. This is heavy duty stuff, so it's tackled in *MORE Microsoft Windows Me For Dummies* (IDG Books Worldwide, Inc.).

Internet Connection Wizard

Designed to simplify one of the most terrifying tasks, Microsoft created the Internet Connection Wizard. After a bit of interrogation, the Wizard helps you and your computer connect to your Internet Service Provider (ISP) so you can Web surf like the best of them. Here's the checklist to get started:

✔ **Find an Internet Service Provider.** This company provides a connection to the Internet. Ask a friend, coworker, or teenager for a recommendation. Don't know which ISP to choose? The Internet Connection Wizard will find one for you that's in your own area.

✔ **Look up your user name, password, and phone number for your current Internet Service Provider.** Don't have an ISP? If the Wizard finds you a service provider, it will dish out those three items, so grab a pencil and paper.

✔ **Find a modem.** Most new computers come with a modem lodged in their innards. To see if one's inside of yours, look for telephone jacks on the back of your computer, near where all the other cables protrude. If a cable modem service is available in your area, go for it. It's a zillion times quicker, and you don't need to tie up your phone line. (Plus, you won't need to pay for a second phone line while Web surfing.)

Now you're ready to start the Internet Connection Wizard by following these steps.

In fact, whenever you encounter difficulties in getting your Internet connection "just right," head here and run through the steps in this section. The Wizard displays your current settings and allows you to change them.

1. **Click the Start button, click Programs, choose Accessories, and load the Internet Connection Wizard from the Communications area.**

2. **Choose one of the three options, as seen in Figure 12-2.**

The Internet
Connection
Wizard
helps you
connect
your
computer to
the Internet.

- **Sign up for a new Internet Account**

  Choose this option if you don't already have an Internet account
  and you want to select one. By choosing this, the Wizard dials a
  number to locate Internet Service Providers in your area and displays their rates and options. Chances are, you can sign up with
  one of several providers, including America Online, Prodigy, AT&T
  WorldNet Service, and Earthlink Internet Services.

  After you choose a provider, the Wizard makes you fill out your
  name, address, and credit card information before leaving you at
  Step 3.

- **Transfer your existing Internet account to your computer**

  Already have an Internet account? Click here to set up your computer to access your existing account. Your modem still dials a
  Microsoft phone number to find local providers in your area. It
  only finds providers who've told Microsoft that they're around,
  though, and your provider may not be listed.

  Tell the form your provider isn't listed, and Windows guides you
  through setting up the Internet connection process manually —
  the same as the next step.

- **Set up your existing Internet account manually or through a
  network**

  After selecting this, click Next to continue along these steps. You
  introduce your computer to your existing Internet account by filling out forms and punching buttons.

3. **Tell Windows Me whether you connect through a phone line or a network.**

   If you use a network, find a techno-savvy teenager for help or check out this book's sequel, *MORE Microsoft Windows Me For Dummies*. Networks are too complicated for this book. The rest of these steps are for a phone line.

4. **Enter the phone number for your Internet Service Provider; click Next and enter your User name and Password.**

   Your provider should have given you these three things. Call them if these three magical tidbits of information aren't in your possession.

5. **Type a name for your Internet provider.**

   Type My Provider or the name of your provider.

6. **Set up a mail account.**

   On the next page, say you want to set up an Internet mail account. In the coming pages, type your name, your user name, and your e-mail address. This is usually your user name, the @ sign, and the name of your provider. If your provider is www.agony.com, and your user name is flower, type flower@agony.com.

   The next page has the most confusing part. Unless your Internet provider tells you otherwise, simply type the word **mail** in the Incoming Mail and Outgoing Mail server boxes.

   On the next page, type your account name. Still using the above example, you type flower. Then type your password in the box below. If you want to log on automatically without entering your password each time, check the Remember Password box. Because this eliminates a need for a password, however, anybody can read your e-mail.

   Check the Secure Password Authentication box only if your Internet provider asks you to.

7. **Click the Finish button.**

   You're done. The latest Internet browser in Windows Me, Internet Explorer 5.5, automatically leaps into action and uses your settings to call your Internet provider.

If everything goes correctly, you're logged onto the Internet and ready to browse. Need a place to go for a quick test? Log onto www.andyrathbone.com and see what happens. Or head to Chapter 13 for an introduction to the land known as the Internet's World Wide Web.

Some versions of Windows may not have the Internet Connection Wizard on your Start menu. To find it, right-click on your Internet Explorer icon, choose Properties, click the Connections tab, and click the Setup button.

ISDN Connection Wizard

ISDN, a special super-speedy phone line for super-speedy modems, warrants its own connection wizard, found right here.

MSN Messenger Service

The *MSN Messenger Service* is a combination doorbell/peephole for the Internet. When a friend logs onto the Internet, your bell rings automatically and a window pops up, ready for you to bug your friend with a message.

Then, when your friends keep bugging you, you search for a way to turn off the darn thing. (Right-click on the little "people" icon in the bottom-right corner of your screen near the clock, and choose Exit.)

NetMeeting

What it does: Want to see who you're dealing with, even though you're in California and they're in New York? If your computer's set up for it, NetMeeting allows Internet-relayed teleconferences with sound, video, and the sharing of files.

Why bother with it: If you're dealing with other techies, go ahead and impress 'em. But you may be marked as a nerd and blow the deal if you're not sure the other folks are techies, too. (If your mom's a computer nerd, use it to talk to her when she winters in Florida.)

Phone Dialer

It's kind of cute. Phone Dialer lets you assign your most frequently dialed phone numbers to push buttons: Just click the button, and Phone Dialer dials the number, as shown in Figure 12-3.

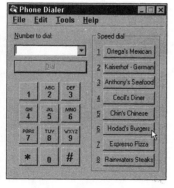

Figure 12-3: The Phone Dialer uses your modem to dial; then it tracks the conversation's length.

Best yet, Phone Dialer keeps track of calls you make by using the program.

Normally, the program works just like a telephone: You click the buttons to dial the number. After a few seconds, you hear the phone ring and somebody say "Hello?" through your modem's speaker. Pick up your phone and start talking.

The fun part comes when you store the number of your favorite relative, radio station, or pizza delivery service (or whatever) into the Phone Dialer.

1. **Click one of the buttons along the program's right side.**

   The button on the top is probably handiest. A box appears, ready for you to type the name and phone number of the place you're calling.

2. **Type the name of the place you're calling into the Name box; then press Tab and type the place's phone number into the Number to Dial box.**

   Start typing the place's name, and the letters appear in the top box. Press Tab to move the cursor to the second box, where you can type the phone number. Use the numbers on your keyboard's numeric keypad or the ones along the top of your keyboard, whichever you prefer. (The Function keys won't work, however.)

3. **Click the Save button.**

   The Phone Dialer reappears, showing its newly configured dial button. To dial the number, click the button.

✔ Can't remember whether you made that important call yesterday morning? Choose Show Log from the Tools menu, and you see a list of the phone numbers you've dialed, when you dialed them, and how long the conversation lasted.

✔ The Phone Dialer is handy for complicated long-distance calls with too many digits to remember.

✔ Are you using Phone Dialer on your laptop in the hotel room? Phone Dialer automatically sets up your call for dozens of countries, from Albania to Zambia (and Afghanistan and Zimbabwe, too) — lots of international stuff in Windows Me.

✔ Now the bad news: If you're using a network modem, cable modem, or a second, dedicated phone line for your modem, Phone Dialer doesn't work correctly. It only works on the telephone line that's actually plugged into your modem.

Entertainment

Windows Me is a bachelor's pad entertainment center, complete with controls for your computer's CD player, DVD player, and TV card. Microsoft has tossed in the software. Pick up a modem and a bag of microwave popcorn, and a modern young couple's plans are set for the evening.

Here's what you find in the Windows Me stereo cabinet of entertainment goodies.

Sound Recorder

A remnant from times past, the lowly Sound Recorder hasn't kept up. It records up to 60 seconds of sound. Most of the time, it's meant to record messages for embedding into documents or attaching to e-mail: Your boss hears a subliminal "Give me a raise" message as she reads your correspondence.

Chances are, you'll never use it.

Volume control

Ignore this one — too many menus to wade through. Instead, click the little speaker in the corner of your taskbar. (See it in the bottom-right corner of your screen?) When the control pops up, just slide it up or down to change your volume.

A double-click on that little speaker brings up the master volume, where you control the mix of your computer's media devices. For example, a CD Player shows up here, as well as general sound (wav), music (MIDI), or peripherals, such as TV cards or video capture cards (Line-in).

Windows Media Player

It's hip, it's happening, and it's huge. Windows' formerly tiny Media Player now fills your entire screen with '60s-era pulsating lights, as shown in Figure 12-4.

As the lights dance, Windows Media Player plays and creates *MP3 files* — computerized versions of songs from your favorite CDs.

That's not all. Media Player grabs sound and video from the Internet. It plays your DVDs and CDs. It categorizes your sound and video, from CDs to movie trailers to radio station presets to favorite playlists.

Bought a PocketPC, one of those cool palmtops? Here's where you go to convert MP3s into a smaller music format and dump them into the toy.

Finally, Windows Media Player meshes with Windows Me's new MovieMaker video-editing program for extra vacation excitement.

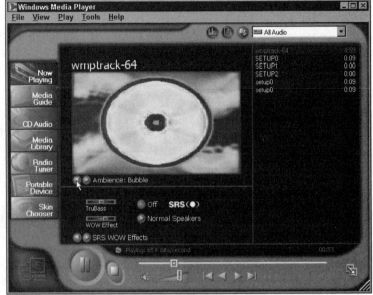

Figure 12-4:
Media
Player, a
gargantuan
monster of
sound and
video, plays
CDs,
converts
them to MP3
files, plays
and stores
videos,
plays
Internet
radio, and
handles
other media
chores.

WebTV for Windows

Windows Me lets users watch TV on their computer screens (see Figure 12-5). Best yet, by shrinking the WebTV for Windows into a window, you can watch old movies while working on Important Business Documents.

Figure 12-5:
With a TV
card
installed,
Windows
Me displays
TV channels
on your
computer
screen.

✔ Don't get excited yet. Windows Me can't show TV unless your computer has a TV card — which costs from $50–$200. Luckily, most TV cards come with a normal video card's circuitry inside, sparing you the expense of two cards.

- WebTV for Windows also comes with a built-in TV guide program. By connecting to the Internet, the program gathers information about the current week's TV shows in your area. It then displays a TV show listing with a search program, letting you ferret out any upcoming favorites.

- Don't want to miss a show? Rev up the TV guide, search for any upcoming episodes, and click the Remind button. WebTV for Windows automatically reminds you five minutes before the show begins.

- Here's the ugly truth, however, and you heard it here first: The Windows Me WebTV software is absolutely *awful* compared to the competition. Skip it, and use the TV-viewing program that comes in the box with your TV card. The TV controller in ATI's All-In-Wonder Pro, for instance, is much more reliable, faster, easier to use, and offers many more features. Don't want to miss anything about the stock market on CNN? Tell ATI's card to listen for the word "stock." When the card finds the word, it brings up the TV screen, ready for instant viewing. Now *that's* TV software.

System Tools

Windows Me comes with several technical programs designed to make the nerd feel at home. They're certainly not designed for the normal user. In fact, the Windows Me installation program doesn't even install all of these programs unless you ask.

If any of these programs strikes your fancy — and they're not on your System Tools menu — grab your Windows Me disc and head for Chapter 14. That chapter explains how to use the Control Panel's Add/Remove Programs feature to make Windows Me toss a few more goodies onto your hard drive.

Meanwhile, the next few sections describe some of the more technical programs in Windows Me.

Character Map (Adding the à in voilà)

What it does: Character Map lets you add weird foreign characters, such as à, £, or even ß, into your document.

Why bother with it: Why? Because Character Map makes it so easy to give your documents that extra shine *à la belle étoile*. A click on the System Tool's Character Map option unleashes a box like the one shown in Figure 12-6, listing every available character and symbol.

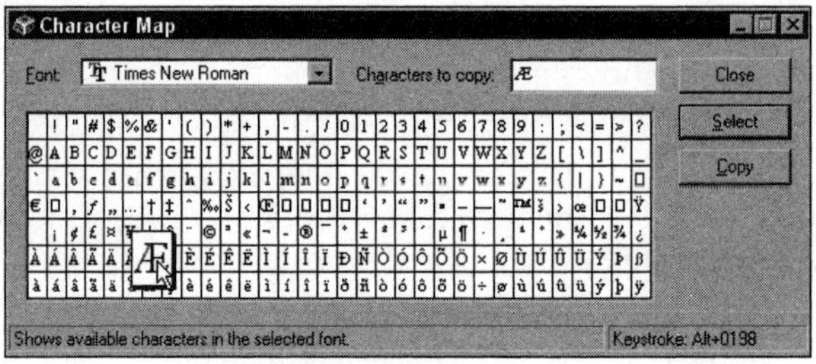

Figure 12-6:
Character
Map finds
foreign
characters
for your font
to place in
your work.

Follow these steps to put a foreign character in your work:

1. **Make sure that the current font — the name for the style of the characters on the page — shows in the Font box.**

   If the current font is not showing, click the down arrow and click the font when it appears in the drop-down list.

2. **Scan the Character Map box until you see the symbol you're after; then pounce on that character with a double-click.**

   The symbol appears in the Characters to Copy box.

3. **Click Copy to send the character to the Clipboard.**

4. **Click the Close button to close the Character Map.**

5. **Click in the document where you want the new symbol or character to appear.**

6. **Press Ctrl+V, and the new character pops right in there.**

   (Give it a second. Sometimes it's slow.)

The symbols in the Character Map box are easier to see if you hold down the mouse button and move the pointer over them.

✔ When working with foreign words, keep the Character Map handy as an icon, ready for consultation.

✔ For some fun symbols like ♋, ♌, ♍, ♎, ♏, ♐, ♑, or ♒, switch to the Wingdings font. It's full of little doodads to spice up your work.

✔ You can grab several characters at a time by double-clicking each of them and then copying them into your work as a chunk. You don't have to keep returning to the Character Map for each one.

TIP

It's weird, but it works

In the bottom right-hand corner, Character Map flashes numbers after the words *Keystroke: Alt+.* Those numbers hail back to the stone-tablet days of adding foreign characters when word processing. Back then, people had to look up a character's code number in the back of a boring manual.

If you remember the code numbers for your favorite symbols or foreign character, however, you can bypass Character Map and add them directly to documents. For example, the code number listed in the bottom corner for é is 0233.

Here's the trick: Turn on your Num Lock keys and, while holding down the Alt key, type **0233** with the numeric keypad. Let go of the Alt key, and the é symbol appears.

If you constantly use one special character, this method may be faster than using Character Map. (Press and release the Num Lock key after you're finished.)

Clipboard Viewer

What it does: This little window lets you view whatever doodad you've just cut or copied from a file. It makes it very easy to see what you've copied.

Why bother with it: Chapter 8, the "cut and paste" chapter, has the dirt on this handy little program. I keep Clipboard Viewer up and running all the time.

Disk Cleanup

What it is: Like the backseat of a car, Windows Me accumulates junk: files temporarily grabbed from the Internet, deleted files from the Recycle Bin, and other space-wasters. Disk Cleanup automatically gathers these programs and lets you delete them.

Why bother with it: When you need a little more room on the hard drive in order to install a program, unleash Disk Cleanup. It's an easy way to purge your system of files you'll never miss.

For best results, delete everything listed in the Disk Cleanup box. If you've been using Windows Me for a few months and if you like it enough to keep it, delete any saved Windows 98 uninstall information, too.

Disk Defragmenter

What it does: When a computer reads and writes files to and from a hard drive, it's working like a liquor store stock clerk after a Labor Day weekend. It has to reorganize the store, moving all the misplaced beer cans out of the wine aisles. The same disorganization happens with computer files. When the computer moves files around, it tends to break the files into chunks and spread them across your hard drive. The computer can still find all the pieces, but it takes more time. Disk Defragmenter reorganizes the hard drive, making sure that all the files' pieces are next to each other for quick and easy grabbing.

Why bother with it: Your hard drive can grab files more quickly if all the files' pieces are stored next to each other. The Disk Defragmenter organizes the files, speeding up access times. When the program pops up, click the drive you want defragmented. The program looks at the drive and tells you whether the drive needs any work. Take the program's advice. (You probably won't have to use the program more than every couple of months, depending on how often you use your computer.)

DriveSpace

What it does: A data cruncher, DriveSpace compresses information so you can pack more programs and software onto your hard drive.

Why bother with it: Don't bother with any disk compression program — buy a bigger hard drive instead. Hard drives are downright inexpensive right now and are a lot more reliable than the older models. Compressed hard drives make it that much more difficult to retrieve stuff when something goes wrong.

Maintenance Wizard

What it does: This offers a chance to automate the three main Windows Me maintenance/repair tools: ScanDisk, Disk Cleanup, and Disk Defragmenter.

Why bother with it: If you make Windows Me automatically perform all of these chores at 3 a.m. while you're snoozing, your computer always runs more smoothly during the day.

Net Watcher

What it is: This lets computer snoops play spy on the network. Net Watcher lets you see who's connected to your computer and whether they're rooting through your files.

Why bother with it: Not much reason, really. If a network administrator has set up your computer for network access, there's not much you can do about it. Plus, you can usually tell when somebody in another cubicle accesses your computer because its hard drive revs up and makes a pestered sound.

Resource Meter

Yawn. A little meter mumbles something about resources. (This stuff attracts the same crowd that enjoys watching oscilloscopes.)

ScanDisk

What it does: Sometimes, a computer goofs and loses track of where it has stored information on a hard drive. ScanDisk examines a hard drive for any errors and, if it finds anything suspicious, offers to fix the problem.

Why bother with it: ScanDisk not only finds hard drive errors, but if you click in the Automatically Fix Errors box, it fixes them.

To bring ScanDisk to work, follow these steps:

1. **Click the Start button and choose Accessories from the Programs menu. Select System Tools and choose ScanDisk.**
2. **Select the drive that you want to check.**
3. **Click the Automatically Fix Errors box.**

   A check mark appears.
4. **Choose the Standard option and click the Start button.**

If you still have problems, rerun the program, but choose the Thorough option instead of the Standard option in Step 4. That makes ScanDisk work a little harder, but it takes its time in the process.

Scheduled Tasks

What it does: Windows Me can run programs when you're not around to supervise, whether you're sleeping at night or away from the home computer during the day. Scheduled Tasks plans the schedule of your computer's routine, telling it which programs to run, when, and for how long.

Why bother with it: Don't bother, actually. Maintenance Wizard requires less thinking.

You can purge any automated tasks by double-clicking the Scheduled Tasks icon in the bottom-right corner of your screen. (The icon is a tiny square with a little clock in one corner and an open book in the other.) Click on the offensive task, press the Delete key, and click the Yes button to send that task to the Recycle Bin.

System Information

What it does: Compiles vast technical charts about your computer's innards.

Why bother with it: Don't. It's a fix-it tool for the mechanics.

System Monitor

What it does: Makes technical charts that reveal performance statistics.

Why bother with it: Don't, unless you just want to see the cool little graphs. Actually, this program slows down your computer because it spends so much time gauging performance and turning it into bar charts.

System Restore

Finally, something new and exciting from a new release of Windows. When your computer's running well — and you wish it would always work that well — open System Restore and click next to the Create a restore point option, as shown in Figure 12-7.

Windows looks at itself and takes a snapshot of all its settings. Then, if something awful happens a few days later, you have an out: Head back to the System Restore area and choose Restore My Computer to an Earlier Time. Choose a restore point you saved back when everything was just ducky, and, when Windows restores your pre-disaster settings, your computer will perform swimmingly.

Figure 12-7:
Use System
Restore to
take system
"snapshots"
both before
and after
installing
new
programs
so your
computer
can be
restored to
its previous
state.

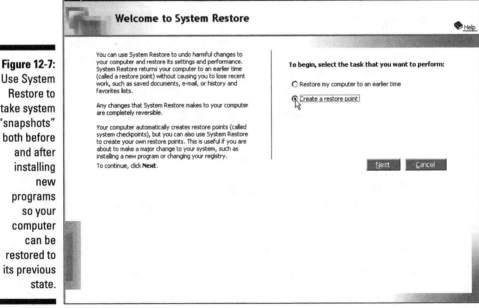

✔ There's a big problem. When System Restore brings back your earlier, faithful Windows setup, it will most likely leave out any of the programs you've installed since then. You have to reinstall them.

✔ System Restore won't touch any files you've stored in the My Documents folder. It swears it won't touch any of your other data files, either. But to be on the safe side, keep your most savored data in the My Documents folder.

✔ If you use System Restore, use it often. Use it both before and after installing any new program, for instance, or when making any major tweaks to your system settings. That way, System Restore can bring up a reasonably current version of your work — not the way it looked six or eight months ago.

✔ If you goof and restore something that made your computer worse than ever, undo the restoration. Call up System Restore and choose Undo My Last Restoration.

Address Book

If you use Outlook Express to send and receive your e-mail, all those names and e-mail addresses will turn up in Address Book, as shown in Figure 12-8.

Figure 12-8:
Windows
Me includes
an address
book for
storing
e-mail
addresses
and other
information.

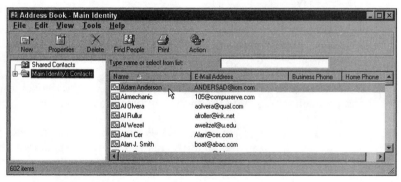

Feel free to flesh out the cards by adding people's home and work addresses, phone and fax numbers, birthdays, and important information like whether they sent you a holiday card last December.

Calculator

Calculator is, well, a calculator. It looks simple enough, and it really is — unless you mistakenly set it for Scientific mode and see some nightmarish logarithmic stuff. To bring the calculator back to normal, choose Standard from the View menu.

To punch in numbers and equations, click the little buttons, just as if it were a normal calculator. When you press the equals sign (=), the answer appears at the top. For an extra measure of handiness, you can copy the answers to the Clipboard by pressing Ctrl+C (holding down the Ctrl key while pressing C). Then click in the window where you want the answer to appear and press Ctrl+V. That method is easier than retyping a number like 2.449489742783.

- Unlike in other Windows programs, you can't copy the Calculator's answer by running the mouse pointer over the numbers. You have to press Ctrl+C or choose Copy from the Edit menu.
- The * is to multiply, and the / is to divide. The Enter key means total.
- If the mouse action is too slow, press the Num Lock key and punch in numbers with the numeric keypad.

Imaging

You've probably noticed how greeting cards and party fliers are getting increasingly elaborate. It's not just the fancy borders and cartoons, although they've never been more colorful. No, it's the embedded color pictures.

Chances are, a scanner copied that photo and sent it to the computer, where computer software turned the picture information into a file.

Imaging, by Kodak, lets Windows Me talk to scanners; it then manipulates and saves the image in a variety of file formats. It's a handy program. But chances are, the software that came with your scanner already does a better job.

MS-DOS Prompt

This remnant lets old-time computer users boss their computers around by typing in a command. It brings up an MS-DOS window, ready to run old DOS programs (and games). In fact, it will even run Windows programs if you're bored enough to type in the program's name and press the Enter key.

Notepad

Windows comes with two word processors, WordPad and Notepad. WordPad is for the letters you're sprucing up for other people to see. Notepad is for stuff you're going to keep for yourself.

Notepad is quicker than WordPad. Double-click its icon, and it leaps to the screen more quickly than you can reach for a notepad in your back pocket. You can type some quick words and save them on the fly.

Understanding Notepad's limitations

Notepad's speed comes at a price, however. Notepad stores only words and numbers. It doesn't store any special formatting, such as italicized letters, and you can't paste any pictures into it, as you can with WordPad. Notepad is a quick, throw-together program for your quick, throw-together thoughts.

- ✓ **Unfortunately, Notepad tosses you into instant confusion:** All the sentences head right off the edge of the screen. To turn those single-line, runaway sentences into normal paragraphs, turn on the *word wrap* feature by choosing Word Wrap from the Edit menu. (After you change this option the first time, strangely enough, Windows Me remembers your preference and uses it each time you use Notepad in the future.)

- ✓ **Notepad prints kind of funny, too:** It prints the file's name at the top of every page. To combat this nonsense, choose Page Setup from the File menu. A box appears, with a funny code word in the Header box. Delete the word and click OK. If you want to get rid of the automatic page numbering, clear out the Footer box as well.

- ✓ **Here's another printing problem:** Notepad doesn't print exactly what you see on-screen. Instead, it prints according to the margins you set in Page Setup from the File menu. This quirk can lead to unpredictable results.

Turning Notepad into a logbook

Although Notepad leans toward simplicity, it has one fancy feature that not even WordPad can match. Notepad can automatically stamp the current time and date at the bottom of a file whenever you open it. Just type **.LOG** in the very top left-hand corner of a file and save the file. Then, whenever you open that file again, you can jot down some current notes and have Notepad stamp it with the time and date. The result looks similar to what is shown in Figure 12-9.

Figure 12-9:
Add the
word **.LOG**
to the top of
the file, and
Notepad
stamps it
with the
time and
date
whenever
you open it.

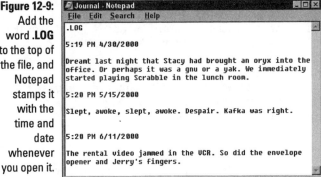

Figure 12-9:
Add the word **.LOG** to the top of the file, and Notepad stamps it with the time and date whenever you open it.

✔ Don't try the .LOG trick by using lowercase letters, and don't omit the period. It doesn't work.

✔ To stick in the date and time manually, press F5. The time and date appear, just as they do in the .LOG trick.

Painting in Paint

Do you love the smell of paint and a fresh canvas? Then you'll hate Paint. After working with real fibers and pigments, you'll find the computerized painting program that comes with Windows Me to be a little sterile. But at least there's no mess. Paint creates pictures and graphics to stick into other programs. The icon for Paint is a picture of a palette, found in the Accessories menu (which leaps out from the Start menu's Programs menu).

Paint offers more than just a paintbrush. It has a can of spray paint for that *airbrushed* look, several pencils of different widths, a paint roller for gobbing on a bunch of paint, and an eraser for when things get out of hand. Figure 12-10 was drawn with Paint.

In addition to capturing your artistic flair, Paint can team up with a digital camera or scanner to touch up pictures in your PC. You can create a flashy letterhead to stick into WordPad letters. You can even create maps to paste into your party fliers.

✔ You can copy drawings and pictures from Paint and paste them into just about any other Windows Me program.

✔ Remember that *cut and paste* stuff from Chapter 8? Well, you can cut out or copy chunks of art from the Paint screen by using the *select* or *free-form select* tools that I describe later in this section. The art goes onto the Windows Me Clipboard, where you can grab it and paste it into any other Windows program. (Paint doesn't support "Scraps," which I cover in Chapter 9.)

✔ Paint enables you to add text and numbers to graphics, so you can add street names to maps, put labels inside drawings, or add the vintage year to your wine labels.

Paint no longer saves files in PCX format. And it saves them only in BMP format. It will open BMP, JPG, and GIF files, though.

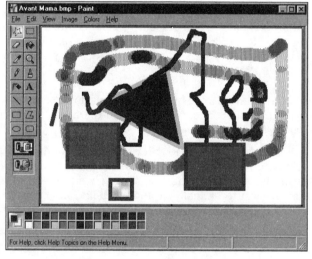

Figure 12-10: Paint can create exotic art, like this picture my mother drew.

Windows Explorer

Windows Explorer provides views of files stored on your computer and lets you copy them from one place to another. I cover this in Chapter 11.

Windows Movie Maker

For years, Windows could only edit words. Eventually, it could edit sounds. Now, Windows Me jumps into the Millennium with a program to edit movies from video cameras. It lets you arrange your clips any way you want and add soundtracks or voiceovers. It's cool, it's catchy, it's complicated, and it requires a special camcorder and a special video card. That's why it's covered in *MORE Microsoft Windows Me For Dummies* (IDG Books Worldwide, Inc.).

Word processing with WordPad

WordPad wears a fancy icon — a distinguished-looking fountain pen, like the ones that get ink on your hands.

Although its icon is fancy, WordPad isn't quite as fancy as some of the more expensive word processors on the market. You can't create tables or multiple columns, like the ones in newspapers or newsletters, nor can you double-space your reports. Ferget the spell checker, too.

But WordPad's great for quick letters, simple reports, and other basic stuff. You can change the fonts around to get reasonably fancy, too, as shown in Figure 12-11.

WordPad can handle Windows *TrueType fonts* — that font technology that shapes how characters appear on-screen. You can create an elegant document by using some fancy TrueType fonts and mail it on a disk to somebody else. That person can view your letter in WordPad, and it looks the same as when you created it.

✔ WordPad handles most word-processing needs: letters, reports, or term papers on philosophers with weird last names. Unless you're a lousy speller, you'll find WordPad easy to use, and you'll enjoy its excellent price.

✔ If you've just ditched your typewriter for Windows, remember this: On an electric typewriter, you have to press the Return key at the end of each line or else you start typing off the edge of the paper. Computers avoid that. They automatically drop down a line and continue the sentence. (Hip computer nerds call this phenomenon *word wrap*.)

Press Enter only when you're finished typing a paragraph and want to start a new one. Press Enter twice to leave a blank line between paragraphs.

Figure 12-11: WordPad may lack a spell checker, but it can churn out some fairly fancy pages.

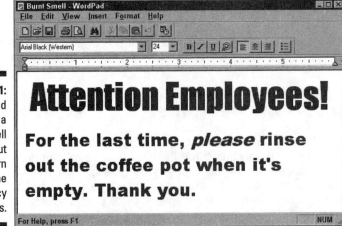

Opening and saving a file

In a refreshing change of pace, all Windows Me programs enable you to open and save a file in exactly the same way: Choose File at the top of the program's window, and a menu tumbles down. Choose Open or Save, depending on your whim. A box pops up, listing the files in the current folder. Select the name of the file you want to open (click it) or type the name of a new file. Click Open or Save, and you're through!

- ✔ If you want to open a file listed in a Windows Explorer or My Computer window, double-click the file's name. Windows Me yanks the file into the correct program and brings both the program and the file to the screen.

- ✔ You can find more explicit instructions on opening a file in Chapter 5.

- ✔ I browbeat folders and equally mind-numbing concepts in Chapter 11.

- ✔ When you save a file for the first time, you have to choose a name for it, as well as a folder to put it in. (My Documents is fine.) WordPad subsequently remembers the file's name and chosen folder, so you don't have to keep typing them each time you save your current progress.

- ✔ WordPad can save files in several formats, from plain text to something weird called Unicode. I cover all these formats in the next section.

- ✔ Sometimes, you open a file, change it, and want to save it with a different name or in a different folder. Choose Save As, not Save. WordPad treats your work as if you are saving it for the first time — it asks you to type in a new name and a location.

- ✔ Did you choose the Save option from the WordPad File menu, but then decide to save your masterpiece in a new folder at the last minute? Right-click in the middle of the Save As box, choose New, and then choose Create Folder. Your new folder appears, ready for a name and some new files.

Saving a WordPad file in different formats

Just as you can't drop a Ford engine into a Volvo, you can't drop a WordPad file into another company's word processor. All brands of word processors save their information in different ways in order to confuse the competition.

WordPad can read and write in several file formats. As soon as you try to create a new file, WordPad forces you to choose between four formats: Word 6 Document, Rich Text Document, Text Document, and Unicode Text Document. Each format meets different needs.

- ✔ **Word 6 Document:** This format creates files that can be read by Microsoft's *real* (and expensive) word processor, Microsoft Word. Many of the most popular competing word processors can read Word 6 files, too. You'll probably be safe with this format. (In fact, WordPad chooses it automatically if you can't make up your mind on a format and simply press the Enter key.)

✔ **Rich Text Format:** A wide variety of word processors can read these files. Rich Text documents can store **boldfaced** and *italicized* words, as well as other special formatting. These files can be *huge,* however. Don't choose this format unless it's the only format your friend's word processor accepts.

✔ **Text Document:** Almost all brands of word processors can read plain old text, making Text Document the safest format when exchanging files with friends. Unfortunately, these text-only documents can't have any **boldface** type, *italic* type, columns, or any other fancy stuff. ***Nerdly note:*** Many word processors refer to Text files as *ASCII* files (pronounced *ASK-ee*).

✔ **Text Document — MS-DOS Format:** This is the same as a Text Document, for the most part, but even simpler — if you can believe that.

✔ **Unicode:** Great for travelers! This lets you include text from many of the world's writing systems, including Roman, Greek, Cyrillic, Chinese, hiragana, and katakana.

If somebody asks you to save a WordPad file in a different format, choose Save As from the File menu. Click the arrow next to the Save As Type box and choose the new format from the drop-down list. Type a new name for the file into the File Name box and press Enter. *Voilà!* You've saved your file in the new format.

✔ The other word processor that comes with Windows Me, Notepad, can't handle anything but the plainest Text files. Notepad can't load WordPad's Word 6 files, and if it opens the Rich Text Format documents, the files look really weird. (WordPad can easily read Notepad's files, though.) Notepad gets its due earlier in this chapter.

✔ Although most word processors can read and write ASCII files, problems still occur. You lose any formatting, such as italicized words, special indents, or embedded pictures of apples.

✔ ASCII stands for American Standard Code for Information Interchange. A bunch of technoids created it when they got tired of other technoids saving their information in different ways. Today, most programs grudgingly read or write information using the ASCII format. In fact, ASCII files can even be exchanged with computers from different home planets, such as Apple Macintosh and UNIX workstations, with only minor technical glitches.

Other WordPad stuff

✔ A faster way to open a file is to press and release the Alt key and then press **F** and then **O**. If you memorize the keyboard commands, you won't have to trudge through all the menus with the mouse. If you don't remember the key commands, check out the handy chart in Table 12-1. I list other time-savers there as well.

✔ To open a file, feel free to "drag" its name from the Windows Explorer or My Computer window and drop the name directly into WordPad's open window. Whoosh! WordPad immediately sucks the file's contents into the open window.

✔ Want to change your page margins? Choose Page Setup from the File menu. The Page Layout dialog box lets you specify top, bottom, and side margins.

Table 12-1	WordPad Shortcut Keys
To Do This	*Do This*
Open a file	Press Alt, F, and O (or Ctrl+O).
Save a file	Press Alt, F, and S (or Ctrl+S).
Save a file under a new name	Press Alt, F, and A.
Print a file	Press Alt, F, and P (or Ctrl+P).
Select the entire document	Click rapidly three times in the left margin or press Ctrl+A.
Select one word	Double-click it.
Add *italics* to selected text	Press Ctrl+I.
Add **boldface** to selected text	Press Ctrl+B.
Add <u>underline</u> to selected text	Press Ctrl+U.

Games

Playtime! The best way to figure out mouse-pushing tactics in Windows Me is in a low-stress environment. So, Microsoft tossed plenty of games into the Windows Me mix. Some of the games already came packaged with last year's version of Windows; they're nothing new. But then again, card games never get old, do they?

Windows Me often leaves out the games when it's first installed. To install them, click the Start button, choose Settings, and load Control Panel. Double-click the Add/Remove Programs icon and click the Windows Setup tab. Double-click the Accessories option from the list and click the box next to Games until a check mark appears.

Click OK on the next two screens, and Windows Me will install the games listed in this section. (You may need to insert your Windows Me CD.)

Classic Hearts

Windows Me has no shortage of card games, that's for sure. If you're tired of Solitaire and FreeCell, give Hearts a try — especially if you're on a network. It lets you play cards with networked computers all across the office.

Shown in Figure 12-12, the game works just like *real* Hearts. One person tosses a card onto the table, everybody else tosses down a card of the same suit, and the person with the highest card grabs the pile. What's the tricky part? You want the *lowest* score — any card with a heart is one point, and the queen of spades is worth 13 points.

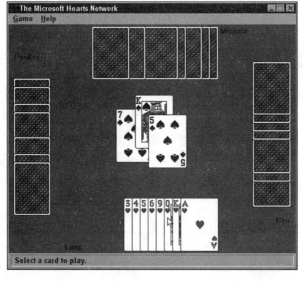

Figure 12-12:
Designed for play on networks and the Internet, Hearts can also substitute computerized opponents if nobody's on the network.

✔ There's a catch: If one player grabs all the hearts and the queen of spades, that player doesn't get any points, and all the other players are penalized 26 points. (That's called "Shooting the Moon.")

✔ If nobody is around at the office network, choose the dealer option and then press F2; the computer fills in for the other three players. You don't need a network to play Hearts.

✔ *Cheat alert:* The computer automatically sorts your cards by suit at the screen's bottom. However, it doesn't sort the cards that represent the other players' hands — the cards around the edges. Therefore, you can't get an idea of what cards the other players have by watching the position of their cards.

✔ Classic Hearts can play with people across a network at home or an office. To play hearts with players over the Internet, choose Internet Hearts, described in the upcoming Internet games section.

Classic Solitaire

Windows Me Solitaire works just like the card game, so here are just a few pointers for the computerized version:

- ✔ When the boss comes by, click the minimize button, that underscore-looking thing in a box in the upper-right corner. If you can't move the mouse quickly enough, hold down the Alt key and press the spacebar, followed by the letter *N*. In either case, Solitaire turns into an icon at the bottom of the screen. Double-click the icon to resume play when the boss passes.

- ✔ When you're in three-card mode — and Solitaire flips the cards over three at a time — you can cheat to make Solitaire temporarily flip the cards one by one. Just hold down the Ctrl, Alt, and Shift keys simultaneously as you click.

- ✔ Sharp-eyed players will notice some background fun: The bats flap their wings, the sun sticks out its tongue, and a card slides in and out of a dealer's sleeve. These shenanigans only occur when you play in *timed* mode. To start the fun, choose Options from the Game menu and make sure that you put an X in the Timed Game box.

FreeCell

Although FreeCell looks a lot like Solitaire, described previously, it plays a lot differently. For instance, FreeCell works with double-clicks: Instead of making you drag the cards around, FreeCell simply jumps them into place.

FreeCell works just like the card game: Sort the cards in order by suit and number from Ace to King on the four upper-right-hand squares. While moving the cards up there, you can move other cards temporarily to the four *free cells* — temporary card-storage areas — on the left-hand side.

- ✔ FreeCell comes with 32,000 different games. So far, only one of them has been proven unbeatable. (That leaves plenty of winnable games.)

- ✔ Press F4, and FreeCell reveals your win/loss ratio. To make it look like you win all your games, cheat: Whenever you're about to lose a game, hold down the Ctrl and Shift keys simultaneously, and press F10. A box appears, offering you three options: Abort, but still win the game, Retry and lose the game, or Ignore and pretend you didn't press those keys. Press Abort, double-click on any card, and you automatically win. Sneaky, eh?

- ✔ Moved the wrong card? Quick — press F10. That's the Undo button, but only if you press it before clicking another card.

- ✔ After you've won 65,535 games, FreeCell resets your winning streak statistics to zero. Be forewarned.

Internet games

Windows Me lets you find opponents on the Internet for Backgammon, Checkers, Hearts, Reversi, and Spades. (No poker.) Click on any of those five games, and Windows seeks out players on the Internet waiting for opponents just like you.

Don't be disappointed if the Internet games don't work through your network at work. The games are easily thwarted by computing security systems. (Plus, when nobody's hanging around to play, you'll think that your computer is broken.)

Minesweeper

Despite the name, Minesweeper does not cause any explosions, even if you accidentally uncover a mine. And it works better on laptops than Solitaire does. Minesweeper is more of a math game than anything else — no jumping little men here.

Start by clicking a random square; some numbers appear in one or more of the little squares. The number states how many mines are hidden in the squares surrounding that square.

Each square is surrounded by eight other squares. (Unless it's on the edge; then there are only five. And only three squares surround corner squares.) If, through the process of elimination, you're sure that a mine exists beneath a certain square, click it with the right mouse button to put a little flag there.

Eventually, through logical deduction (or just mindless pointing and clicking), an accidental click on a mine blows you up, or you mark all the mine squares with flags and win the game.

The object of the game is to win as quickly as you can.

Ready to cheat? To stop the clock, hold down both the left and right mouse buttons and press the Escape key. To change your high scores, head for your Windows folder and use Notepad to open a file called `winmine.ini`. Then edit the high score list, changing the names and times to anything you want.

Pinball

When the pinball machine appears on your screen but flipper buttons don't appear on the sides of your keyboard, check out Table 12-2.

Table 12-2	Keyboard Controls for Pinball
To	**Press**
Move left flipper	z
Move right flipper	/
Nudge table to right	x
Nudge table to the left	.
Nudge the table up	Up-arrow key
Launch the ball	Spacebar

In addition to groovy graphics and sounds, Pinball lets you change the keyboard controls to other keys, should you find them awkward. To really get serious, click the Advanced Play sections and read how to rack up a high score.

When playing at work, mute the sound and music: Choose Options from the top menu and click both the words *Sounds* and *Music* from the drop-down menu. When the check mark disappears by their names, the sound disappears as well.

Spider Solitaire

Spider Solitaire is lots of fun and similar to FreeCell in appearance, but certainly not in the way you play it. In fact, suddenly switching between the two games causes immediate confusion. In Solitaire, you can place cards on their own suits or other suits (as a last resort). In FreeCell, you always place opposite suits onto each other.

Try to line up the cards in numerical order, even if you have to insert cards of different suits into the rows. Try desperately to line up a complete row in one suit, from King to Ace. That removes the entire stack, leaving more room to work with.

Also, create as many empty stacks as you can for moving cards around. But you must temporarily fill those stacks again before Spider will deal you the next round of cards. It's a tad confusing at first, but stay with the Easy game until you're ready to move on to the Two Suit game. (Ignore the sadistically difficult Four Suit game unless you're setting it up for a wiseacre friend.)

Although delightfully addictive, Spider isn't always winnable — even if you play a perfect game. At least you know you can eventually win FreeCell if you play the same game long enough.

The Online Services

Most people have heard about *online services,* where you can hook your computer up to the phone lines and, under the pretense of making direct-deposit payments through your checking account, swap pictures of your cat wearing a beret with newfound friends on the Cat Forum.

The latest version of Windows Me comes with icons that access a bundle of online services and networks. You can point and click your way to The Microsoft Network, CompuServe, America Online, Prodigy, and AT&T WorldNet. Here's a look at what's what.

Before signing up with any of these ISPs on the spot, check 'em out: Take this book to a friend's place and try out the Web links listed for each ISP. Take note of the ones with the most busy signals and dropped connections.

America Online

America Online (www.aol.com) uses splashy graphics, easy-to-use buttons, and a huge marketing campaign to propel its subscription past 23 million people. If you're looking for a cushioned way to enter the Internet, America Online may be your best bet.

- America Online's flat monthly fee provides unlimited access to the Internet, as well as entrance to *forums* — message areas — open only to other America Online members.

- America Online can be an easy way to start experiencing online life. It provides a free trial period to see if online living suits your constitution.

- The rigid construction of America Online isn't all for the good, unfortunately. America Online's software isn't standard with many other services. Many users can't download pictures that are attached to their e-mail. America Online's mail system lacks the details found in Outlook Express, Windows' built-in e-mail program. Many America Online users eventually move onto a more full-featured Internet Service Provider.

AT&T WorldNet

One of the newest entrants to the online service business, AT&T set a new pricing standard when it muscled its way into the Internet Service Provider ring in March 1996. Whereas most companies charged people an hourly rate for Web surfing, AT&T WorldNet (www.att.net) let its long-distance customers access the Internet all they wanted for a flat fee of $19.95.

Everybody else started offering the same deal, so AT&T extended its flat-fee offer to *everyone* — not just its long-distance customers. Since then, it's grown to about 1.5 million users.

Earthlink Internet Services

They don't display banners on blimps or give away free CDs in the mail, but Earthlink Internet Services (www.earthlink.net) has quietly served as ISP for more than three million people. With twice as many customers as AT&T WorldNet, they must be doing something right. I've never tried 'em.

Prodigy

IBM's Prodigy (www.prodigy.com), one of the Internet's first providers, nearly died from its clunky graphics and stodgy management: Every publicly posted message ran before an IBM censor before posting; messages took hours to appear.

Under new management, Prodigy's back on track and at the front of the line with the first bilingual ISP. A few mouse clicks transfers the words from Spanish to English, or vice versa. Toss in a Web page builder, a price cheaper than America Online, and Prodigy's become quite appealing to the Hispanic market.

MSN (Microsoft Network)

Microsoft, always smelling cash, saw people making lots of money through online services. So it created its own online service — Microsoft Network, or MSN (www.msn.com). Then Microsoft tried to elbow past the competition by doing something sneaky: Microsoft stuck the signup icon for MSN directly onto Windows' desktop, just a click away.

Talk about free advertising! A curious Windows Me user merely clicked the MSN icon, and the program took over, slyly grasping its prey by the arms and telling the user exactly how to install the system and begin enjoying the pleasures of online life.

Needless to say, competing online services were outraged and headed for the courts, claiming unfair competition. Microsoft, eager to keep things from getting *too* ugly, struck a deal: It would include icons for the other online services with Windows, too. However, they were sequestered into a desktop folder called Online Services.

StartUp

The StartUp folder, which I cover in Chapter 10, lists programs that start automatically when Windows Me loads itself for a day's work.

Internet Explorer and Outlook Express

Internet Explorer, the door to the Internet and its hodgepodge of Web sites, gets its own section in Chapter 13. It comes with a handful of other programs for putting together Web pages, sorting e-mail, chatting with other Internet surfers around the world, and performing other Internet-related tricks.

The Internet Explorer companion e-mail program, Outlook Express, gets a rundown in Chapter 13 as well.

Windows Media Player

Microsoft puts this one in here twice. The Entertainment section holds the description, because that's the first place Microsoft lists it on the menu.

My Version of Windows Me Doesn't Have the Right Programs!

Depending on the buttons you punched when you installed Windows Me, you find different varieties of programs installed on your hard drive. Very few people get all the programs installed. If you feel left out and want some of the optional programs mentioned in this chapter, follow these steps. Beware, however; a few of the programs in this chapter only come with Windows Me.

1. **Double-click the Control Panel's Add/Remove Programs icon.**

   You can load the Control Panel by clicking Settings in the Start menu.

2. **Click the Windows Setup tab.**

   It's the middle tab among the three top tabs. A box appears showing the various components of Windows Me, as well as the amount of space they need to elbow onto your computer's hard drive.

3. **Click in the little box by the programs or accessories you want to add.**

   A check mark appears in the box of the items you select. To select part of a category — a portion of the accessories, for example — click the category's name and click the Details button. Windows Me lists the items available in that category so that you can select the ones you want. If you clicked the Details button, click OK to continue back at the main categories list.

4. **Click OK and insert your Windows Me CD when asked.**

   Windows Me copies the necessary files from your CD onto your hard drive. You can remove Windows Me accessories the same way, but by *removing* the check mark from the box next to their names.

A black check mark means that you've already selected all of the available programs in that program category. A gray check mark means you've grabbed only some of them. Empty check marks mean that you aren't using any of those programs.

Chapter 13

Cruising the Web, Sending E-Mail, and Using Newsgroups

● ●

In This Chapter

▶ Understanding the Internet and World Wide Web

▶ Understanding differences between the Internet and online services

▶ Knowing how to access the World Wide Web

▶ Using the Microsoft Internet Explorer Web browser

▶ Navigating the World Wide Web

▶ Upgrading with downloaded plug-ins

▶ Sending and receiving e-mail with Outlook Express

▶ Using Newsgroups with Outlook Express

● ●

*T*he family photo album is disappearing. A friend of mine visited with his family the other day. He brought his new digital camera and took pictures of the vacation.

Each evening, he used the telephone and his laptop to send the camera's pictures to his Web site, and then he tweaked his Web site's settings to create a daily pictorial journal of the day's events. There's not a black photo album in his closet; he's sharing his life with anyone who cares to look.

Other Web sites go to even greater extremes. A cab driver in New York has a digital camera hooked up to a cellular phone; every few minutes, the camera takes a picture of the bustling streets and automatically sends the photo to the cabby's Web site.

You needn't be as elaborate with your own Web site. In fact, you don't *need* to have a Web site at all. This chapter shows how to peek at all the other sites out there, though, should you get the urge.

What's the Difference between the Internet, the World Wide Web, and a Web Browser?

The *Internet* is a rapidly growing collection of computers linked around the globe through wires and satellites. Millions of people of all ages swap information with other computers via the Internet.

The *World Wide Web* (known as "The Web," to be cool) runs on the Internet to let computers display *Web sites* — electronic, interactive software that often resembles magazine pages with pretty pictures.

A *Web browser* lets you flip through a Web site's different pages, just like you flip the pages of a magazine. Best yet, the Web browser lets you jump from Web site to Web site. You can read newspapers at one site and order books or take-out food at another site.

Internet Explorer, the free browser that comes with Windows Me, makes the Web look like a kiosk in a hotel or airport lobby. Internet Explorer fills your screen with buttons and pictures. But instead of touching the pictures and buttons, like you do at the airport or hotel lobby, you use the mouse to point and click on-screen buttons. By doing so, you can view museums, cameras, pizza menus, guitar shops, city maps, and more. (You can also find the right rental car.)

✔ Just as a television channel surfer flips from channel to channel, sampling the wares, a Web surfer moves from page to page, sampling the vast and esoteric piles of information.

✔ Just about anybody can set up a Web site, but doing so usually involves some programming skills using a language called *HTML* (HyperText Markup Language). Surfing the pages is much easier than building the wave. That's why most people remain Web surfers.

✔ Because setting up a Web site on the Internet is fairly easy for programmers, thousands of just plain wacky sites exist. If you're flabbergasted by flying saucers, for example, head for `www.fsreview.net/` to read the Flying Saucer Review. Another fellow's well-documented site tests the durability of the pink and white "Marshmallow Bunnies" sold in drug stores. Head to `www.pcola.gulf.net/~irving/bunnies/` and watch the Laser Exposure Test!

Who Can Use the Internet and World Wide Web?

Gosh, everybody who *doesn't* use the Internet is forced to hear everybody else talk about it at parties and on TV commercials, and read about it in magazines, newspapers, and billboards.

Here are a few of the Internet's most enthusiastic subscribers:

- ✔ Universities, corporations, government entities, and millions of plain ol' normal folk use the Internet every day. Many users simply send messages back and forth — *electronic mail* or *e-mail.* Other users swap programs, pictures, or sounds — anything that can be stored as data inside of a computer.

- ✔ The United States government loves the Internet. The FBI posts pictures of its ten most wanted criminals (www.fbi.gov) for public viewing, for example, and the Internal Revenue Service (www.irs.ustreasgov/prod/cover.html) lets Internet users make free copies of tax forms 24 hours a day.

- ✔ Universities love the network, too. Departments can file grant forms more quickly than ever. Worried about the goo coagulating in the center of your bromeliads? The Internet's famed botanical site (www.botany.net/IDB) enables researchers to move quickly from 24 Canoe Plants of Ancient Hawaii to the Zoosporic Fungi database.

- ✔ Many computer companies support their products on the Internet. Visitors to the Web site can leave messages to technicians in hopes that the technicians can figure out why their latest computer doodads aren't working. After posting messages back and forth, callers can often download a software cure or patch to fix the problem.

- ✔ Businesses, spotting a new way to advertise, quickly jumped aboard the Web. Some vintage guitar dealers (www.choiceguitar.com), for example, display photos of their classic guitars, like the one shown in Figure 13-1, hoping to snag potential buyers. Some sites even let you click a picture to hear the howl of a '67 Stratocaster.

- ✔ Curious about Volkswagen Beetles? Head for the Volkswagen Web site (www.vw.com) and start flipping through the pages of the Volkswagen "point and clickable" brochure on the "new" Beetle. (See Figure 13-2.)

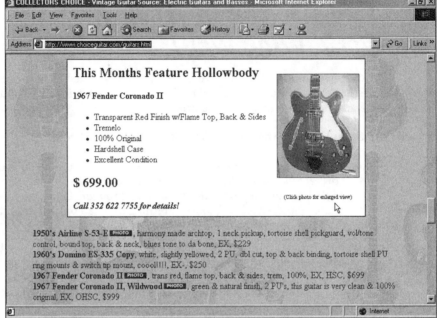

Figure 13-1:
World Wide
Web sites let
you shop
for nearly
everything —
even
guitars.

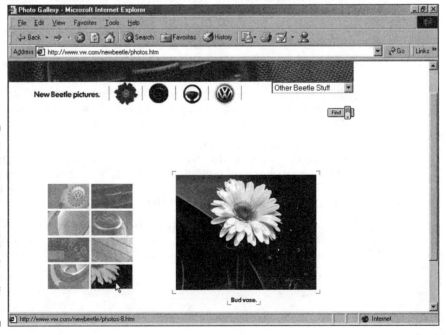

Figure 13-2:
The
Volkswagen's
"point and
clickable"
brochure
lets
computer
users view
online
close-ups of
their cars.

What's an ISP and Do I Need One?

Signals for television channels come wafting through the air to your TV set for free. Unless you're paying for cable or satellite TV, you can watch *Dawson's Creek* for free.

The Internet ain't free, though. You need to pay for Internet signals, just like you pay for gas and electricity. For the privilege of surfing the Web, you do business with an *Internet Service Provider* known by the hip computing crowd as an *ISP.* You pay the ISP for a password and phone number to call. When your computer modem dials the number and connects to your ISP's network, you type your password and grab your surfboard: You've entered the Web.

✔ Some ISPs charge for each minute you're connected; others provide a flat fee for unlimited service. The going rate seems to be stabilizing at around $20 a month for unlimited service. Make sure that you find out your rate before hopping aboard, or you may be surprised at the end of the month.

✔ Good thing you glanced at the Tip icon: You *can* access the Internet for free, because some sites aren't charging anything at all. Freewwweb (www.freewwweb.com), one of the first freebie ISPs, lets users dial up from nearly anywhere in the United States and Canada. Then users can access the Web and send or receive e-mail.

✔ If you're computer-inclined, some ISPs provide hard disk space on their computers so that you can create *your* own Web pages for other Internet members to visit. Show the world pictures of your kids and cats, share your favorite recipes, talk about your favorite car waxes, or swap tips on constructing fishing flies!

✔ Different ISPs let you connect in different ways. The slowest ISPs connect through the phone lines with a modem. Faster still are special DSL lines that some phone companies provide. Some ISPs send their signals through satellites; some of the fastest come from your cable TV company. With the speedy ISPs, your location often determines your options.

What Do I Need to Access the World Wide Web?

A first-timer needs a computer, Internet browser software, a modem, and an ISP to connect to the Web. You have the computer, and the Internet Explorer Web browser comes wedged into almost every menu and crevice of Windows Me.

You can find an ISP listed in your local Yellow Pages under *Computers —
Online Services & Internet* or *Telecommunications.* Or ask your local computer
dealer for names and numbers. If you're desperate, double-click on the Setup
MSN Internet Account icon on the desktop of Windows Me to sign up for an
account. You may even find offers in your mailbox.

Open the Online Services folder on your desktop to choose between four
ISPs, including the popular America Online.

✔ Blatant Endorsement Department: If you use the Internet a lot, please
check with your cable provider to see if it offers cable modem service.
No more thumb-twiddling: Pictures, graphics, and animation simply pop
onto the screen. I love mine.

✔ Because techies created the Internet, it's often cumbersome for new
users to enter and navigate. Sometimes, your computer can slip into the
Internet just as easily as a crooked politician can. Other times, your
computer makes you fill out many forms and enter a lot of numbers
before you can access the Internet. Don't be afraid to ask a friend for
help the first time you connect to your ISP.

✔ Don't be afraid to bug your ISP for help, too. The best ISPs come with
technical support lines. A member of the support staff can talk you
through the installation process.

✔ Life rolls along much easier once you're aboard the Internet. The Web is
enormous, but it contains speedy indexes known as *search engines* that
ferret out your favorite goodies. Type in a subject, and the search engine
spits out bunches of applicable places to visit.

✔ Because Windows Me can run so many things in the background, forget-
ting to disconnect your Internet connection is an easy thing to do. If
you're being charged by the hour, keep a watchful eye on your Internet
browser and make sure that you log off when you no longer need to
access the service.

What Is a Web Browser?

Your Web browser is your Internet surfboard — your transportation to the
computers strewn along the Web. One browser, Internet Explorer 5.5, comes
free with Windows Me. Other people use a competing browser called
Netscape Communicator. People with too much time on their hands switch
back and forth between the two programs.

Both browsers work basically the same way. Every Web page comes with a
specific address, just like houses do. When you type that address into the
browser, the browser takes you there like a veteran cabby — unless you
make a typo when you're typing in the address.

To avoid typing laborious addresses (those www things), Web browsers allow for a lazy flipping through of Web pages. Web browsers read *hypertext*, or *Web links*. Web page owners embed addresses of other Web pages into their own Web pages. For example, the Web Museum Network in Paris (`www.sunsite.unc.edu/louvre/`) lets you visit museums from Australia to Singapore by simply clicking the museums' names.

Today's Web browsers come with little add-on bits of software for spicing things up. They can handle animated cartoons, voices, sounds, music, scrolling marquees, and other flashy goodies. If you kind of squint — and your computer's powerful enough — it looks like your computer's turning more and more into a TV.

- ✔ If your browser takes you to a boring Web page, there's a quick way to go back to the previous page. Click the big Back button at the top of your Web browser (on the top-left corner of Internet Explorer). Your Web browser immediately scurries back to the previous location.

- ✔ Many people use their Web sites to display collections of links to certain hobby areas, such as growing vegetables, weaving, or making cigars.

- ✔ Web sites come with *hyperlinks* — highlighted words or buttons that are linked to certain addresses of other computers on the Web. Click the button or highlighted word (usually underlined or a different color), and your Web browser takes you to the Web page with that address.

- ✔ Web site addresses look pretty strange. They usually start with the letters www and end with something even weirder looking, like `winespectator.com`. Now you know what all of those strange-looking words in parenthesis mean throughout this chapter. Other addresses skip the `www` and use `http://` instead. Yes, it's confusing.

- ✔ Sometimes, clicking on a Web address doesn't take you to the page. For example, if a friend e-mails you an address, you may need to type it in by hand. But here's how to avoid any misspellings: Highlight the Web address by holding down your mouse button and sliding the pointer over the address. Then hold down the Ctrl key and press C. (That copies the address.) Now, click in your browser's address box and, while holding down the Ctrl key, press V. By doing so, you paste the address in the address box. Press Enter, and your browser should whisk you off to that new site.

How Do I Navigate the Web with Microsoft Internet Explorer?

After you've chosen and set up your Internet Service Provider — either by choosing The Microsoft Network (MSN), America Online, AT&T WorldNet, Prodigy, or somebody *not* included in the Windows Me Online Services folder — you're ready to cruise the Internet.

Although Windows Me makes it easier than ever to hook up with an Internet provider, tweaking the settings can be a drag. First, try using the Internet Connection Wizard using the step-by-step process that I outline in Chapter 12. That cures most of the basic problems.

If you're still having trouble getting your computer set up for the Internet or you need more customized settings, a book like *The Internet For Dummies,* 7th Edition by John R. Levine, Carol Baroudi, and Margaret Levine Young, may help (published by IDG Books Worldwide, Inc.).

After you bring Internet Explorer to the screen, as shown in Figure 13-3, you can put it to work. The next few sections show how.

What's a Home page?

Just as your television set always shows a channel when you turn it on, your Web browser automatically displays a certain portion of the Internet.

This first Web page you see when a Web browser comes to life is called your *Home page.* Your browser's Home page is simply a Web page that always appears when the browser is first loaded. It's always the same Web site.

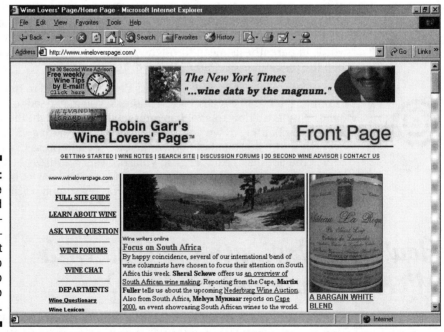

Figure 13-3: Click on the underlined words — *hyperlinks* — in Internet Explorer to head to other Web sites.

A Home page of a Web site, however, is a little different. It's like the cover of a magazine that lists the contents. Whenever you jump to a new Web site, you usually jump to the Home page of that site.

After you load your own Home page, you can move around the Internet, searching for topics by looking in indexes or simply pointing and clicking from topic to topic.

✔ Most Web browsers come with their own Home page preinstalled. After you install Internet Explorer and first log on to the Web, for example, you're whisked away to the Microsoft Home page. The competing company's browser, Netscape Navigator, takes you to the Netscape Home page.

✔ You can turn *any* Web site into your Home page — the first site that you see when you load your browser. Call up your favorite page in Internet Explorer and choose Internet Options from the Internet Explorer Tools menu. Click the General tab (that page usually opens automatically) and click the button marked Use Current. (It's the top-left button.) Click OK to save your efforts and return to browsing.

✔ To return to your Home page quickly while you're connected to the Internet, click the Home button along the top of Internet Explorer. (The Home button is at the very top of Figure 13-3, where the arrow is pointing.)

How do I move from Web page to Web page?

Internet Explorer lets you move from page to page in three different ways:

✔ Pointing and clicking a button or link that automatically whisks you away to another page

✔ Typing a complicated string of code words into the Address box of the Web browser and pressing Enter

✔ Clicking the navigation buttons along a browser's menu

The first way is the easiest. Look for *links* — highlighted words or pictures on a page — and click them. See the list of topics along the left side of Figure 13-3? Clicking "Learn About Wine" takes you to the Web page where Robin Garr offers basic education about his favorite beverage. Notice how those words are underlined. All of the other underlined words on his site are also links; clicking on any of them takes you to different pages dealing with that link's particular subject.

The second way is the most difficult. If a friend gives you a napkin with a cool Web page's address written on it, there's nothing to click. You need to type the Web site's address into your browser's Address box yourself. That's fairly easy, as long as you don't misspell anything. See the Web site address for the Wine page along the top of Figure 13-3? I typed www.wineloverspage.com into the Address box and pressed Enter; Internet Explorer scooted me to Robin Garr's Wine Lovers' Page. To head for the Volkswagen Web site, type in www.vw.com and press Enter. By pointing and clicking your way to that site's page with pictures of cars, you see the site in Figure 13-2.

Finally, you can maneuver through the Internet by clicking various parts of Internet Explorer itself. Clicking the Favorites button along the top reveals a folder where you can stash buttons leading to your favorite Web sites. Click History from the top-most menu to return to any page that you visited in the past few weeks.

Feel free to explore the Internet by simply clicking the buttons. You really can't get into any trouble; if you get stuck, you can always click the Home button along the top to move back into familiar territory.

✔ The easiest way to start surfing the Internet is to be a button pusher, so remember this bit o' wisdom: Watch how your mouse pointer changes shape as you move it over a Web page. If the pointer changes into a little hand, you're hovering over a button that aches to be pressed.

✔ Why the caution over buttons? Because Web page manufacturers get mighty creative these days, and it's often hard to tell where to point and click. Some buttons look like sturdy elevator buttons; others look more like fuzzy dice or vegetables. But when you click a button, the browser takes you to the page relating to that button. Clicking the fuzzy dice may bring up a betting odds sheet for local casinos, for example.

✔ Pointed and clicked yourself into a dead end? Click the Back button along the top, left-hand corner to head for the last Web page you visited. If you click the Back button long enough, you wind up back at the Home page, where you began.

✔ It's easy to copy text from the Internet. Slide your mouse pointer over the text while holding down the mouse button, just as if you were in a word processing program. When Internet Explorer highlights the text, press Ctrl+C to copy the text to the Clipboard. To copy a picture, right-click on the picture and select Save Picture As from the menu that appears.

How can I revisit my favorite places?

Sooner or later, you'll stumble across a Web page that's indescribably delicious. To make sure that you can find it again later, add it to your favorite pages folder. Click the folder marked Favorites from the top of the Internet Explorer menu and choose the Add to Favorites option after the menu tumbles down. Click OK to save your efforts.

To return to the page, click the Favorites folder along the top of the screen again, and then click the name of the link you want to revisit.

Librarian-types like to click the Organize Favorites button when the Favorites menu drops down. By doing so, they can create new folders for storing similar links and move related links from folder to folder.

What's an index or search engine?

Just as it is nearly impossible to find a book in a library without a card catalog, it is nearly impossible to find a Web site on the Internet without a good index. Luckily, several exist.

To find one, click the Internet Explorer Search button along the top of the menu. The Internet Explorer Search page appears, as shown in Figure 13-4.

Figure 13-4: Internet Explorer can access a search engine that scours the Web for any subject.

Type the name of the subject you're searching for — Cher, in this case — in the search box on the left and click the Search button. After a few seconds, Internet Explorer brings up a list of Web sites dealing with that subject. Click on any site that looks appealing, and Internet Explorer brings that page onto your computer screen.

- ✓ The Search page also searches for addresses, businesses, and maps. Click the More button to look up word definitions or locate pictures on the Internet. Click the Find in Newsgroups button to discover what people have been saying about your particular subject on the Internet's huge *bulletin boards* known as *Newsgroups*. (I cover Newsgroups later in this chapter.)

- ✓ Head for the bottom of the Search box to locate files or folders, computers on a network, or people logged into networked computers.

- ✓ Although the Search box is handy, it's just one way of finding information. The Internet's loaded with other search engines. To use a different search engine, type its Web address in the address box.

- ✓ My favorite search engine is www.alltheweb.com. It's zippedeedoodah-speedy. My second favorite is www.dogpile.com. This site takes your words and pours them in almost a dozen other search engines and then tells you what each search engine has located. Finally, www.google.com is the current rave. Give all three a try to see which search engine fits your needs.

- ✓ Searches usually come up with hundreds, or even thousands, of hits relating to your subject. If you come up with too many, try again, but be more specific.

How Does Windows Me Improve Internet Access?

Windows Me doesn't improve Internet access as much as it makes it more accessible by piling it onto menus. It includes a free Web browser — Internet Explorer — in addition to a bunch of free programs for chatting and video-conferencing over the Net, faster video access, more secure online transactions, and other exciting technojabber.

If you're typing in a long-and-laborious Web address — one you just typed in last night — Windows Me recognizes the address and types it in for you.

Although many of these goodies are already available in earlier versions of Windows through handfuls of upgrades, Windows Me provides an all-in-one package that's bound to be the standard. (Check out Chapter 17 to see some of the coolest goodies added to Windows Me.)

It Doesn't Work!

Don't feel bad. The Internet's been around for a while, but this whole Web thing is relatively new and quickly becoming overburdened. It's not supposed to work smoothly yet. Here are some of the most common problems and some possible solutions.

I can't get it to install!

Installing Internet Explorer isn't all that difficult; the hard part is telling Internet Explorer how to connect to your Internet Service Provider — the company that's providing the phone connection to the Internet.

Check out the Internet Connection Wizard described in Chapter 12. It displays your current settings and allows you to change them, if needed.

Because the ISPs all use slightly different ways to connect, your best bet is to call their tech support number and ask for help. (Be sure to call your Internet Service Provider, not Microsoft.)

Yeah, connecting to your ISP is a pain, but remember — you only have to connect to the thing once. After Internet Explorer has locked arms with your ISP, you can simply click a button to make it dial up the connection and start surfing.

I keep getting busy signals!

This problem means that your Internet Service Provider is probably offering a great deal — unlimited access to the Internet for one low price — or for nothing at all. Unfortunately, a bargain means that many people are going to be calling at the same time as you, leading to busy signals.

What's the answer? Reassess your priorities. Are you looking to save money or find a reliable connection to the Internet? You may be able to find a better deal with a different provider.

The Web page says it needs [insert name of weird plug-in thing here]!

Computer programmers abandoned their boring old TV sets and turned to their exciting new computers for entertainment. Now, they're trying to turn their computers back into TV sets. They're using fancy programming techniques called *Java, Shockwave, RealPlayer, QuickTime,* and other goodies to add animation and other gizmos to the Internet.

Programmers are also adding little software tidbits called "plug-ins" that increase your computer's capability to display flashy advertisements along the top of your screen.

What's the problem? New versions of these plug-ins follow the seasons. If your computer says it needs a plug-in or its latest version, click the button on the Web page that takes you to its download area.

Close down all your software (except for the Web browser), download the software, and install it. The next time you open your Web browser, the advertisements will have never looked better.

The Web page says that it's optimized for Navigator, not Explorer!

Many Web surfers use Netscape Navigator, not Internet Explorer. So, many programmers optimize their Web pages for the Navigator program.

Usually, this doesn't matter. Internet Explorer can usually display the page just as well as Netscape Navigator. Other times, the differences won't even be noticeable. In fact, many Web programmers put that line on their page just because they don't like Microsoft.

I can't figure any of this stuff out!

The Internet and its World Wide Web can be rough for beginners to figure out — and it's much too complex to be stuffed into a single chapter of this book. To pick up more information on the Internet and its wealth of information, head for the bookstore and pick up a copy of *The Internet Directory For Dummies,* 3rd Edition, by Brad Hill published by IDG Books Worldwide, Inc.

Managing E-Mail with Outlook Express

Internet Explorer merely flips through the Web pages stuffed onto the Internet, letting you jump from page to page.

Outlook Express, on the other hand, uses the Internet as a post office, letting you send letters and files to anybody with an Internet account. Best yet, the recipients of your e-mail don't have to use Outlook Express to view and respond to them: Almost any e-mail program can talk to almost any other one. (Some e-mail programs can't receive files well — or at all — but that's another story.)

This section guides you through setting up Outlook Express, writing a letter, sending it, and reading the responses.

Setting up Outlook Express 5.0

Outlook Express usually sends and receives mail through the same service you're using to access Web sites. However, it doesn't always work that way. Outlook Express is designed to work with an industry-standard Internet Service Provider that pipes the Internet signal to your computer without an online service getting in the way.

Outlook Express 5.0, the version included with Windows Me, doesn't work with online services like America Online (AOL). Those online services come with built-in e-mail programs that process mail differently than Outlook Express does. So if you're using America Online, don't bother reading this section. You won't be using Outlook Express 5.0.

If you're using a normal Internet Service Provider, however, you're in luck. Chances are, the Windows Me newly improved Internet Connection Wizard has already configured Outlook Express to send and receive your mail.

Can't get any e-mail, or is your account acting weird? Head back to Chapter 12 and check out the Internet Connection Wizard. You need the user name, phone number, and password given to you by your ISP.

To call up Outlook Express for the first time, double-click on its desktop icon: an envelope surrounded by twirling blue arrows. Or click on the tiny version of that icon next to your Start button. Or click the Start button and choose Outlook Express from Programs. Or . . . well, you get the idea. No matter which button you push, Outlook Express pops onto the screen, looking like Figure 13-5.

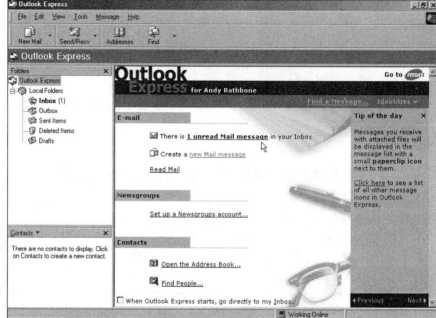

Figure 13-5:
Outlook
Express
sends and
receives
e-mail.

If Outlook Express asks for your name or a password, head back to Chapter 12
and run the Internet Connection Wizard, making sure to type your password
in the correct box. You gotta have that password, or you can't read your mail.
(Nobody else can read it, either — the password protects your e-mail from
prying eyes, no matter how gross that metaphor sounds.)

America Online users can't use Outlook Express 5.0 on their own computers
to send e-mail. However, they can still accept e-mail from somebody using
Outlook Express 5.0 or any other e-mail program.

The Outlook Express screen consists of three main parts: Folders, where you
store your e-mail; Contacts, which displays address book entries; and the
work screen, where you choose whether you'll be looking at e-mail or
Newsgroups. (I talk about Newsgroups later in this chapter.)

Getting ready to send e-mail

To send e-mail to a friend or enemy, you need three things:

> ✔ **A properly configured Outlook Express**
>
> The Internet Connection Wizard, which I describe in Chapter 12, automat-
> ically configures Outlook Express when it sets up Internet Explorer 5.0.

✔ **Your friend or enemy's e-mail address**

You need to find out your friend's e-mail address by simply asking them. There's no way to guess. It consists of a user name (which isn't always his or her real name), followed by the @ sign, followed by the name of the Internet Service Provider, be it America Online, Juno, or any of the thousands of other ISPs. The e-mail address of somebody with the user name of Jeff9435 who subscribes to America Online would be `jeff9435@aol.com`.

✔ **Your message**

Here's where the fun part starts: typing your letter. After you type in the e-mail address and the letter, you're ready to send your message along its merry way.

You can find e-mail addresses on business cards, Web sites, and even return addresses: Whenever anybody sends you some e-mail, you can see his or her e-mail address for responding.

It doesn't matter if you capitalize part of an e-mail address or not. The message still arrives there. But any misspellings in the address can make the message "bounce" back to your own mailbox with a confusing "undeliverable" message attached.

Composing a letter

Ready to send your first letter? Follow these steps to compose your letter and to drop it in the electronic mailbox, sending it through virtual space to your friend's electronic mailbox.

New Mail

1. **Click the New Mail icon in the upper-left corner of Outlook Express.**

   A New Message window appears, as shown in Figure 13-6.

2. **Type your friend's e-mail address into the To: box.**

   Type whatever the person's e-mail happens to be.

3. **Fill in the Subject: box.**

   This one's optional, but it helps your friend know what your e-mail is about so that he or she can choose to respond right away or file it in the "I'll respond when I get around to it" box.

4. **Type your message in the large box at the box's bottom.**

   Type whatever you want, and for as long as you want. There's very little limit on the size of a text file.

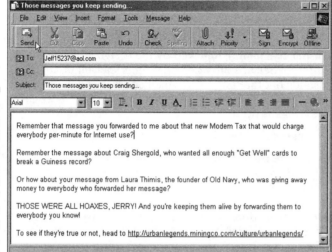

Figure 13-6:
Type an
e-mail
address in
the To: box,
and type
your
message in
the big box
below.

5. **Click the Send button in the box's top, left corner.**

   Whoosh! Outlook Express whisks your message through the Internet pipelines to your friend's mailbox. Depending on the speed of the Internet connections, mail arrives anywhere within 15 seconds to 5 days, with a few minutes being the average.

   Not too good of a speler? Then click the spellcheck button from the icons along the top. Or click on Tools and choose Spelling from the menu that appears. Or push your F7 key. Or grab a dictionary off the shelf. (Pressing F7 is quicker.)

   Microsoft pulled a dirty trick on the spell checker. Outlook Express borrows the spellchecker that comes with Microsoft Word, Microsoft Excel, or Microsoft PowerPoint. If you don't have any of those programs, the spell checker won't work. (That's why the Spelling button is grayed out in Figure 13-6.)

   Want to attach a file to your message? After completing Step 4, click the paper clip icon. Windows Me brings up a box straight out of My Computer. Navigate through the folders to reach the file that you want to send and then double-click on its name. When you click the Send button in Step 5, Outlook Express sends your message — and the attached file — to your friend. (Most ISPs balk at sending files larger than about 4MB, though.)

Reading a received letter

If you keep Outlook Express running 24 hours a day, you'll know when a new letter drops into your mailbox. Most computers make a breezy little sound to notify you of its arrival. You'll also spot a tiny Outlook Express icon sitting in the bottom-right corner of your desktop, right next to the digital clock.

To check for any new mail if Outlook Express isn't running, load it from the Start menu, toolbar, or any other way that's convenient.

Then follow these steps to read your letter and either respond or file it away into one of Outlook Express' convenient folders.

1. **Open Outlook Express.**

   When Outlook Express fills the screen, it says you have an unread mail message in your Inbox, as shown in Figure 13-7.

2. **Click on the words *Read Mail* to read your new message.**

   The new message appears, as shown in Figure 13-8, ready for you to read.

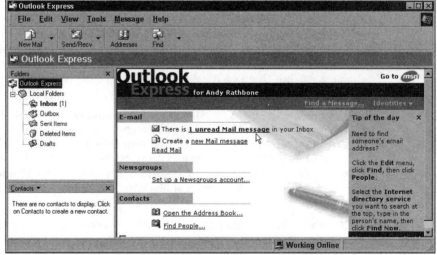

Figure 13-7:
Click in Outlook Express to unveil your newly received message.

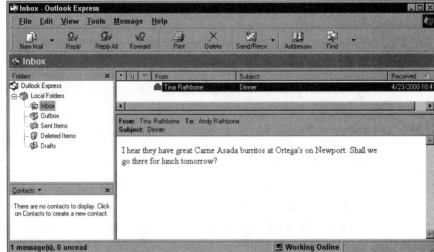

Figure 13-8:
Read your
new
message.

From here, Outlook Express leaves you with many options, each described below.

- ✔ You can do nothing. The message stays in your Inbox folder until you delete it.

- ✔ You can respond to the message. Click the Reply icon along the top of Outlook Express, and a new box appears, ready for you to type in a message. The box is just like the one that appears when you first compose a message, but there's a big difference: This box is preaddressed with the recipient's name and the subject.

- ✔ You can file the message. Use the Folders window on the left. Right-click on Local Folders, choose New Folder, and type a name like Personal or Business into the Folder name box. Your newly created folder is listed beneath Local Folders. Drag and drop the message's header — the line with a little envelope next to the sender's name — to that folder for organized safekeeping. It works just like Windows Explorer, which I cover in Chapter 11.

- ✔ You can print the message. Click the Print icon along the menu's top, and Outlook Express shoots your message to the printer to make a paper copy.

- ✔ Outlook Express can be confusing when you file a message: As you drag the message over to the folders, the little envelope icon turns into a circle with a diagonal line through it. Don't fret. That menacing circle disappears when the mouse rests over a folder that's ready to accept a message.

- ✔ Outlook Express can handle more complicated tasks, but these basic steps enable you to send and receive e-mail to your friends and congressional leaders.

What does the "News" area do?

Thousands of people with similar interests yak it up on the Internet through something called *Newsgroups*. Newsgroups work sort of like mail that everybody gets to read.

A Newsgroup is like a public bulletin board. One person posts a message or file, and then everybody can read it and post their own replies, which spawns more replies.

To keep Newsgroups on track, they are divided by subject — usually more than 30,000 of them — and Outlook Express can display all the subjects on your screen when you double-click on the word News or choose Subscribe to Newsgroups on the main window, as shown in Figure 13-9.

When you first subscribe to the Newsgroups, Outlook Express searches for names of *all* the Newsgroups carried by your Internet Service Provider and displays them on the screen. Collecting the names and descriptions of thousands of Newsgroups takes some time, as shown in Figure 13-10, so play FreeCell for awhile. Luckily, Outlook only searches for the Newsgroups once, and then it remembers them all.

Figure 13-9:
Double-click the word *News* or choose *Subscribe to Newsgroups* to see all the Newsgroups on the Internet.

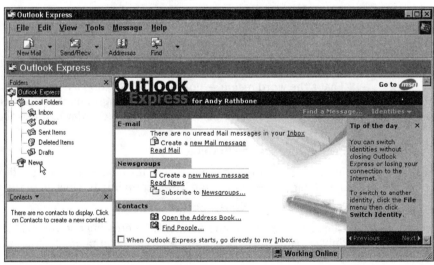

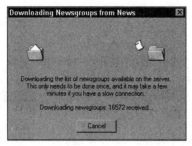

Finding and reading a Newsgroup

With many thousands of Newsgroups, how can you find the right one? Well, start by making Outlook Express find it for you. For example, here's how to find and subscribe to a Newsgroup with discussions on recipes.

1. **Make Outlook Express gather a list of Newsgroup names.**

   Discussed in the preceding section, the searching for Newsgroup names must only be conducted once. (Thank goodness, because it can take a l-o-n-g time.)

2. **Type** `recipe` **in the box named Display Newsgroups Which Contain.**

   That's the word *recipe* — nothing else. As soon as you begin to type, Outlook Express begins weeding out Newsgroups that don't contain the letters of the word *recipe*. Eventually, only the Newsgroups that deal with recipes remain on your screen.

3. **Search through the findings.**

   In this case, a dozen or so Newsgroups deal with recipes. Click on the scroll bar to the right of the Newsgroup box to view all of the findings.

4. **Subscribe to the Newsgroup you want.**

   Click a Newsgroup name that looks interesting and then click the Subscribe button to the right. A little icon appears beside the name to let you know that you've subscribed. Subscribe to as many or as few Newsgroups as you want.

5. **After subscribing to your chosen Newsgroups, click the OK button.**

   Your newly chosen Newsgroups now appear at the very bottom of the folders on the left side of the Outlook Express window.

6. Click one of your recently subscribed names.

A list of postings in that particular Newsgroup appears on the right side of the screen, as shown in Figure 13-11.

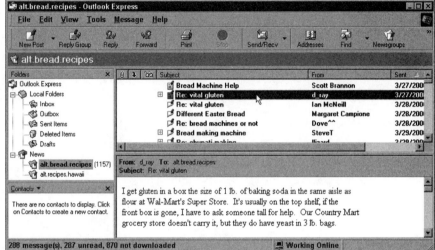

Figure 13-11: After subscribing to Newsgroups, click on one of their names to see the postings.

7. Finally, click one of the postings to see what that person has written about the topic.

In Figure 13-11, for example, you click on Re: vital gluten, and Outlook Express brings up the message in a window, just as if it were e-mail. (The "Re:" in front of vital gluten means that message is a response to somebody's message about vital gluten.)

That's it; you've subscribed to the wacky world of Newsgroups, where you can find people chatting about nearly every subject imaginable — and some unimaginable ones as well.

✔ To respond to a Newsgroup post, treat it as if it were e-mail. Click the Reply button at the top of the window, type your response, and click the Send button.

✔ Newsgroups are public information, as opposed to e-mail, which is private. Don't say anything on a Newsgroup that might hurt your chances for public office. (And don't write anything that you wouldn't want your parents, spouse, boss, or next-door neighbor to read.)

✔ Some of the information on Newsgroups deals with very adult-oriented content. Make sure that you know what Newsgroups your kids are reading.

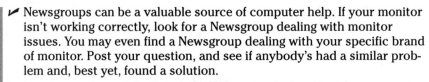

✔ Newsgroups can be a valuable source of computer help. If your monitor isn't working correctly, look for a Newsgroup dealing with monitor issues. You may even find a Newsgroup dealing with your specific brand of monitor. Post your question, and see if anybody's had a similar problem and, best yet, found a solution.

✔ Many people who hang out on Newsgroups view themselves as "old-timers" who resent any encroachment on their territory. Before posting, spend some time "lurking" on a Newsgroup to get a taste of its particular flavor and decorum. Read the current posts for a few days to catch the group's flavor before adding your own spice.

Part IV
Help!

The 5th Wave   By Rich Tennant

"GENTLEMEN, I SAY RATHER THAN FIX THE 'BUGS', WE CHANGE THE DOCUMENTATION AND CALL THEM 'FEATURES'."

In this part . . .

*W*indows Me can do hundreds of tasks in dozens of ways. This means that approximately one million things can fail at any given time.

Some problems are easy to fix. For example, one misplaced pair of clicks in the taskbar makes all your programs disappear. Yet one more click in the right place puts them all back.

Other problems are far more complex, requiring teams of computer surgeons to diagnose, remedy, and bill accordingly.

This part helps you separate the big problems from the little ones. You'll know whether you can fix it yourself with a few clicks and a kick. If your situation's worse, you'll know when it's time to call in the surgeons.

Chapter 14

The Case of the Broken Window

Sometimes, you just have a sense that something's wrong. The computer makes quiet grumbling noises, or Windows Me starts running more slowly than Congress. Other times, something's obviously wrong. Pressing any key triggers a beeping noise, menus keep shooting at you, or Windows Me greets you with a cheery error message when you first turn it on.

Many of the biggest-looking problems are solved by the smallest-looking solutions. This chapter may be able to point you to the right one.

Making a Startup Disk

Unless you grab a spare floppy right now, this information won't do you any good. See, Windows Me can make a startup disk for emergencies. When Windows Me refuses to load, you can pop the disk into your computer's mouth, push the reset button, and a bare-bones version of Windows Me comes to the screen. That bare-bones version may be enough to get you started. At the very least, it can make it easier for a computer guru friend to get your computer started.

So grab a floppy disk that's blank or doesn't have important information on it. This procedure erases the disk's contents, and there's no turning back.

1. **Double-click the Control Panel's Add/Remove Programs icon.**

   You can load the Control Panel by clicking Settings in the Start menu.

2. **Click the Windows Startup Disk tab.**

   It's the rightmost tab of the three along the top.

3. **Click the Create Disk button.**

   After grunting a little bit, Windows Me tells you to insert a disk into drive A. Before pushing the disk into the drive, grab a felt-tip pen and write Emergency Startup Disk on the floppy disk's label.

4. **Insert a blank disk into drive A when told; then click the OK button.**

   Windows Me formats the blank disk and copies special files onto it, allowing it to start your computer in the worst of situations. Put the disk in a safe place and hope you never have to use it.

   • In an emergency, put the disk in drive A and push your computer's reset button — that "last resort" button that's one step shy of turning the power switch on and off. The computer "boots" off the floppy disk; that is, the computer comes to life, even though its hard drive isn't working.

   • When loaded from the floppy disk, Windows Me comes up in "DOS prompt" mode. It won't look anything like the real Windows Me, but a computer guru may be able to use the DOS prompt as a doorway to fix whatever's gone wrong.

Restoring Calm with System Restore

It has happened to everybody. Windows works fine until something happens; then it's all over. For instance, you delete a program and Windows begins hitting you up with an error message each time it loads.

Or you install a new program, which promptly disconnects your scanner, digital camera, modem, or all three.

Wouldn't you love to go back in time to when Windows worked right?

When your system is working fine, open System Restore. (Choose Programs from the Start menu, choose Accessories, open System Tools, and click System Restore.) Push the System Restore button that saves your system's current settings. Also, before installing a program, push the computer's "save" button to save its current state of mind.

You can save many System Restore settings — each one is a snapshot of your computer's configuration.

By thinking ahead and saving your computer's mental condition when things are fine, you'll be able to return it to that frame of mind if Windows starts misbehaving.

My Mouse Doesn't Work Right

Sometimes, the mouse doesn't work at all; other times, the mouse pointer hops across the screen like a flea. Here are a few things to look for:

- ✔ If no mouse arrow is on the screen when you start Windows, make sure that the mouse's tail is plugged snugly into the computer's rump. Then exit and restart Windows Me.

- ✔ If the mouse arrow is on-screen but won't move, Windows may be mistaking your brand of mouse for a different brand. You can make sure that Windows Me recognizes the correct type of mouse by following the steps on adding new hardware, as described in Chapter 9.

- ✔ A mouse pointer can jump around on-screen if it's dirty. First, turn the mouse upside-down and clean off any visible dirt stuck to the bottom. Then twist the little round cover until the mouse ball pops out. Wipe off any crud and blow any dust out of the hole. Pull any stray hairs, dust, and goo off the little rollers and stick the ball back inside the mouse. If you wear wool sweaters (or have a cat that sleeps on the mouse pad), you may have to clean the ball every week or so.

- ✔ If the mouse was working fine and now the buttons seem to be reversed, you've probably changed the right- or left-handed button configuration setting in the Control Panel. Double-click the Control Panel's Mouse icon and make sure that the configuration is set up to match your needs. (That's covered in Chapter 9, by the way.)

I'm Stuck in Menu Land

If your keystrokes don't appear in your work but instead make a bunch of menus shoot out from the top of the window, you're stuck in Menu Land. Somehow, you've pressed and released Alt, an innocent-looking key that's easy to hit accidentally.

When you press and release Alt, Windows turns its attention away from your work and toward the menus along the top of the window.

To get back to work, press and release Alt one more time. Alternatively, press Esc. One or the other is your ticket out of Menu Land.

I'm Supposed to Install a New Driver

When you buy a new toy for the computer, it usually comes with a piece of software called a *driver*. A driver is a sort of translator that lets Windows know how to boss around the new toy. If you buy a new keyboard, sound card, compact disc player, printer, mouse, monitor, or almost any other computer toy, you usually need to install its driver in Windows. Luckily, it's a fairly painless process covered in the section on adding new hardware in Chapter 9.

✔ Companies constantly update drivers, fixing problems or making the drivers communicate better. If the computer device is misbehaving, a newer driver may calm it down. Call the manufacturer and ask for the latest version. Or if you've entered the world of the Internet, fire up your modem and head for the manufacturer's Web page so that you can grab a free copy.

✔ To find the company's Web page, rev up Internet Explorer, head to the www.yahoo.com Web site, and type the company's name. Chances are, Yahoo! can dig it up and let you head there with a mouse click.

✔ Not all computer toys work with Windows Me. In fact, some games don't even work with some sound cards, and some software won't work with certain CD-ROM drives. Bring a list of your computer's parts to the store and check them with the requirements listed on the side of a computer toy's box before setting down the cash.

✔ To get a list of your computer's parts, right-click the My Computer icon and click the Device Manager tab. Click the Print button and click OK. You might not be able to make sense of the detailed computer information, but the folks at the store can decipher the numbers.

✔ After you've registered Windows Me, a program called Windows Update handles many chores for keeping Windows Me up to date. Windows Update dials a special place on the Internet and downloads updated information your computer might need.

His Version of Windows Me Has More Programs Than Mine!

Windows Me installs itself differently on different types of computers. As it copies itself over to a hard drive, it brings different files with it. If installed on a laptop, for example, Windows Me brings along programs that help a laptop transfer files and keep track of its battery life.

Computers with smaller hard drives will probably get the minimum files Windows Me needs to run. Chapter 12 describes some of the programs and accessories Windows Me comes with; here's how to copy them to your computer if Windows Me left them off the first time.

1. **Double-click the Control Panel's Add/Remove Programs icon.**

   You can load the Control Panel by clicking Settings in the Start menu.

2. **Click the Windows Setup tab.**

   It's the tab in the middle of the three along the top; after a moment of thumb-twiddling, a box appears that shows the various components of Windows Me, as well as the amount of space they need to nestle onto your computer's hard drive.

3. **Click in the little box by the programs or accessories you want to add.**

   A check mark appears in the box of the items you've selected. To select part of a category — a portion of the accessories, for example — click the category's name and click the Details button. Windows Me lists the items available in that category, so you can only click the ones you want. If you clicked the Details button, click the OK button to continue back at the main categories list.

4. **Click the OK button and insert your installation disks when asked.**

   Windows Me copies the necessary files from your installation disks onto your hard drive. You can remove a Windows Me accessory by *removing* the check mark from the box next to its name.

Windows Me comes with some pretty weird stuff, so don't get carried away and copy *all* of it over — especially stuff that you're not even going to use.

I Clicked the Wrong Button (But Haven't Lifted My Finger Yet)

Clicking the mouse takes two steps: a push and a release. If you click the wrong button on-screen and haven't lifted your finger yet, press the Esc button and slowly slide the mouse pointer off the button on-screen. Then take your finger off the mouse.

The screen button pops back up, and Windows Me pretends nothing happened. Thankfully.

My Computer Is Frozen Up Solid

Every once in a while, Windows just drops the ball and wanders off somewhere to sit under a tree. You're left looking at a computer that just looks back. Panicked clicks don't do anything. Pressing every key on the keyboard doesn't do anything — or worse yet, the computer starts to beep at every key press.

When nothing on-screen moves except the mouse pointer, the computer is frozen up solid. Try the following approaches, in the following order, to correct the problem:

Approach 1: Press Esc twice.

That action usually doesn't work, but give it a shot anyway.

Approach 2: Press Ctrl, Alt, and Delete all at the same time.

If you're lucky, Windows flashes an error message saying that you've discovered an "unresponsive application" and lists the names of currently running programs — including the one that's not responding. Click the name of the program that's causing the mess and click the End Task button. You lose any unsaved work in it, of course, but you should be used to that. (If you somehow stumbled onto the Ctrl+Alt+Delete combination by accident, press Esc at the unresponsive-application message to return to Windows.)

If that still doesn't do the trick, try clicking the Shut Down button that's next to the End Task button (pressing Ctrl+Esc, then U and S), or pressing Ctrl+Alt+Delete again. That shuts down your computer and lets you start over.

Approach 3: If the preceding approaches don't work, push the computer's reset button.

The screen is cleared, and the computer acts like you turned it off and on again. When the dust settles, Windows Me should return to life.

Approach 4: If not even the reset button works, turn the computer off, wait 30 seconds, and then turn it back on again.

Don't ever flip the computer off and on again quickly. Doing so can damage its internal organs.

The Printer Isn't Working Right

If the printer's not working right, start with the simplest solution first: Make sure that it's plugged into the wall and turned on. Surprisingly, this step fixes about half the problems with printers. Next, make sure that the printer cable is snugly nestled in the ports on both the printer and the computer. Then check to make sure that it has enough paper — and that the paper isn't jammed in the mechanism.

Then try printing from different programs, such as WordPad and Notepad, to see whether the problem's with the printer, Windows Me, or a particular Windows program. Try printing the document by using different fonts. All these chores help pinpoint the culprit.

Could your printer be out of ink or toner? Sometimes these calamities can stop a printer from working.

For a quick test of a printer, choose Printers from the Start button's Settings menu. Right-click on your printer's icon, choose Properties, and click the Print Test Page button. If your printer sends you a nicely printed page, the problem is probably with the software, not the printer.

The Windows Help program can also pitch in; click Help from the Start menu, click the Index tab, and type the word **printers** into the box. Press Enter to find the printers help section; then choose the printer's troubleshooting program to figure out why the printer's goofing off.

If you don't have access to the Internet, call the printer's manufacturer and ask for a new Windows driver. When the disk comes in the mail, follow the instructions in the printer section of Chapter 9.

If you can get on the Internet, head to the printer manufacturer's Web site and look for the latest driver. Chances are, you'll find the manufacturer listed at Yahoo! (www.yahoo.com), a huge Internet search engine that's particularly efficient at finding businesses.

My Double-Clicks Are Now Single-Clicks!

In an effort to make things easier, Windows Me lets people choose whether a single-click or a double-click should open a file or folder.

But if you're not satisfied with the click method Windows Me uses, here's how to change it:

1. **Open the Control Panel from the Start button's Settings menu and choose Folder Options.**

2. **Choose your click preference in the Click Items As Follows section.**

3. **Click OK to save your preferences.**

Don't like to follow steps? Just click the Folder Options' Restore Defaults button, and Windows will bring back double-clicking.

Chapter 15

Error Messages (What You Did Does Not Compute)

*M*ost people don't have any trouble understanding error messages. A car's pleasant beeping tone means that you've left your keys in the ignition. An electronic stuttering sound from the stereo means that your compact disc has problems.

Things are different with Windows Me, however. The error messages in Windows Me could have been written by a Senate subcommittee, if only they weren't so brief. When Windows Me tosses an error message your way, it's usually just a single sentence. Windows Me rarely describes what you did to cause the error, and even worse, hardly ever tells you how to make the error go away.

Here are some of the phrases that you'll find in the most common error messages that Windows Me throws in your face. This chapter explains what Windows Me is trying to say, why it's saying it, and just what the heck it expects you to do.

Not Enough Memory

Meaning: Windows Me is running out of the room it needs to operate.

Probable cause: You have too many windows opened on the screen.

Solutions: A short-term solution is to close some of the windows. Also, make sure that you're not using a large color picture of a peacock for wallpaper. A single large picture consumes lots of memory. Windows devotes much less memory when tiling small pictures across the screen (see Chapter 9 for information about tiling windows). If Windows Me still acts sluggish, click the Start button, select Shut Down, and select the Restart the Computer option.

For a long-term solution, make sure that you have plenty of empty space on your hard drive so that Windows has room to read and write information. Delete any files or programs that you don't use.

The Disk Cleanup program, which I describe in Chapter 12, rummages through your hard drive and automatically clears it of file detritus. For best results, keep your hard drive less than ¾ full.

Finally, consider buying some more memory. Windows works much better with 64MB of memory than with 32MB of memory. And 128MB of memory is better still. Today, people are walking out the door with 256MB of memory in their laptops, and nobody's laughing. In fact, the old timers are crying because memory costs about one-tenth of what it did five years ago.

Whenever you cut or copy a large amount of information to the Clipboard, that information stays there, taking up memory — even after you paste it into another application. To clear out the Clipboard after a large paste operation, copy a single word to the Clipboard. Doing so replaces the earlier, memory-hogging chunk, freeing some memory for other programs.

Please Insert a Disk into Drive A:

Meaning: Windows can't find a floppy disk in drive A.

Probable cause: No floppy disk is in drive A.

Solution: Slide a disk in and wish all errors were this easy to fix. (Click the Cancel button if you don't have a floppy disk and want Windows Me to stop waiting for one.)

The Disk in the Destination Drive Is Full

Meaning: Windows Me has run out of room on a floppy disk or on the hard drive to store something.

Probable cause: Windows Me tried saving something to a disk file, but it ran out of space.

Solution: Clear more room on that disk before saving your work. Delete any junk files on the hard disk. Try running the Disk Cleanup program that I describe in Chapter 12. Use the Control Panel's Add/Remove programs feature to delete any programs you don't use anymore. Also, in this era when the most rowdy computer games often require 2GB of hard drive space, it may be time for you to upgrade to a larger hard drive.

Confidential to Sue in Illinois: When Windows says the disk is full, it stops copying the file. Windows won't break your large file in half at that point and copy the file's second half to a different floppy disk.

The File or Folder That This Shortcut Refers to Can't Be Found

Meaning: Windows Me can't find the program, file, or folder that's supposed to be attached to a Shortcut icon.

Probable cause: You may have moved, renamed, or deleted a program, file, or folder after a shortcut was attached to it.

Solution: Try using the Windows Me Search program, which I describe in Chapter 7. If the Search program can't find it, double-click the Recycle Bin to see if the missing program is in there and can be salvaged. Or, if you're sure the shortcut's program, file, or folder is gone for good, right-click the shortcut and choose Delete to get rid of it.

This Filename Is Not Valid

Meaning: Windows Me refuses to accept your choice of filename.

Probable cause: You've tried to name a file by using one or more of the forbidden characters.

Solution: Turn to the section about renaming a file in Chapter 11 and make sure that you're not naming a file something you shouldn't.

This File Is a Program. If You Remove It, You Will No Longer Be Able to Run This Program or Edit Some Documents.

Meaning: You're trying to delete a file containing a program.

Probable cause: You're clearing off some hard disk space to make room for incoming programs. You may have accidentally tried to delete something you shouldn't have.

Solution: Click the No button to say, no, you don't want to delete the file. In the future, try to figure out what you're deleting before sending it to the slaughterhouse. (Right-click the file and choose Properties, for instance, to read the file's vital statistics.)

Make sure that you have the program's box sitting on the shelf so you can reinstall it if you decide you need it after all.

Above all, use the Control Panel's Add/Remove Programs icon if you're intentionally trying to remove a program.

Open with . . .

Meaning: Windows Me doesn't know what program created the file that you've double-clicked, so it's asking *you* to figure it out. Click Open With, and Windows Me places a list of programs on the screen and asks you to choose the right one.

Probable cause: Windows Me usually sticks secret hidden codes, known as *file extensions,* onto the ends of filenames. Notepad, for example, uses the letters TXT. When you double-click the Notepad icon, Windows Me spots the secret, hidden TXT letters and uses the Notepad program to open the file. If Windows doesn't recognize the secret code letters, however, it complains with this error message.

Solution: This problem's a little rough, so you may have to experiment. If you know what program created that file, choose it from the list of programs. Then select the Always Use This Program To Open These Files check box. Finally, click the OK button, and your problem should be solved.

Don't have the foggiest idea which program should open that file? Notepad's always a good start. Choose Notepad, click the OK button, and double-click your mystery file again. If your screen fills with legible text, you're saved! Close Notepad and double-click the mischievous file again. This time, however, select the Always Use This Program To Open This File check box so that Windows Me learns that Notepad should always open that type of file.

You Must Type a Filename

Meaning: Windows Me insists that you type a filename into the box.

Probable cause: You've chosen (accidentally or otherwise) the Rename command from a menu or clicked an icon's title in *just the right way*. Now the file's original name has disappeared, your cursor is stuck in the filename box, and you can't escape this dreadful error message.

Solution: Type in a new filename — consisting of mostly numbers and letters — to describe the file. If you've been trapped inside the rename box by mistake, press your keyboard's Esc key. The Rename box resumes its old filename and sets you free.

Cannot Open Internet . . . A Connection to the Server Could Not Be Established.

Meaning: Your Internet browser can't connect to your Internet Service Provider.

Probable cause: Your Internet Service Provider may be turned off temporarily, but most likely your Internet Browser's settings are probably configured incorrectly.

Solution: Use the Internet Connection Wizard that I describe in Chapter 12. If that doesn't work or proves too frustrating, wait awhile. Play cards. Sniff flowers in the garden. Paint a watercolor picture of your shoes. Sometimes, an ISP goes down to preserve its users' mental health.

Have to get online *right now?* Head for www.freewwweb.com, which I describe in Chapter 12, and sign up for a new (and free) ISP account, on the spot. By juggling several different ISPs, you can usually stay online, even through national disasters.

My Computer Keeps Saying That Windows Me Wasn't Properly Shut Down!

Meaning: You probably turned your computer off without giving Windows time to "brace itself."

Probable cause: If your computer complains that it wasn't properly shut down when you first turn it on to begin work, that usually means you succumbed to temptation: You just flipped the computer's Off switch when you were done working. That's a Compu-No-No.

Solution: When you want to turn off your computer, click the Start button and choose Shut Down from the menu that shoots up. When Windows Me says it's okay to turn off your computer, it's okay to reach for the Off switch.

Chapter 16

Help on the Windows Me Help System

*W*hen you raise your hand in just the right way, Windows Me walks over and offers you some help.

In many instances, it has so much help to offer, it throws it at you in big chunks. The Windows Help program rarely gives you a straight answer. Instead, it prefers to direct you to another location, a horrible computerized answering machine sending you from computerized location to location.

This chapter squeezes some helpful tidbits on using the Windows Help system.

Get Me Some Help, and Fast!

Don't bother plowing through this whole chapter if you don't need to: Here are the quickest ways to make Windows Me dish out helpful information when you're stumped. I explain each tip more fully later in this chapter.

Press F1

When you're confused in Windows Me, press the F1 key or choose Help from the Start button's menu. The F1 key always stands for "Help!" Most of the time, Windows Me checks to see what program you're using and fetches some helpful information about that particular program or your current situation. Other times, pressing F1 brings up a huge Help program, which gets its own section later in this chapter.

Click the right mouse button on the confusing part

Windows Me constantly flings confusing questions onto the screen, expecting you to come up with an answer. If you know where to tackle the program, however, you can often shake loose some helpful chunks of information.

When a particular button, setting, box, or menu item has your creativity stifled, click it with your right (the opposite of left) mouse button. A What's This? box often appears, as shown in Figure 16-1, letting you know that Windows Me can offer help about that particular area. Click the What's This? box, and Windows Me tosses extra information onto the screen, as shown in Figure 16-2, explaining the confusing area you clicked on.

Figure 16-1: Click a confusing button with the right mouse button to get the What's This? button.

When confused about something on-screen, make Windows Me explain it: Click the confusing item with your right mouse button and click the What's This? box that pops up.

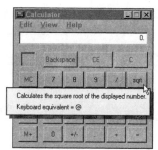

Figure 16-2:
Clicking the
What's
This? button
brings more
information
your way.

Choose Help from the main menu

If pressing F1 doesn't get you anywhere, look for the word Help in the menu along the top of the confusing program. Click Help, and a menu drops down, usually listing two words: Help Topics and About. Click Help Topics to make the Windows Me Help program leap to the screen and bring assistance to your dilemma. (Clicking About just brings a version number to the screen, which can be dangerously irritating when you're looking for something a little more helpful.)

Sending in the Troubleshooters

Sometimes, the Windows Me Help program scores big: It tells you exactly how to solve your particular problem. Unfortunately, however, the Help program occasionally says you need to load a *different* program to solve your problem. (Don't get grumpy, though: Save your real angst for long touch-tone menus.)

To let Windows Me fix its own problems, follow these steps:

1. **Choose Help from the Start menu.**

2. **Choose Troubleshooting from the What Would You Like Help With? menu.**

   As you can see in Figure 16-3, a torrent of computer subjects tumbles from the menu, from Audio-visual problems to Problems with programs.

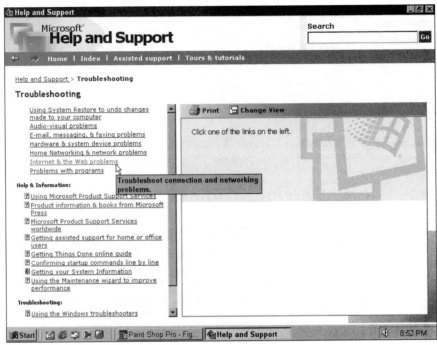

Figure 16-3:
The
Troubleshooter
programs
help solve a
wide variety
of problems.

3. Click the subject that troubles you.

Click Internet & the Web problems, for example, if the Web is being weird, and Windows unveils its Troubleshooter "robots" designed for different problems. Choose the Modem Troubleshooter if that's your problem.

4. Answer the Troubleshooter's questions.

As you answer the questions, shown in Figure 16-4, Windows narrows down your problem until it decides whether it can fix things itself, or whether the situation requires outside intervention. (In which case, you need to beg assistance from the computer store or manufacturer, the computer guy at work, or a neighboring 12-year-old.)

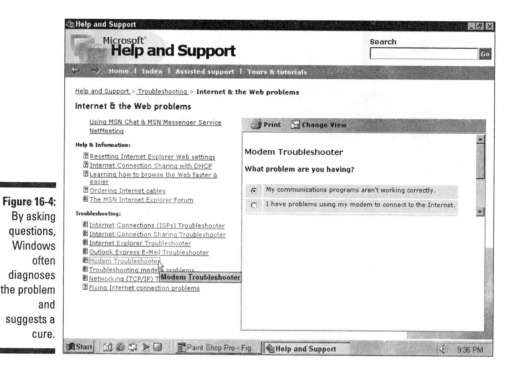

Figure 16-4:
By asking
questions,
Windows
often
diagnoses
the problem
and
suggests a
cure.

Consulting the Windows Me Built-In Computer Guru

Almost every Windows program has the word Help in its top menu. Click
Help, and the Windows Me built-in computer guru rushes to your aid. For
example, click Help in Paint, and you see the menu shown in Figure 16-5.

Figure 16-5:
Click Help
when you
need
"Help!"

To pick the computer guru's brain, click Help Topics, and Windows Me pops up the box shown in Figure 16-6. This box is the table of contents for all the help information Windows Me can offer on the Paint program.

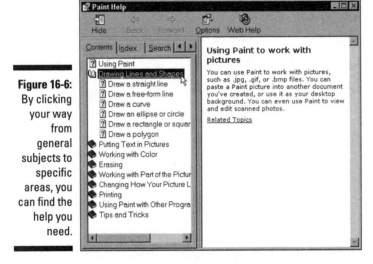

Figure 16-6: By clicking your way from general subjects to specific areas, you can find the help you need.

See any subject that covers what you're confused about? Then choose it. For example, if Erasing has you stumped, choose the word *Erasing;* the Help program then shows what additional help it can offer, as shown in Figure 16-7.

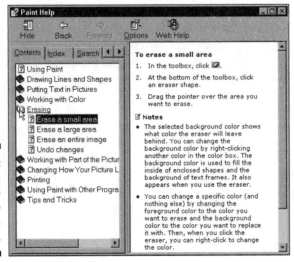

Figure 16-7: Choose a topic to see more specific help areas.

Want to see more information on erasing an entire image? Click that listed subject, and a new window pops up, as shown in Figure 16-8, bringing even more detailed information to the screen.

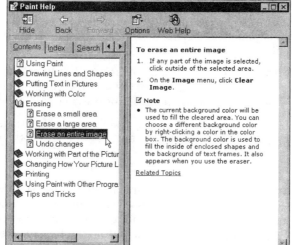

Figure 16-8: Click on items bearing a question mark to see information about those items.

Windows Me can offer help with any underlined topic. As the mouse pointer nears an underlined topic, the pointer turns into a little hand. When the hand points at the phrase that has you stumped, click the mouse button. For example, click Related Topics in the Paint Help box, and Windows Me displays more help on similar subjects, as shown in Figure 16-9.

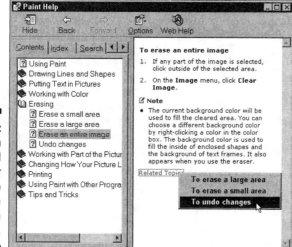

Figure 16-9: Click on underlined words or topics to see more information about them.

The Windows Me Help system is sometimes a lot of work, forcing you to wade through increasingly detailed menus to find specific information. Still, it can be much faster than paging through the awkward Windows Me manual. And it's often much faster than tracking down the newly pocket-protected neighbor who's just announced himself to be a "computer expert."

✔ The quickest way to find help in any Windows Me program is to press F1. Windows automatically jumps to the table of contents page for the help information it has for the current program.

✔ Windows Me packs a lot of information into its Help boxes; some of the words usually scroll off the bottom of the window. To see them, click the scroll bar, which I describe in Chapter 5, or press PgDn.

✔ Sometimes, you click the wrong topic, and Windows Me brings up something really dumb. Click the Contents button at the top of the window, and Windows Me scoots back to the contents page. From there, click a different topic to move in a different direction.

✔ Underlined phrases and words appear throughout the Windows Me Help system. Whenever you click something that's underlined, Windows Me brings up a definition or jumps to a spot that has information about that subject. Click the Help Topics or Back button to return to where you jumped from.

✔ If you're impressed with a particularly helpful page, send it to the printer: Click the right mouse button and choose Print Topic from the menu that appears. Windows Me shoots that page to the printer so you can keep it handy until you lose it.

✔ To grab a help message and stick it in your own work, highlight the text with your mouse and choose Copy from the menu. Windows then lets you highlight the helpful words you want to copy to the Clipboard. I dunno why anybody would want to do this, but you can do it.

Finding Help for Your Problem

If you don't see your problem listed in the particular table of contents page that you access, there's another way to find help (although it takes a little more time and effort). Click the Search tab at the top of any help window, as shown in Figure 16-10. Type a few words describing your problem and click the Go button. Windows Me actively ferrets out anything helpful about your topic.

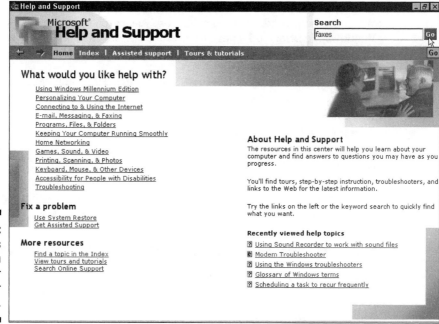

Figure 16-10:
Windows
Me lets you
search for
particular
subjects.

If Windows matches what you type with an appropriate topic, click the topic that looks the most pertinent and then click the Display button. Windows jumps to the page of information that describes that particular subject the best.

A quicker way to find help is to click the scroll bar or press PgUp and PgDn to see what subjects Windows is willing to explain. If you see a subject that even remotely resembles what you're confused about, double-click it. Windows Me brings up that page of help information.

From there, you can jump around by clicking underlined words and phrases. Sooner or later, you stumble onto the right page of information.

Windows searches alphabetically and, unfortunately, isn't very smart. So, if you're looking for help on margins, for example, don't type **adding margins** or **changing margins.** Instead, type **margins** so that Windows jumps to the words beginning with M.

Finding Help on the Web

The Help system built into Windows Me is better than ever, and finding help for a particular trouble is relatively painless. Now, however, the Help system has grown past windows and programs. In fact, it's grown past your computer and now lives on the Internet.

To find Internet help for Windows Me, choose Help from the Start menu. When the Help window appears, choose Assisted support from the top menu. Windows Me brings up a page of Internet options, as shown in Figure 16-11, and asks you to choose the most helpful one.

The Web page offers help in several ways; I describe each next.

Contact Support

Got a problem? Click here to send Microsoft a letter about it. Of course, there's no saying when or if they'll get back to you, although some people get form letter responses. But if you want to submit an "online incident," this is where to click.

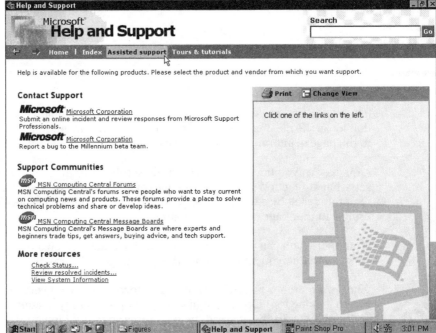

Figure 16-11: Internet users click on Assisted support to locate potential Web help with their problems.

MSN Computing Central Forums

Click here to take your first step down the computer techie road. This is a collection of online magazines dealing with all aspects of computers: hardware, software, desktop publishing, Internet Explorer, or other mostly Windows-related items.

From here, you can read the articles, download the files, or join the message boards, which I describe next.

MSN Computing Central Message Boards

Head for the message boards to write about your particular problem. The message appears on the Web site, where everybody can read it. Lots of 12-year-old kids like to polish their egos by hanging out on the message boards and answering everybody's questions.

However, you often don't need to post anything to find out the answer. If you're suffering from a computing problem, chances are that other people are, too. And they've probably already asked the same question. In fact, many questions appear over and over. So, to find an answer, try this trick:

Look to see where somebody's already asked your question: Printer prints in red ink, for instance. Then, look for subjects titled, "Re: Printer prints in red ink." That "Re:" means that somebody is answering the question. By clicking on the subjects beginning with "Re:", you can skip all the questions and just find the answers.

Taking a Tour and Tutorial

Wish Windows would just take you by the hand and show you how to do something? Click on Tours & Tutorials at the top of the Help screen, and Windows Me displays its list of available tours and tutorials, as shown in Figure 16-12.

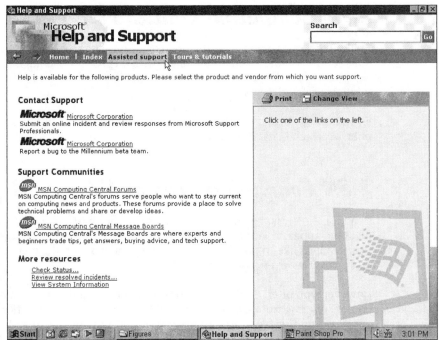

Figure 16-12:
Windows
Me offers
lots of tours
and tutorials
for teaching
the hard
stuff.

Click on a tour dealing with something you find confusing — the Plug and Play tour, for instance — and Windows leads you through the procedure, pointing out the things you need to do to get stuff done.

Part V
The Part of Tens

The 5th Wave   By Rich Tennant

"It still bothers me that I'm paying a lot of REAL dollars to a REAL university so you can get a degree in ARTIFICIAL intelligence."

In this part . . .

Everybody likes to read top tens in magazines — especially in the grocery store checkout aisle when you're stuck behind someone who's just pulled a rubber band off a thick stack of double coupons and the checker can't find the right validation stamp.

Unlike the reading material at the grocery store, the chapters in this part of the book don't list ten new aerobic bounces or ten ways to stop your kids from making explosives with kitchen cleansers. Instead, you find lists of ways to make Windows Me more efficient — or at least not as hostile. You find a few tips, tricks, and explanations of Windows Me icons and what they do.

Some lists have more than ten items; others have fewer. But who's counting, besides the guy wading through all those double coupons?

Chapter 17

Ten New Windows Me Goodies

*J*ust bought a new PC? You're stuck with Windows Me. It almost always comes preinstalled.

Current PC owners have a choice. After reading the Windows Me box in computer stores, they can decide whether or not to upgrade.

To keep you from squinting at fine print in the computer store, here are the ten most interesting new things in Windows Me.

Using PC Health

Windows Me brings a happier world than its predecessors. The error messages aren't as lurching. The icons look friendlier. The computer starts up faster — more eager to meet you. And it doesn't seem to stall quite as often.

A series of Windows Me programs called "PC Health" help keep a PC crash-free by protecting files, automatically installing patches and fixes through the Internet, and stopping unruly programs before they rock the boat.

Best yet, the action takes place behind the curtain where you don't have to mess with it.

✔ In the past, Windows often crashed after a new program was installed. That's because the incoming software elbows other files out of the way — occasionally overwriting existing files in the process. PC Health's System File Protection (SFP) aims to track a file's lineage more accurately, keeping incomers from beating up on the old-timers.

✔ System Restore, as I describe in Chapter 12 and that you can see in Figure 17-1, saves "snapshots" of Windows current condition. By taking a snapshot before installing a program, a user can fix up a botched installation by restoring the snapshot.

Installing Digital Cameras and Scanners

Sometimes, Windows Me recognizes your newly installed computer part, begins speaking to it in the correct language, and starts a relationship that's beneficial to everyone. Other times, it pretends it doesn't exist.

If Windows doesn't recognize your new digital camera or scanner, head for the Control Panel, open the Scanners and Camera's icon, and run the handy new Scanner and Camera wizard.

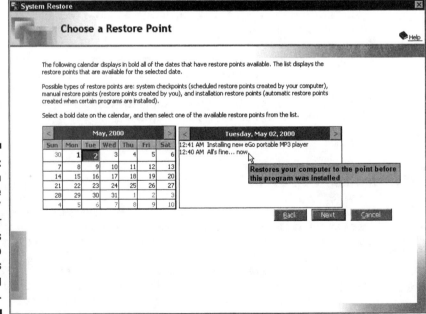

Figure 17-1: System Restore "rolls back" your computer's settings to when it was working well.

The wizard places an icon for your new camera or scanner into My Computer, and creates a folder for your incoming picture album: the My Pictures folder in the My Documents window.

To check out a camera's pictures, open the My Pictures folder and click the words *scanner or camera,* as shown in Figure 17-2.

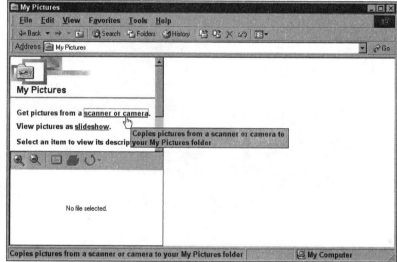

Figure 17-2:
Windows
Me works
better with
digital
cameras
and
scanners.

The Scanner and Camera wizard begins extracting tiny previews of your camera's photos, letting you rotate them and select the ones to grab. Finally, the Wizard whisks the selected pictures out of the camera and onto your hard drive, storing them conveniently in a folder with the current date.

Open the new folder to access the images, create a slideshow, or just preview them, as shown in Figure 17-3.

✔ Windows Me supports cameras and scanners from the major brands, including Agfa, Canon, Casio, Hewlett Packard, Kodak, Nikon, and Olympus.

✔ The Scanner and Camera wizard grabs cameras that aren't normally picked up by Windows' Plug and Play technology. (Many of these devices plug into serial ports.)

✔ Newly downloaded photos are stored in a folder with the day's date. After downloading, immediately rename the folder with a descriptive word or two. 2000-09-01 isn't as easy to remember as 2000-09-01 — Jacob's Toad Farm.

Figure 17-3:
Click on a
picture to
see its
preview.

Using Help

Windows' occasional doling out of helpful information tidbits has exploded into a full-screen Help page. Resembling a Web site, Windows Me's Help program gathers all your potentially helpful sources of information into one place.

The newly redesigned Help page contains more robotic troubleshooters than ever, for instance. A Search button at the screen's top, right corner lets you quickly zoom in on troubling topics. Internet users can search the Web for solutions, or head to Microsoft's Central Message Boards: Internet gathering spots where confused users try to answer each other's questions.

Windows Me's new Help system gets its own coverage in Chapter 16.

Playing Online Games

Have fond memories of childhood videogames? Windows Me includes socially acceptable videogames like Hearts, Backgammon, Reversi, and others. But there's a new twist.

When you tire of playing against the computer, you can play for free against friendly folk on the Internet.

✔ The action takes place at Microsoft's MSN Gaming Zone www.zone. msn.com, a long-time hangout for Internet game players. Head there for lots more information than Windows Me has to offer.

✔ Windows Me's Internet games don't care for firewalls or proxy servers, two items commonly found on networks and cable modems. You may find your best luck with a plain old dial-up connection and a plain 56K modem.

Editing Video with Windows Movie Maker

Hoping to please today's credit-card generation and its digicams, Windows Me includes a free video-editing package. When digicam owners install video capture cards into their computers, they can now capture the action from their video camera, digital camera, or Web Cam and edit it.

As shown in Figure 17-4, Movie Maker imports several common video formats, including MPG and AVI. Unfortunately, Microsoft only saves the movies in its own ASX format.

Figure 17-4: Edit your home movies or imported videos with Windows Me's bundled Movie Maker.

When importing video, either from a camera, live feed or another file, Windows Movie Maker splits it into short clips. By rearranging the clips onto a line, users edit their work into shape. After you rearrange everything into the correct order — and the bad parts are left out — the software records your new version, letting you create a new soundtrack for accompaniment.

Windows Me provides the software, but you need the other, more expensive stuff: a video recorder and a powerful computer with a video capture card and a huge hard drive.

Taming Media Player

Once a small boombox of a program (Figure 17-5), Media Player has grown into a large home theater system (Figure 17-6). Through Media Player, Windows Me computers now play and record music and videos.

Figure 17-5:
The old
version of
Media
Player was
tiny.

For instance, few newspaper readers have escaped the word "MP3 technology," the media's current techno-basketball. With MP3, people make computer copies of their CDs' tunes, play them through portable players, and swap the songs on the Internet.

Sensing the fervor in the music marketplace, Microsoft upgraded its Media Player to create and store music files from CDs, too. Shunning MP3, Microsoft stores songs in its own competing WMA format. WMA songs still play in the most chic MP3 players, but it holds license restrictions: Often, you can't play the songs on other computers.

Media Player also works as a media cleaning service. It roots through your computer's folders, grabbing any sound or video. It can even search the Internet, if you'd like. Then it presents its findings on a list, organized for easy playback.

It seeks out and plays Internet radio stations from around the world. Best of all, it puts on a customized light show while playing back your tunes.

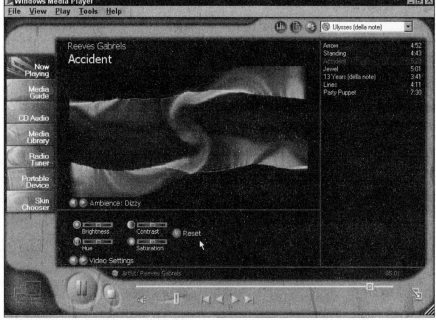

Figure 17-6:
Windows
Me
expanded
Media
Player in
size and
capacity,
adding
swirling
colors and
other frills.

✔ Just as Windows Me connects seamlessly to digital cameras, Media
Player connects to MP3 players, copying tunes into Lyra, WinJam, and
others. It also sends music to PDAs such as Windows CE palmtops and
PocketPCs.

✔ Unlike its predecessor, the new Windows Media Player offers bunches of
details. Choose Options from the Tools menu, for instance, to make
Media Player constantly look for upgrades over the Internet.

The Icons Are Different

Okay, not everything's an earth shaker, but this is probably the most noticeable to former Windows 98 users. The most-used icons on Windows Me's
desktop have changed — for the better.

The My Computer and Recycle Bin icons, as shown in Figure 17-7, took a course
in Feng Shui. Both icons have shed their hard, angular edges. Now, their soft,
little replacements face the *center* of the screen — unlike their predecessors,
which constantly peered away from the action in haughty indifference.

Figure 17-7:
The icons
for
Windows
Me (right)
seem
friendlier
than the
icons from
Windows'
older
versions (left).

✔ The Control Panel boasts a few new icons as well. Most of the newcomers provide one-button access to heavy-use decision areas. For instance, clicking the new Folder Options icon allows quick changes to a folder's behavior. (Before, users needed to call up a folder and fumble with its menus to change its settings.)

✔ The My Computer window looks pretty bare; icons for your drives hung around, but nearly all the others headed for the Control Panel. When in doubt, look inside the Control Panel first.

✔ Actually, Windows Me recycled many of its new icons from its older brother, Windows 2000. (Windows 2000 replaces Windows NT, while Windows Millennium Edition replaces Windows 98.)

Keeping Windows Me Up-to-Date through "Windows Update"

Face it: The computer industry moves so quickly that even your brand-new copy of Windows Me is probably out of date in some way or another. The answer? Until Windows Me, frustrated users had to search through the Internet for the "magic fix," hoping to find the up-to-date, newly improved file that would cure their systems and make Windows act normally.

Windows Me makes searching for fixes much easier with its newly improved Windows Update program. Click Windows Update from the top of the Start menu, and Windows Me heads for the Windows Update site on the Internet.

After you connect, little Web site gremlins diagnose your computer and present you with a list of needed repairs. You click the updates you want, and the program installs them automatically. Quick and easy.

✔ Best yet, the program remembers what it did so it can reverse its actions if it made things even *worse.*

✔ Windows Update is nothing new; it started in Windows 98. However, it's been improved so it doesn't keep sending out false "update" alarms to users, telling them an update is waiting — only to have that update disappear when the user arrives to pick it up.

Chapter 18

Ten Aggravating Things about Windows Me (And How to Fix Them)

· ·

In This Chapter

▶ Finding out your computer's version of Windows

▶ Wanting to double-click instead of click (or vice versa)!

▶ Bypassing the menus

▶ Reattaching fallen button bars

▶ Keeping track of multiple windows

▶ Finding a missing taskbar

▶ Fixing the Print Screen key

▶ Installing a missing program

▶ Lining up two windows on the screen

▶ Updating a floppy disk's contents in the Windows Explorer or My Computer program

▶ Turning off that annoying Active Desktop

▶ Turning off the Channel bar

· ·

*W*indows Me would be great if only . . . (insert your pet peeve here). If you find yourself thinking (or saying) this frequently, this chapter is for you. This chapter not only lists the most aggravating things about Windows Me, but it also explains how you can fix them.

What Version of Windows Do I Have?

Windows has been sold in more than a dozen flavors since its debut in November 1985. How do you know if your new computer *really* comes with Windows Me?

Right-click on My Computer and choose Properties. Click the General tab, if that page isn't already showing.

Under the word System, Windows displays its version and version number.

I Want to Click instead of Double-Click (Or Vice Versa!)

Slowly but surely, Windows Me is stretching away from your desktop and onto the Internet's *World Wide Web:* a huge, worldwide network of computers stuffed with everything from movie previews to groups of people discussing eggnog recipes.

When accessing the Internet, users click *once* on icons — not twice, the way Windows users have grown accustomed. To see how your computer's currently set up, open the Control Panel from within My Computer and open the Folder Options icon.

The last option, titled Click items as follows, lets you choose between single-clicking and double-clicking. Select the one you want and click OK to make your change.

When maneuvering through the options listed in the Start menu, you only need to click once, no matter how your mouse is set up: Just click the Start button to bring the Start menu to life. All the other menus contained in the Start menu pop up automatically as the mouse pointer hovers over them. When you spot the program or choice you're after, click it, and the Start menu loads that program or choice.

I Don't Like the Mouse!

Look closely at the words on the menu bar, along the top of each window. Somewhere in almost every word, you can spot a single underlined letter. Press and release the Alt key and then press one of the underlined letters you see in a word. Try pressing the F in File, for example. Presto! The File menu leaps into place. Look for underlined letters on the newly displayed File menu. For example, press S for Save. Presto again! Windows Me saves the current file, without a single mouse click.

To save a file in nearly any Windows Me program, press and release the Alt key, press F, and then press S. It's that simple (after you memorize the combination, that is).

You find these underlined letters everywhere in Windows Me. *Note:* I include a list of the most commonly used key combinations in the Cheat Sheet at the front of this book.

- ✔ To move from box to box while filling out a form, press the Tab key. Each press of the Tab key takes you to a new part of the form to fill out. Ecstasy! There's more: Hold down Shift while pressing the Tab key to go backwards.

- ✔ For some keys, you hold the Alt key while pressing a function key. For example, to close any Windows Me program, hold down the Alt key and press F4 (Alt+F4).

- ✔ If you accidentally press the Alt key and are stuck in Menu Land, press the Alt key again. Alternatively, press the Esc key and bark loudly until it lets you out.

My Bar Full of Buttons Just Fell Off!

It's happened to the best of us. We reach up to click a button from the row of buttons along the top of a program, when all of a sudden something awful happens.

The entire row of buttons falls off and appears as a bar in the middle of your program. What did you do wrong? Nothing, it turns out. Microsoft figures that some people enjoy the versatility of placing their buttons in the middle of their work. So, it lets people "drag" the button bar off the program and place it someplace else.

To place it back where it started, place the mouse pointer on the bar, hold down your right mouse button, and drag the bar back where it belongs. Release the mouse button, and the bar reattaches itself.

Or, if that's not working right, try double-clicking the bar. It often reattaches itself automatically.

It's Too Hard to Keep Track of All Those Windows

You don't *have* to keep track of all those windows. Windows Me does it for you with the taskbar. Hold the Ctrl key and press the Esc key, and the taskbar rises to the forefront. (If it doesn't, see the very next section.)

The taskbar, which I cover in Chapter 10, has a separate box listing the name of every window currently open. Click the name of the window you want, and that window hops to the top of the pile.

Even better, shrink all the open windows into icons except for the window you're currently working on. Then click the taskbar with your right mouse button and click one of the two tile commands to line everything up neatly on the screen.

In Chapter 7, you find more soldiers to enlist in the battle against misplaced windows, files, and programs.

The Taskbar Keeps Disappearing!

The taskbar's a handy Windows Me program that's always running. Usually, it sits along the bottom of your screen — if you can just find the darn thing. It sometimes vanishes from the screen. Here are a few ways to bring it back.

First, try holding down the Ctrl key and pressing the Esc key. Sometimes this effort makes the taskbar appear, but sometimes it only brings up the Start menu.

Still no taskbar? Try putting your mouse pointer on the very edge of your screen, stopping for a second or two at each of the four sides. If you point at the correct side, some specially configured taskbars stop goofing around and come back to the screen.

If you can only see a slim edge of the taskbar — the rest of it hangs off the edge of the screen, for example — place the mouse pointer on the edge you *can* see. After the mouse pointer turns into a two-headed arrow, hold down your mouse button and move the mouse toward the screen's center to drag the taskbar back into view.

- ✔ If your taskbar disappears whenever you're not specifically pointing at it, turn off its Auto Hide feature: Click a blank part of the taskbar with your right mouse button and choose Properties from the pop-up menu. When the Taskbar and Start Menu Properties window appears, click in the Auto Hide box until a little check mark disappears. (Or, to turn on the Auto Hide feature, add the check mark.)

- ✔ While you're in the Taskbar's Properties window, make sure that a check mark appears in the Always On Top box. That way, the taskbar always rides visibly on the desktop, making it much easier to spot.

- ✔ Running two monitors? Don't forget the taskbar can be on any monitor's edge — that includes the second monitor. Make sure that you point at every edge before giving up.

My Print Screen Key Doesn't Work

Windows Me takes over the Print Screen key (labeled PrtSc, PrtScr, or something even more supernatural on some keyboards). Instead of sending the stuff on the screen to the printer, the Print Screen key sends it to the Windows Me Clipboard, where you can paste it into other windows.

  ✔ If you hold the Alt key while pressing the Print Screen key, Windows Me sends the current *window* — not the entire screen — to the Clipboard.

  ✔ If you *really* want a printout of the screen, press the Print Screen button to send a picture of the screen to the Clipboard. Paste the contents of the Clipboard into Paint and print from there. (Chapter 12 explains that process.)

  ✔ Some very, very old keyboards make you hold the Shift key while pressing the Print Screen key. You may need to hold the Shift key and the Print Screen key to send a picture of the screen to the Clipboard.

Windows Me Didn't Install All the Programs Listed on the Box

In an attempt to make friends with everybody, Windows Me comes with gobs of programs — more than anybody would ever want. So, to keep from making enemies of everybody, Windows Me doesn't fill up everybody's hard drive with every possible program.

For example, Windows Me comes with sounds that make your computer sound like a robot or squawking bird. But it doesn't automatically install those sounds, nor does it tell you about them. If you want to add those sounds, you must go back and do it yourself.

Start by double-clicking the Add/Remove Programs icon in the Control Panel and then click the Windows Setup tab along the top. Windows Me lists the programs it can install and offers to install them for you — a process that I describe in Chapter 12. To install the robot sounds, double-click the Multimedia option and choose Multimedia Sound Schemes from the next window. Click OK, and click OK again to close the next window. Windows installs the Multimedia Sound Schemes — one of the many options it originally left out of its Multimedia offerings.

(To hear the newly installed robot sounds, double-click the Control Panel's Sounds and Multimedia icon, and choose Robotz Sound Scheme. The birds and frogs hang out in the Jungle Sound Scheme. Beware, however: Some employers may have already deleted these fun files from your computer.)

It's Too Hard to Line Up Two Windows on the Screen

With all its cut-and-paste stuff, Windows Me makes it easy for you to grab information from one program and slap it into another. With its drag-and-drop stuff, you can grab an address from a database and drag it into a letter in your word processor.

The hard part of Windows Me is lining up two windows on the screen, side by side. That's where you need to call in the taskbar. First, open the two windows and place them anywhere on the screen. Then turn all the other windows into icons (minimize them) by clicking the button with the little line that lives in the top-right corners of those windows.

Now, click a blank area of the taskbar with your right mouse button and click one of the two Tile commands listed on the menu. The two windows line up on the screen perfectly.

The My Computer and Windows Explorer Programs Show the Wrong Stuff on My Floppy Disk

The My Computer and Windows Explorer programs sometimes get confused and don't always list the files currently sitting on a disk drive. To prod the programs into taking a second look, simply press the F5 key along the top of your keyboard.

Turning Off That Annoying Active Desktop

You may have noticed the symptoms. Your computer may ignore your selection of wallpaper, for instance, and instead display a Web page on your desktop. Sometimes, your desktop becomes embedded with strange moving things: stock market tickers, twirling clocks, or other bits of weirdness.

Or perhaps you turned on the Active Desktop feature out of curiosity and headed to Microsoft's Active Desktop Gallery Web site to check out the goodies. You then discovered that many of the offerings don't work any more because Microsoft hasn't updated its Gallery for two years.

Simply put, Microsoft seems to be abandoning the Active Desktop, but has left it in Windows Me to remain compatible with earlier versions of Windows.

To turn off the Active Desktop, click the desktop with your right mouse button and choose Customize My Desktop from the Active Desktop menu. When the next window appears, click the box marked Show Web Content on My Active Desktop. The little box's check mark disappears. Finally, click OK to turn the thing off.

If you hear your modem dialing places when you're nowhere near your computer, chances are it's trying to keep parts of your Active Desktop up-to-date. To make it stop, turn off all parts of your Active Desktop and delete any options listed on your Customize my Desktop area.

Turning the Ugly Channel Bar On or Off

If you installed Windows Me over an earlier version of Windows, your desktop may contain a large black totem pole called the Channel bar. It's an ugly, black bar that looks like a misplaced TV remote control. It's a confusing, Microsoft-devised way to reach the Internet without using a Web browser.

Unfortunately, the Channel bar takes up a lot of desktop space. To get rid of it, click the little X resting at the very top of the bar. Poof! The Channels bar disappears, leaving a question: Do you want the Channel bar to be displayed next time you restart your computer?

Click the No button, and you've banished the bar. Good riddance.

- Windows Me no longer installs the Channel bar. If your computer came with Windows Me already installed, you'll never see the bar.

- Actually, Microsoft took all the Channel bar's contents and stuck them on an Internet menu. Open Internet Explorer, choose Favorites from the menu, and look under the Media section to see the sites from Microsoft's favorite corporate conglomerates.

Chapter 19

Ten Expensive Things You Can Do to Make Windows Me Run Better

*G*ive a Ford Fairlane to the right teenage boy, and he'll get right to work: boring out the cylinders, putting in a high-lift cam, and adding a double-roller timing chain . . . and replacing the exhaust system with headers, if his cash holds out.

Computer nerds feel the same way about getting under the hood of their computers. They add a few new parts, flip a few switches, and tweak a few things here and there to make Windows Me scream.

Even if you're not a computer nerd, you can still soup up Windows Me a bit. Take the computer back to the store and have the *store's* computer nerd get under the hood.

This chapter talks about what parts to ask for so that you don't end up with high-lift cams rather than more memory.

Buy More Memory

When you bought your new computer, the salesperson probably tried to talk you into buying more memory, or RAM. Windows Me probably talks just as loudly about this issue as the salesperson.

See, Windows Me can read and write information to RAM very quickly. The phrase *lightning quick* comes to mind. But when Windows Me runs out of RAM, it starts using the hard drive for storage. Compared with RAM, hard drives are slow, mechanical dinosaurs. If you're short on memory, you can hear the hard drive grinding away as you switch between programs and Windows Me frantically tries to make room for everything.

Windows Me runs very slowly on a computer with only 32MB of RAM, the amount recommended on the Windows Me box. Even Microsoft winks and says that "More memory improves performance."

For instance, to use Windows Me's Media Player or Movie Editor, Microsoft says to bump it up to 64MB of RAM. Doubling that figure certainly won't be going overboard.

With 128MB of RAM, Windows Me juggles programs more quickly (and without dropping them as often).

If you're tired of waiting for Windows Me, toss the computer in the back seat, take it back to the computer store, and have the store people put some more RAM inside. (The price has dropped since the last time you shopped.)

Different computers hold different amounts of RAM. And some computers make you yank the old memory chips before you can install the newer, higher-capacity chips. Before buying more memory, check with your dealer to make sure that your computer can handle it. (You'll find that type of memory information and more in my book, *Upgrading and Fixing PCs For Dummies,* 5th Edition, from IDG Books Worldwide, Inc. Don't bother buying the book, just read Chapter 11 at the bookstore.)

Shell Out the Bucks for a Bigger Hard Drive

To install every part of Windows Me, you'll need about 700MB of hard drive space. That's for Windows Me and no other programs.

If you buy the latest version of Microsoft Word for Windows, however, that program wants at least 150MB of hard drive space, too. Using e-mail? Games? The Internet? Add a few other hoggy Windows programs, and your hard drive can run out of room quickly.

If you're planning on using Windows Me's video editor, add an extra 2GB of hard drive space for storing video.

In fact, it's important to leave part of the hard drive empty so that Windows Me has room to shuffle information around.

The moral is to shop for the biggest hard drive you can afford. Then borrow some money and buy one that's slightly bigger. A hard drive that's 8GB is a good starting size these days. If you can afford a larger one, go for it. And if you're planning on editing videos, buy a drive that's larger than 20GB.

Order a Faster Pentium Computer

Windows Me works on a fast Pentium computer, but not as well as it could. In fact, the Windows Video Editor needs a speedy 300MHz Pentium II or equivalent computer.

As programs incorporate more and more sound and graphics, computers are becoming more and more burdened with computing chores. That's why you want a fast Pentium II or Pentium III to keep the information flowing smoothly across the screen. Balance your need for speed with your checking account balance.

You can find this computer model/Pentium stuff thrashed out in Chapter 2.

Put a 3-D Graphics Accelerator Card on the Credit Card

When tossing boxes and bars around, Windows Me puts a big strain on the computer's *graphics card,* the gizmo that tells the monitor what information to put on-screen.

Windows Me also puts a strain on the computer's *microprocessor,* the gizmo that tells the graphics card what to tell the monitor.

A *3-D graphics accelerator card* eases the burden on both parties. Simply put, a graphics accelerator is a hot-rod graphics card. It replaces the VGA or Super VGA card and contains a special chip that handles the dirty work of filling the monitor with pretty pictures.

The result? Dialog boxes that shoot on-screen almost instantly. You no longer have to wait for Windows Me to repaint the screen when you move windows around. Everything just looks snappier.

- ✔ You probably don't need to upgrade the monitor when buying an accelerator card. Monitors always work fast; it's the cards that slow them down.

- ✔ Upgrading the computer to a faster Pentium also speeds up the graphics, even if you don't buy a 3-D accelerator card. (Graphics cards are cheaper and easier to install, though.)

- ✔ Computers with special *PCI* or *AGP* slots can speed up 3-D graphics the fastest. These slots can accept the speedy PCI and AGP video cards. Anything else is obsolete.

- ✔ In fact, only PCI cards and AGP slots work with the Windows Me multi-monitor feature. If your computer doesn't have those type of slots, you can't use more than one monitor with it. Best bet: Use an AGP slot for your main monitor, and a PCI slot for your second monitor.

Beg for, or Borrow, a Bigger Monitor (Or Two)

Part of the problem with the Windows Me stack-of-windows approach to computing is the size of the screen. The Windows Me desktop is the size of the monitor: a little larger than one square foot. That's why everything constantly covers up everything else.

To get a bigger desktop, buy a bigger monitor. The 17-inch monitors offer almost twice the elbowroom as the standard 14-inchers. You have more room to put windows side by side on the screen, as well as more room to spread icons along the bottom. The new 20-inchers give you an executive-sized desktop, but at a mahogany price.

- ✔ If you have a stack of phone books holding up one side of your desk, buy a new desk when you buy the new monitor. Those big monitors can weigh 50 pounds or more.

- ✔ That last tip holds particularly true if you're buying into the Windows Me multi-monitor plan and you want to use two or more monitors with your computer.

✔ To cut down the weight — and increase the amount of space on your desktop — consider buying one of those way-cool LCD panel screens. They only weigh a few pounds, they're about 2 or 3 inches thick, and they can actually pack more information onto the screen than a "normal" monitor of the same size. Plus, there's less eyestrain and the picture's clearer. Unfortunately, they cost a lot more. . . .

Buy a CD-RW Drive

Software companies have just about given up on floppy disks. Their programs are simply too big to fit on one disk, and nobody wants to feed their computer handfuls of disks in order to install the program.

The solution? Package the program on a compact disc, which can hold the equivalent of hundreds of floppies.

And if you're getting tired of packing your own information onto those tiny floppies, check out those CD Read/Write drives. They not only read information from normal CDs, but they also write information onto special CDs costing a dollar or two.

✔ CD Read/Write drives can write information once onto those dollar discs. But they can erase the information and write new information onto more expensive discs costing about ten times as much. The more expensive discs that can read and write many times are dubbed CD-RW; the cheaper, write-once discs are called CD-R.

✔ CD drives are always slower at writing information to a disc than they are at reading that information.

✔ Today, CD-RW drives don't cost much more than CD drives that can only read information. However, they're usually a lot slower. Expect that to change as the technology continues.

Buy a TV Tuner Card

Admittedly, a TV Tuner card could be considered an extravagance. You can often buy a small TV set for the cost of a TV Tuner card.

Nevertheless, few things in life compare to watching *Three's Company* in the corner of your Windows Me screen. And Windows Me makes it sinfully easily. It'll even keep a running download of your area's TV programming information, so it can alert you to the next airing of *Green Acres*.

You can find more information about the TV Tuner in Chapter 17, as well as in this book's more advanced sequel, *MORE Windows Me For Dummies,* published by IDG Books Worldwide, Inc.

- ✔ Good news: Many video cards today toss on a TV tuner for just a few dollars more. Hurray! Now you just need to connect them to a cable TV outlet or rooftop TV antenna to get a decent picture.

- ✔ If you're using a computer for business, convince the boss you need the TV Tuner card for watching CNN business information on the stock market.

- ✔ If your computer's staying at home, a TV Tuner card means you'll have to upgrade your home/office chair into a lounge chair.

Snap Up a Faster Modem

Face it: The Internet isn't going to disappear, even after all the hullabaloo has died down. With the Internet's World Wide Web software, you won't have to leave the house to go to the library, read newspapers and magazines, meet people, research trips, and join I Hate Barney User Groups. You can even have food delivered while you tap the keyboard.

- ✔ If you find yourself using the Internet a lot, make sure that you're using a 56 Kbps or faster modem.

- ✔ If you find yourself using the Internet a *super* lot, call up your phone company and Internet Service Provider to see if they offer something called DSL (digital subscriber line) service. DSL can spew out the information a super lot faster — but at a higher price (especially because DSL service requires special, DSL modems — your old modem won't work).

- ✔ ISDN lines are another fast-modem word to mention when looking to speed up your access.

- ✔ If your cable company offers it, look into the costs of a super-speedy 500 Kbps cable modem. Most offer 24-hour access through your cable line, freeing up the cost of a second phone line. Plus, you can still watch TV — even on your computer — while surfing the Net. No more thumb-twiddling while waiting for weather maps!

Chapter 20

Ten (Or so) Windows Me Icons and What They Do

● ●

In This Chapter

Windows Me uses different icons to stand for different types of files. That arrangement means that the program is packed with enough icons to befuddle the most experienced iconographer.

● ●

*T*able 20-1 shows pictures of the most common icons built into Windows Me and what the icons are supposed to represent. Double-click the icon to open it or launch it into action.

Table 20-1	Windows Me Icons
What It Looks Like	*What It Stands For*
	3½-inch floppy drive
	3½-inch floppy drive shared on a network
	Hard drive
	Hard drive shared on a network
	CD-ROM drive
	CD-ROM drive shared on a network
	Audio CD; a CD with music currently inserted in your CD-ROM drive

(continued)

Table 20-1 *(continued)*

What It Looks Like	What It Stands For
	Audio CD; a CD with music available to anyone on the network
	Batch file; a collection of DOS commands for the computer to run automatically
	Bitmap file; graphics usually created by Paint
	Cabinet file; a compressed collection of Windows Me installation files; open with Explorer
	Camera attached through serial port
	DOS program
	Folder or directory; a computerized storage area for files
	Fonts; stored in a TrueType format that can be easily shrunk or enlarged
	Fonts; stored in an older, fixed-size format
	Help file; contains instructions stored in a special format for the Windows Me Help system
	The gray, washed-out look means it's a hidden information file; Windows keeps these important system files invisible unless the user flips a secret switch.
	Internet information; usually a map to a Web site
	Internet HTML file; opened by Internet Explorer, these look just like a Web page.
	Media; a file containing a movie, sound, MP3 or MIDI song, or anything else playable in Media Player
	Outlook Express mail; a piece of e-mail that's been cut or copied from Outlook Express and pasted to your desktop or another folder

What It Looks Like	What It Stands For
	Scrap; scraps are dabs of information dragged and dropped onto the desktop: a paragraph from WordPad, for example.
	System file; technical files for Windows Me to use
	Text file; settings information for a computer program or part
	Text; usually created by Notepad
	Word processor file; a file usually created by either WordPad or Microsoft Word
	A file Windows Me doesn't think it recognizes

Chapter 21

Ten Most Frequently Asked Windows Questions

*H*ere they are, all in one place: the most frequently asked questions about Windows Me.

If you don't find your answer here, check out Chapter 18. That shows how to cure the most aggravating things about Windows, and plenty of people are asking how to do that.

How Can I Remember All the Stuff I Can Do to a File?

Windows lets you do zillions of things to a file in a zillion different ways. How do you remember what your options are when dealing with a file? By just remembering this one thing:

Right-click on the file. A menu pops up, listing all your available options, as shown in Figure 21-1.

Here's a quick explanation of what those options accomplish.

- ✔ **Open:** This opens the program that's linked to the file; it then places the file inside the program, ready for playing or editing.

- ✔ **Print:** Send the file to the printer by choosing this.

- ✔ **Open With:** Choose this, and a list appears. It contains most of the programs on your computer. Select one of the programs, and Windows will use that program to open your file. *Note:* Make sure that there's no check mark in the box labeled Always Use This Program to Open These Files.

- ✔ **Send To:** Choosing this option lists several commonly used programs. You can immediately send the program to your floppy drive, convert it to a shortcut and send it to the desktop, mail it to somebody, or store it in your My Documents area.

- ✔ **Cut:** This transfers the file to your Clipboard, ready to be pasted into another program or area.

- ✔ **Copy:** This transfers a copy of the file to your Clipboard, ready for pasting.

- ✔ **Create Shortcut:** Click here to create a shortcut in the same folder. Then you can copy the shortcut to a new location.

- ✔ **Delete:** Poof! It's sent to the Recycle Bin.

- ✔ **Rename:** This highlights the file's name, ready for you to type in a new name.

- ✔ **Properties:** Click here to see the file's size, creation date, and other vital statistics.

If you drag a file while holding down your right mouse button, a similar menu appears, letting you choose whether you'd like to copy the file, move it, create a shortcut, or cancel your drag.

Should I Upgrade to Windows 2000 Instead of Windows Me?

Windows Me, the replacement for Windows 98, is designed for home users. "Consumers" is what Microsoft likes to call them.

Windows 2000, by contrast, replaces a version of Windows called Windows NT. It's designed for business users — small businesses and corporations that need more-advanced network support.

Windows 2000 is a sturdier program, but that's not always good. If a program pushes Windows 2000 too hard — an unruly game, for example, or the latest type of computer toy from CompUSA — Windows 2000 simply won't run it. Windows Me gives its programs a little more leeway and can run more new hardware straight out of the box. That lets Windows Me run more programs, but that also means that it can crash more often.

So, it's a tradeoff. With Windows 2000, you get a sturdy operating system that won't crash, but it won't run a lot of the newest hardware or difficult programs. Windows Me, on the other hand, runs a wider variety of computer programs and accessories, but its flexibility leads it to crash occasionally.

- ✔ People who need Windows 2000 may be tired of all the crashes in Windows 98 or Windows Me. They want more advanced networking, and they're not afraid of learning how to handle a new operating system with a lot more bells and whistles.

- ✔ People who stick with Windows Me don't want to pay more than $200 for Windows 2000. They may not have the required 64MB or more of RAM and a super speedy Pentium with a Windows 2000-capable BIOS. Windows 2000 may not support their favorite software or computer parts. These people are reasonably happy with the Windows Me program's stability and its home networking system. Finally, they don't want to spend time learning a new operating system and figuring out all the new settings.

How Do I Make Windows Stop Asking for a Password When It Starts?

When Windows Me starts on your computer each day, it often bases its relationship on mistrust. It asks for a password, as shown in Figure 21-2.

Figure 21-2:
Windows
Me often
starts the
day with an
annoying
password
request.

How can you get rid of that darn thing? Well, sometimes it's not possible. In fact, Windows must check your identity for two main reasons.

1. If your computer is part of a network — it's linked to other computers so you can share files — Windows Me wants to make sure that *you're* the one using the computer. It doesn't want just anybody to sit down at the computer and start meddling with all the files on any computer connected to the network.

2. Some people share their computer with other people. They set up the computer so everybody has their own wallpaper, for instance, or they each have access to their own programs. (They do this through the Control Panel's Users icon.)

If your computer isn't connected to a network of other computers (the Internet doesn't count) and everybody that uses the computer doesn't mind using the same desktop, you can safely turn off the password request by following these instructions:

1. **Open the Control Panel from the My Computer folder and open the Network icon.**

2. **Click the little downward-pointing arrow next to the Primary Network Logon box and choose Windows Logon instead of Client for Microsoft Networks.**

3. **Your computer will probably want to restart, so let it.**

Now, make sure that all the computer's users work with the same desktop by removing any personalization.

1. **Open the Control Panel from the My Computer folder and open the Passwords icon.**

2. **When the Passwords Properties dialog box appears, click the User Profiles tab.**

   It's the last tab to the right.

3. **Click the button that says All Users of This Computer Use the Same Preferences and Desktop Settings.**

4. **Click OK.**

Windows should no longer have any reason to ask for a password each time it restarts or loads up in the morning.

How Can I See Previews of My Pictures?

Windows Me has made it easier than ever to peek inside your graphics files. Instead of displaying a folder full of bland icons, Windows Me transforms each icon into a thumbnail-sized preview of the file's contents.

That makes it a lot easier to find the picture of Kitty eating the bamboo leaves after you dump 63 cat pictures into the same folder.

To turn on the previews, open the folder with the pictures, click View from its menu, and choose Thumbnails from the drop-down menu. Windows Me immediately replaces the icons with previews of your graphics and photos.

How Can I Make All My Web Pages Open in a Full-Screen Window?

Internet Explorer always opens Web windows to the same size as they were when they were last closed. So, open Internet Explorer and double-click on its title bar — that strip along the top. That makes it fill the screen. Or simply drag the window's edges until it is the size you want. (Chapter 6 explains how to change a window's size.) After Internet Explorer is the size you want, quit the program by clicking the little X in its upper-right corner.

When you restart Internet Explorer, it should always open to its previously set size.

(This trick works for many other programs, too.)

What Will I Miss If I Don't Use the Internet with Windows Me?

I certainly won't tell anybody. In fact, many people won't notice. Despite the media hype, plenty of people don't use the Internet. Don't get me wrong; I use it an awful lot to look up subjects like determining the manufacture dates of potentiometers and finding out if I should be feeding the neighborhood blue jays raw or roasted peanuts.

I also read the news, check the weather, and listen to Chinese radio stations. Yep, there's a lot of information floating around on the Internet, but it's certainly not everybody's top priority.

My point? Rest assured that Windows Me works fine without the Internet plugged in. You can still write letters, make spreadsheets, and create databases. You can participate on networks, including ones run around the office. You can even send faxes through your modem.

However, Windows Me is designed to run exceptionally well with the Internet. So if you don't sign up for an Internet account, you'll miss the extra Internet goodies tossed into Windows Me.

- ✔ For example, Internet users can use Windows Update, a special place on the Internet that automatically dishes out files for helping your computer stay up-to-date with new improvements to the Windows software. While you're connected, the Update Wizard peers under your computer's hood and examines the way everything's working. Then it recommends or installs any updates your computer might need.

- ✔ Windows Me includes Outlook Express, a freebie program for sending and receiving e-mail — if you have a connection to the Internet.

- ✔ The Windows Me program's feature-packed Media Player plays sound and videos through the Internet. It tunes in radio stations from Argentina to Zimbabwe. It displays movie trailers, news videos, and TV shows.

- ✔ Installed a TV card in your computer? You can download the week's TV program list so you can always know when your favorite shows are on. (You can even set alarms to go off when *The Munsters* TV show begins.)

- ✔ Stayed away from the Internet because it was too hard to use? The Windows Me Internet Connection Wizard makes matters much easier when signing up for Internet service. It automatically handles the software configuration steps necessary for gaining access to the Internet. (It'll still toss you a few jaw-dropping questions that may send you scurrying to Chapter 13, though.)

Appendix A

Installing Windows Me

● ●

In This Chapter

▶ Turning on the computer

▶ Deciding whether to install Windows Me over your old version of Windows

▶ Installing Windows Me

▶ Taking a Windows Me Tutorial

▶ Leaving the Setup program

▶ Turning off the computer

● ●

*I*nstalling software means copying the program from the CD in the software box onto the hard drive inside your PC. Unfortunately, it can also mean hours of tinkering until the newly installed software works correctly with your particular computer, printer, disk drives, and other internal organs. Because of the frustration potential, installation chores should usually be left to a certified computer guru. Gurus like that sort of stuff. (They even like the smell of freshly opened compact disc boxes.)

Luckily, Microsoft took mercy on Windows Me beginners. It designed Windows Me to practically install itself. Just slide the CD into the compact disc drive and click the Setup icon. After that, answer a few questions and put your feet up; Windows Me figures out the rest.

This chapter walks you through the installation process — upgrading to Windows Me from an earlier version of Windows.

Turning On the Computer

The first step is to look for the computer's *power* switch. It's usually the largest switch on the computer. Sometimes, it's red and important looking; other times, it's an itty-bitty "push on, push off" switch near the disk drives.

✔ Put your ear next to the computer's case: If the computer is not making any noise, it's either turned off or broken. Flip its power switch to the opposite direction (or push in the switch), and the computer either jumps to life or stays broken (or stays unplugged, which is why it always works in the repair shop).

✔ Turning the computer off and then turning it on again can send devastating jolts of electricity through the computer's tender internal organs. Turn the computer on in the morning and off when you're finished for the day. Some sensitive people even leave their computers turned on all the time to spare them that morning power jolt.

✔ Never turn the computer off while it's running Windows Me or any other program. Doing so can destroy data and damage your programs. If the computer is doing something weird, like freezing up solid, try the less disastrous disciplinary measures described in Chapter 14.

✔ Turn on your computer's monitor in much the same way: Push in its On switch, and it should jump to life.

✔ Finally, when installing Windows Me, tell it to keep your old version of Windows hanging around, as I describe later in this chapter. Windows Me then compresses your old Windows version and hides it in a secret directory on your hard drive. Later, after you've had time to play with Windows Me, you can tell Windows Me to purge your old version for good. (Or, if Windows Me doesn't meet your needs, you can tell it to resurrect your old version, removing itself in the process. Whichever your choice, it takes place in the Control Panel's Add/Remove Programs area.)

Removing the Wrapper from the Box

Pick up the Windows Me box and look for where the plastic wrap bunches up in the corners. With your incisors, bite into that little chunk of bunched-up plastic and give it a good tug. Repeat this procedure a few times until you've created a finger-sized hole. Then peel back the plastic until the box is free. Be careful of your gums.

Should you install Windows Me over your old version of Windows?

Should you copy this new version of Windows Me over your older, faithful version of Windows — a version that serves you so well except when it crashes?

Yeah, go ahead. The new version won't wipe out the important parts of the old version. The desktop will have the same programs as before. In fact, if you don't install Windows Me over your old version of Windows, you must reinstall all your old programs by hand.

To be safe, make copies of your important data files before you begin. You've probably been backing up your work anyway, so copying the files shouldn't take long.

✔ If you haven't been copying your important files to floppy disks for safekeeping, head to the store and ask for a backup system that's compatible with Windows Me.

✔ When you're ready to delete the old version of Windows and free up some hard drive space, head for the Control Panel's Add/Remove Programs icon.

Upgrading to Windows Me

Forget those awkward experiences setting up metal Christmas trees or listening to your car make funny noises. Windows Me caters to beginners with an installation program that checks under your PC's hood and sets itself up automatically, adjusting the fluid levels as needed.

Here's how to pull into the full-service lane:

First, make sure that your computer is turned on; then make sure that anything plugged into your computer is turned on as well. That includes modems, printers, compact disc drives, eGo MP3 players, yogurt makers, and other goodies. Plug in your joysticks and gamepads, too; Windows Me actually recognizes them. Hurrah!

1. **Start your current version of Windows and put your Windows Me Installation disc into your computer's CD-ROM drive.**

   You may get lucky right away. If your computer has always automatically played songs when you slipped in a CD, then it should start the installation process automatically, too.

   Rejoice, and climb the ladder to Step 3. If the computer just sits there, move to Step 2.

2. **Click the Start button, choose Run from the menu, and type the letters** D:\SETUP **in the Run box that appears. Press Enter.**

   If your CD-ROM drive's letter isn't D, be sure to change the drive letter. For example, if your CD-ROM drive is drive E, type this in the Run dialog box shown in Figure A-1:

   ```
   E:\SETUP
   ```

Figure A-1: If your CD-ROM drive is E, type E:\SETUP into the Run dialog box and click OK.

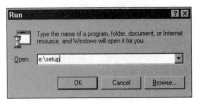

Is all this :\ stuff too much for you? Open My Computer and double-clicking your CD-ROM drive icon (It *looks* like a CD.) Double-click the word *Setup* from its file listings, and the installation wheels start churning.

When Setup begins, the first taste (and sound, in some cases) of Windows Me leaps to the screen. The window merely announces that Windows Me will check your system for any problems before continuing. It also breaks the news that you may be sitting in front of your computer for anywhere from 30 minutes to an hour, depending on how smoothly the installation process goes. Call ahead to pick up a sandwich.

3. **Click Next, and Windows Me examines your computer.**

If Windows Me finds anything wrong with your hard drive, it says so and promptly fixes the problem. If it finds something weird, click the Details button to see what's up. You can usually get away with clicking the Continue button and trudging forward, however.

Windows Me then loads its own Windows Me Setup Wizard program to ensure that everything proceeds without problems.

If Windows Me asks you to close down any currently running programs, do so. The Windows Me Setup Wizard doesn't want mere *programs* mingling at such an important event; the Wizard wants the computer all to itself while replacing the operating system. (**Hint:** Hold down the Alt key and press Tab to cycle between your open programs. Then close each program as it appears.)

Be sure to shut down any virus protection programs that many be running. They'll be startled at the new version of Windows and will cause trouble.

Finally, rustle around for the little envelope that held your Windows Me disc. You'll probably need to type in the envelope's secret "Product ID" code. (Microsoft's afraid that people will make illegal copies of their disc, so they came up with the secret code idea to stop the "bootleggers.")

4. **If asked, click next to the words I Accept the Agreement, and click the Next button.**

   Here's where Microsoft tosses you a stumper, as shown in Figure A-2. Unless you agree to abide by Microsoft's special Windows Me terms, the install process simply stops and leaves the room like a surly bellhop who only got a dollar tip. Promise to play by Microsoft's rules by clicking in the circle where it says I Accept the Agreement.

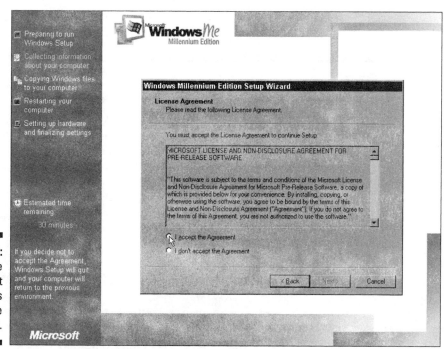

Figure A-2:
Click in the circle next to the words I Accept the Agreement.

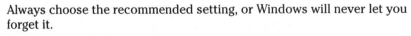

Legal gibberish and licensing terms that leap out during the installation

By choosing the I accept the Agreement option, you're essentially telling Microsoft that you agree to the following things:

- You won't make copies of your software and then rent, sell, or give them away to friends.

- In fact, you don't even own your copy of Windows. You just own the rights to use one copy of it. Microsoft holds the copyright to any images, photographs, animations, video, audio, music, text, programming, and anything else that could possibly have commercial value.

- You won't take Windows Me apart to see how it works, and even if you did, you couldn't make any money off of it.

- It's only guaranteed to work for 90 days.

- Finally, understand that you're the one punching the keyboard, so Microsoft isn't responsible if the software completely destroys your computer, your business, your data, and general sense of happiness.

Welcome to Windows Me!

5. **Enter your Windows Product Key and click Next.**

   Even if you agreed to abide by the License Agreement, Microsoft doesn't trust you. No, you still have to enter a customized Windows Product Key. The secret code containing letters and numbers is usually stamped on the back of your CD's container. Other times, it's stamped on the cover of the software manual.

   Without the key, you're stuck: Windows Me refuses to install. With the key, Windows Me continues its preparations to install itself onto your hard drive.

6. **Click Next.**

   This tells Windows to hop inside your computer and make itself at home wherever it wants.

   Always choose the recommended setting, or Windows will never let you forget it.

   Windows boldly knocks about inside the computer's hard drive, taking measurements and preparing for its big move in.

   See the Back and Next buttons along the bottom of the window? Throughout the next few steps, you can click the Back button to go back to your last step. So don't feel that you've blown it if you accidentally click the Next button before you're ready or if you want to go back and change something. Just click the Back button, and Windows Me goes back a step.

7. **If given the choice, save your System Files and click Next.**

When Windows Me starts shacking up inside your computer, it offers to stuff your old version of Windows into a closet. Then, if Windows Me doesn't work out, a button click brings back your old version of Windows: Everything's back to normal. If only all relationships worked that way.

Go ahead and click Yes to save the system files. You can always delete them if you prefer Windows Me. (In fact, deleting those files frees up plenty of hard drive space.)

8. **Make a Windows Me Startup Disk.**

As you can see in Figure A-3, Windows graciously offers to create emergency medical equipment for itself. The cost? Only a floppy disk. Grab one that doesn't contain anything important — the disk is erased in the process — and label it Windows Me Startup Disk.

Actually, you can write anything you want on the Startup disk's label. However, you *must* insert it into Drive A. No other drive works.

Want to take your chances and not be bothered by creating a Startup Disk? Click OK anyway. The next window gives you a chance to cancel the disk-creation process.

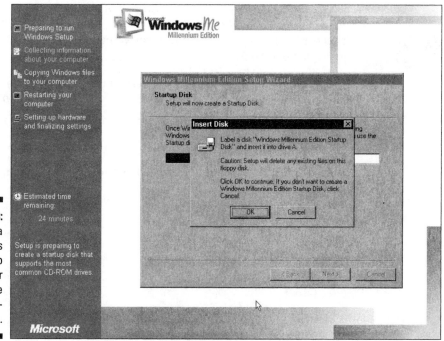

Figure A-3: Create a Windows Me Startup Disk for possible trouble- shooting.

9. **Remove the floppy disk and click OK; then click Finish.**

   Clicking the Finish button tells Windows Me to install itself onto your computer. Windows Me flashes some pictures of happy people on the screen as it begins the laborious chore of extracting, decompressing, and copying every chunk of Windows Me to the hard drive. Now's the time to pick up that sandwich you called ahead for when beginning the Setup process. Windows Me installs itself automatically, leaving you nothing else to do for the next half-hour or so.

   While installing itself, the Windows Wizard kicks the computer's tires a few times, even restarting the computer once or twice as it looks in the windows to see what's installed. After the program figures out the brand names and models of the computer parts, it tries to connect them automatically so they'll talk. (Called "Plug and Play," this bit of educated guessing has improved greatly over the years.)

10. **Sign on to Windows Me.**

    Congratulations! You've installed Windows Me. Type in your user name (add a password to keep out intruders, if you prefer), and Windows Me stretches out, fluffs the pillows, and calls the inside of your computer home.

    Almost. It still hems and haws, updating a few system settings before settling down to a clean desktop.

 New to Windows? Click the Start button and choose Help from the pop-up menu to see the Windows Help program. Click on Tours & Tutorials from the top menu and click on a tutorial that sounds interesting, as shown in Figure A-4.

    Occasionally, Windows Me wants to restart the computer one last time to set things straight. Just click the Yes button and wait patiently.

    You're through, unless something's gotten confusing, in which case it may be mentioned in the next section.

    Also, if something happens where the installation stops or the computer shuts down, turn the computer off. When they turn it back on, choose the Installation Recovery option.

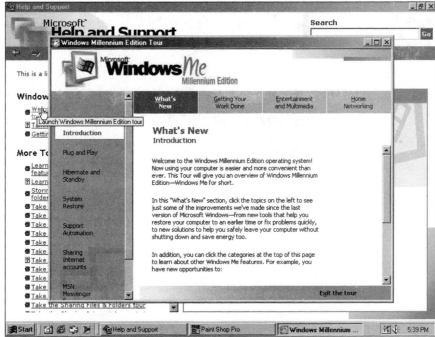

Figure A-4:
Click Tours
& Tutorials
to see the
tours
Windows
Me offers.

Installing Windows on a New Computer

Not everyone will be installing Windows Me over an old version of Windows.
Some will install "straight up" — onto a computer with no other version of
Windows. Here are a few tips for the additional questions they'll encounter.

Choose the Typical Setup option

Windows Me, a huge program, breaks itself into several setup options. You're
an average user, so choose the Typical Setup option. Windows pulls the most
common programs from its arsenal and places them inside your computer.

The Portable option installs software to control devices found on laptops.
Compact leaves out frills in order to nestle onto small hard drives. Computer
nerds choose Custom, honing their computer's operating system to meet
their advanced needs.

None of the setup options "lock" you into anything. Choose Typical, and you can always add the additional parts of Windows through the Control Panel's Add/Remove Programs feature, which I cover in Chapter 9.

Type your name, company, and network information if asked

Windows wants to know your name. The company name is optional, but Windows gets huffy if you don't enter your name. There's not much you can do about it.

If you're installing Windows on a network, Windows will ask for three more things: Your Computer name, Workgroup, and Computer Description.

Make up any computer name: C, Tina, or Zoombah. This is how others on the network will see your computer listed. In the Computer Description box, the least important of the three boxes, type your computer's brand and model number.

Finally, ask the network master for the name of your workgroup. The person who created the network also created that workgroup's name. The workgroup shows which group of computers your computer may chat with. Without the right workgroup, your computer can't talk to the others.

Set your time zone and geographical location

Windows needs to know your geographical information so it can set up the correct time zones, currency, Internet information, and other stuff pertaining to your area.

Make sure the daylight savings time setting matches your particular area.

Leaving Windows Me

After you finish with Windows Me and are ready to turn off your computer, click the Start button, located near the lower-left corner of the screen. When the menu sprouts upward, click the Shut Down option.

A window pops up, leaving four options:

- **Shut down:** Choose this option if you want to turn off your computer for the day and do something more constructive.

- **Restart:** This option works well if Windows Me is acting funny; it tells Windows Me to shut down and then come back to life, hopefully in a better mood.

- **Hibernate:** Offered by some computers, this automatically saves your work, saves the position of everything on your desktop, and turns off your computer. Then, when you restart Windows, your desktop is restored to the same way it looked before you chose Hibernate.

- **Standby:** The most dangerous option, this puts Windows to "sleep" temporarily — while you're on a phone call, for instance. The computer draws less power, like Hibernate, but it doesn't save your work before drifting off to sleep. Be *sure* to save your work before choosing Standby.

If you've chosen the Shut Down button by accident, click Cancel. Windows pretends you never wanted to leave, and all is well.

Turning Off the Computer

If you're finished computing for the day — and you've told Windows Me to shut down — turn off the computer. Find that switch you used to turn it on and flick it the other way. (Or, if it's a push button, give it another push.)

Never turn off the computer while Windows Me is running. Use the Windows Me Shut Down command and wait until Windows Me flashes a message on-screen saying that it's safe to turn off your computer.

Appendix B

Glossary

● ●

*W*indows Me's "easy access" Glossary program leaps to the screen in two ways. First, if you spot an unfamiliar word in the Help program — and the word's underlined — click the word, and Windows Me fetches a definition for you.

The second method is more complicated. Choose Help from the Start button, type Glossary into the Search box, and click Go. When Windows brings up the glossary, click on the stumper, and Windows fills you in on the definition.

If Windows isn't particularly handy, feel free to pick up a definition or two right here.

Active Desktop: A feature enabling Internet Web content to appear directly on the desktop, where it's automatically updated in the background.

active window: The last window you clicked — the one that's currently highlighted — is considered active. Any keys that you press affect this window.

Apply: Click this button, and Windows Me immediately applies and saves any changes you've made from the current list of options.

AUTOEXEC.BAT: A file that old-school MS-DOS computers read when turned on. The file contains instructions that affect any subsequently running MS-DOS programs — and older Windows programs as well. Windows Me no longer needs an AUTOEXEC.BAT file, but it keeps one around in case older programs may need to use it.

bitmap: A graphic consisting of bunches of little dots on-screen. They're saved as bitmap files, which end with the letters BMP. The Windows Me program called *Paint* can create and edit BMP files.

border: The edge of a window; you can move the border in or out to change the window's size.

cache: A storage area where Windows temporarily memorizes recently used files so they can be retrieved quickly if needed.

case-sensitive: A program that knows the difference between uppercase and lowercase letters. For example, a case-sensitive program considers *Pickle* and *pickle* to be two different things.

Classic style: Like Classic Coke, the Windows Classic style forgoes any fancy Windows Me frivolities and makes Windows Me operate like the perpetually crowd-pleasing Windows 95.

click: To push and release a button on the mouse.

Clipboard: A part of Windows Me that keeps track of information you've cut or copied from a program or file. It stores that information so that you can paste it into other programs.

command prompt: The little symbol that looks like C:\> or A:\> or something similar. It's the place where you can type instructions — *commands* — for DOS to carry out.

CONFIG.SYS: A file that your computer reads every time it boots up. The file contains information about how the computer is set up and what it's attached to. Both DOS and Windows programs rely on information contained in the CONFIG.SYS file. Windows Me no longer needs a CONFIG.SYS file, but it keeps one around in case other programs need one.

cursor: The little blinking line that shows where the next letter will appear when you start typing.

default: Choosing the default option enables you to avoid making a more-complicated decision. The *default option* is the one the computer chooses for you when you give up and just press Enter.

defragment: Organizing pieces of files that live on your hard drive so the drive can access them more easily.

desktop: The area on your screen where you move windows and icons around. Most people cover the desktop with *wallpaper* — a pretty picture.

Dial-Up Networking: A way to connect to the Internet through a modem and a telephone line.

directory: A separate *folder* on a hard disk for storing files. Storing related files in a directory makes them easier to find. Windows Me no longer uses the word directory and prefers the word *folder* instead.

document: A file containing information such as text, sound, or graphics. Documents are created or changed from within programs. *See **program**.*

DOS: Short for Disk Operating System, it's an older operating system for running programs. Windows Me can run programs designed for DOS, as well as programs designed for Windows.

double-click: Pushing and releasing the left mouse button twice in rapid succession. (Double-clicking the *right* mouse button doesn't do anything special.)

download: To copy files onto your computer through phone lines or cables.

drag: A four-step mouse process that moves an object across your desktop. First, point at the object — an icon, a highlighted paragraph, or something similar. Second, press and hold your left mouse button. Third, move the mouse pointer to the location to which you want to move that object. Fourth, release the mouse button. The object is dragged to its new location.

drop: Step four of the *drag* technique, described in the preceding entry. *Dropping* is merely letting go of the mouse button and letting your object fall onto something else, be it a new window, directory, or area on your desktop.

DRV: A file ending in DRV usually lets Windows talk to computer gizmos, such as video cards, sound cards, CD-ROM drives, and other stuff. (DRV is short for *driver.*)

FAQ: Short for Frequently Asked Questions, these text files are usually found on online services. Designed to save everyone some time, the files answer questions most frequently asked by new users. The Scanners FAQ explains all about scanners, for example; the Xena FAQ would trace Xena's history, starting with Hercules.

file: A collection of information in a format designed for computer use.

firewall: Specialized hardware or software on a network that keeps unauthorized people from breaking in through the Internet and accessing the network's files. Some firewalls also keep employees from downloading unauthorized material. Because cable modems, in particular, run on a large network, cable modem users should install firewall software to keep hackers from breaking in.

folder: An area for storing files to keep them organized (formerly called a *directory*). Folders can contain other folders for further organization. *See* **subdirectory.**

format: The process of preparing a disk to have files written on it. The disk needs to have "electronic shelves" tacked onto it so that Windows Me can store information on it. Formatting a disk wipes it clean of all previously recorded information.

highlighted: A selected item. Different colors usually appear over a high-lighted object to show that it's been singled out for further action.

icon: The little picture that represents an object — a program, file, or command — making it easier to figure out that object's function.

infrared: A special way for computers to communicate through invisible light beams; infrared ports (IR ports) are found frequently on laptops and printers.

INI: Short for *initialization,* INI usually hangs on the end of files that contain special system settings. The files are for the computer, not users, to mess with.

Internet: A huge collection of computers linked around the world. The *World Wide Web* rides atop the Internet along with other computer transactions. You can connect to the Internet's World Wide Web by paying a fee to an Internet Service Provider — much like paying a monthly phone bill.

lasso: Grabbing a bunch of items simultaneously with the mouse. Point at one corner of the items and, while holding down the left mouse button, point at the opposite corner. Lassoing the items highlights them for further action.

maximize: The act of making a window fill the entire screen. You can maximize a window by double-clicking its title bar — that long strip across its very top. Or you can click its maximize button — that button with the big square inside, located near the window's upper-right corner.

memory: The stuff computers use to store on-the-fly calculations while running.

minimize: The act of shrinking a window down to a tiny icon to get it out of the way temporarily. To minimize a window, click the minimize button — that button with the horizontal bar on it, located near the window's upper-right corner.

multitasking: Running several different programs simultaneously.

network: Connecting computers with cables so that people can share information without getting up from their desks.

operating system: Software that controls how a computer does its most basic stuff: stores files, talks to printers, and performs other gut-level operations. Windows Me is an operating system.

path: A sentence of computerese that tells a computer the precise name and location of a file.

PC card: Used mainly by laptops, PC cards can house modems, memory, network parts, or other handy items.

PDA: Short for Personal Digital Assistant, a PDA is a little computer toy for keeping track of contacts, schedules, and e-mail (and playing Bachman Turner Overdrive tunes).

Plug and Play (PnP): A sprightly phrase used to describe computer parts that Windows Me is supposed to be able to recognize and install automatically.

program: Something that enables you to work on the computer. Spreadsheets, word processors, and games are *programs*. *See* **document**.

RAM: Random-Access Memory. *See* **memory**.

scrap: When you highlight some text or graphics from a program, drag the chunk to the desktop, and drop it, you've created an official Windows *scrap* — a file containing a copy of that information. The scrap can be saved or dragged into other programs.

Shortcut: A Windows Me icon that serves as a push button for doing some-thing — loading a file, starting a program, or playing a sound, for example. Shortcuts have little arrows in their bottom corners so that you can tell them apart from the icons that *really* stand for files and programs.

shortcut button: A button in a Help menu that takes you directly to the area you need to fiddle with.

shortcut key: As opposed to a Shortcut, a shortcut key is an underlined letter in a program's menu that lets you work with the keyboard instead of the mouse. For example, if you see the word <u>H</u>elp in a menu, the underlined H means that you can get help by pressing Alt+H.

Shut Down: The process of telling Windows Me to save all its settings and files so that you can turn off your computer. You must click the Shut Down option, found on the Start menu, before turning off your computer.

Start button: A button in the corner of your screen where you can begin working. Clicking the Start button brings up the Start menu.

Start menu: A menu of options that appears when the Start button is clicked. From the Start menu, you can load programs, load files, change settings, find programs, find help, or shut down your computer so that you can turn it off.

subdirectory: A directory within a directory, used to further organize files. For example, a JUNKFOOD directory may contain subdirectories for CHIPS, PEANUTS, and PRETZELS. (A CELERY subdirectory would be empty.) In Windows Me, a subdirectory is a folder that's inside another folder.

taskbar: The bar in Windows Me that lists all currently running programs and open folders. The Start button lives on one end of the taskbar.

VGA: A popular standard for displaying information on monitors in certain colors and resolutions. It's now being replaced by SVGA — Super VGA — which can display even more colors and even finer resolution.

virtual: A trendy word to describe computer simulations. It's commonly used to describe things that *look* real, but aren't really there. For example, when Windows Me uses *virtual memory,* it's using part of the hard drive for memory, not the actual memory chips.

wallpaper: Graphics spread across the background of your computer screen. The Windows Me Control Panel lets you choose among different wallpaper files.

Web browser: Software for maneuvering through the World Wide Web, visiting Web pages, and examining the wares. The Microsoft Web browser, Internet Explorer, comes free with the latest version of Windows Me or can be downloaded for free from the Microsoft Web page at `www.microsoft.com`.

Web page: Just as televisions can show bunches of different channels, the World Wide Web can show gazillions of different *Web pages*. These screenfuls of information can be set up by anyone: The government can display county meeting schedules; corporations can project flashy marketing propaganda; publications can display online versions of their works. (Or, the Cushmans can put up a Family Page with pictures of the baby at Disneyland.)

window: An on-screen box that contains information for you to look at or work with. Programs run in *windows* on your screen.

Wizard: Helpful Windows program that takes over the chores of program installation and setup.

World Wide Web: Riding atop the Internet's motley collection of cables, the flashy World Wide Web works as a sort of computerized television, letting you jump from channel to channel by pointing and clicking at the pages. Also known simply as "The Web."

Index

• *E* •

• *F* •

● *G* ●

YOUR ONLINE RESOURCE

WWW.DUMMIES.COM

Discover Dummies Online!

The Dummies Web Site is your fun and friendly online resource for the latest information about *For Dummies*® books and your favorite topics. The Web site is the place to communicate with us, exchange ideas with other *For Dummies* readers, chat with authors, and have fun!

Ten Fun and Useful Things You Can Do at www.dummies.com

1. Win free *For Dummies* books and more!
2. Register your book and be entered in a prize drawing.
3. Meet your favorite authors through the IDG Books Worldwide Author Chat Series.
4. Exchange helpful information with other *For Dummies* readers.
5. Discover other great *For Dummies* books you must have!
6. Purchase Dummieswear® exclusively from our Web site.
7. Buy *For Dummies* books online.
8. Talk to us. Make comments, ask questions, get answers!
9. Download free software.
10. Find additional useful resources from authors.

Link directly to these ten fun and useful things at **http://www.dummies.com/10useful**

SURF THE NET

WWW.DUMMIES.COM

For other technology titles from IDG Books Worldwide, go to www.idgbooks.com

Not on the Web yet? It's easy to get started with *Dummies 101*®: *The Internet For Windows*® *98* or *The Internet For Dummies*® at local retailers everywhere.

IDG BOOKS WORLDWIDE®

Find other *For Dummies* books on these topics:
Business • Career • Databases • Food & Beverage • Games • Gardening • Graphics • Hardware
Health & Fitness • Internet and the World Wide Web • Networking • Office Suites
Operating Systems • Personal Finance • Pets • Programming • Recreation • Sports
Spreadsheets • Teacher Resources • Test Prep • Word Processing

IDG BOOKS WORLDWIDE
BOOK REGISTRATION

Register This Book and Win!

We want to hear from you!

Visit **http://my2cents.dummies.com** to register this book and tell us how you liked it!

✔ Get entered in our monthly prize giveaway.

✔ Give us feedback about this book — tell us what you like best, what you like least, or maybe what you'd like to ask the author and us to change!

✔ Let us know any other *For Dummies*® topics that interest you.

Your feedback helps us determine what books to publish, tells us what coverage to add as we revise our books, and lets us know whether we're meeting your needs as a *For Dummies* reader. You're our most valuable resource, and what you have to say is important to us!

Not on the Web yet? It's easy to get started with *Dummies 101*®: *The Internet For Windows*® *98* or *The Internet For Dummies*® at local retailers everywhere.

Or let us know what you think by sending us a letter at the following address:

For Dummies Book Registration
Dummies Press
10475 Crosspoint Blvd.
Indianapolis, IN 46256

...FOR DUMMIES™

BESTSELLING BOOK SERIES